KEYNES' ECONOMICS

METHODOLOGICAL ISSUES

Edited by TONY LAWSON and HASHEM PESARAN
for the *Cambridge Journal of Economics*

CROOM HELM
London & Sydney

© 1985 Tony Lawson and Hashem Pesaran
Croom Helm Ltd, Provident House, Burrell Row,
Beckenham, Kent BR3 1AT
Croom Helm Australia Pty Ltd., First Floor,
139 King Street, Sydney, NSW 20001, Australia

British Library Cataloguing in Publication Data

Keynes' economics: methodological issues.
  1. Keynes, John Maynard   2. Keynesian economics
  3. Macroeconomics   4. Microeconomics
I. Lawson, Tony   II. Pesaran, Hashem
  339.3'092'4   HB99.7

ISBN 0-7099-1680-9

Printed and bound in Great Britain
by Billing & Sons Limited, Worcester.

CONTENTS

BIBLIOGRAPHICAL NOTE

Throughout this volume all references denoted by CW are to *The Collected Writings of John Maynard Keynes*, published on behalf of the Royal Economic Society by Macmillan and Cambridge University Press. Details of the relevant volumes are given below.

I (1971)	Indian Currency and Finance (first published 1913)
II (1971)	The Economic Consequences of the Peace (first published 1919)
III (1971)	A Revision of the Treaty (first published 1922)
IV (1971)	A Tract on Monetary Reform (first published 1923)
V (1971)	A Treatise on Money, 1 The Pure Theory of Money (first published 1930)
VI (1971)	A Treatise on Money, 2 The Applied Theory of Money (first published 1930)
VII (1973)	The General Theory (first published 1936)
VIII (1973)	A Treatise on Probability (first published 1921)
IX (1972)	Essays in Persuasion (full texts with additional essays) (first published 1931)
X (1972)	Essays in Biography (full texts with additional biographical writings) (first published 1933)
XI (1983)	Economic Articles and Correspondence: Academic
XII (1983)	Economic Articles and Correspondence: Investment and Editorial
XIII (1973)	The General Theory and After: Part I, Preparation
XIV (1973)	The General Theory and After: Part II, Defence and Development
XV (1971)	Activities 1906-14: India and Cambridge
XVI (1971)	Activities 1914-19: The Treasury and Versailles
XVII (1978)	Activities 1920-2: Treaty Revision and Reconstruction
XVIII (1978)	Activities 1922-32: The End of Reparations
XIX (1981)	Activities 1922-9: The Return to Gold and Industrial Policy
XX (1981)	Activities 1929-31: Rethinking Employment and Unemployment Policies

1 METHODOLOGICAL ISSUES IN KEYNES' ECONOMICS: AN INTRODUCTION

Tony Lawson and Hashem Pesaran

When a field of study becomes marked by dissatisfaction and disillusionment, methodological analyses and debates tend to become prominent and often provide pointers to fruitful directions for the subject to move in. Economics is currently undergoing just such a period of crisis: the post-war Keynesian orthodoxy has been criticised, only to be replaced by what, to many people, seem to be implausible theories concerning the formation of expectations and the functioning of markets; the value of econometrics as an effective tool for discriminating between competing theories has been seriously questioned; and there are crucial disagreements as to the nature and scope of economics. It seems, therefore, that there may be some benefit to be gained from re-examining the fundamental concepts and methods involved in economics.

Recent books on economic methodology, such as those by Blaug (1980), Boland (1982), Caldwell (1982), Hollis and Nell (1975) and Katouzian (1980), all provide valuable contributions towards this end. None of these, however, deals with Keynes' contribution on methodology in any depth, and yet Keynes' work on methodology was not insignificant. In fact, Keynes' methodological contribution has been neglected generally, being overshadowed by his other work on economic theory and policy analysis. In an attempt, in part, to rectify matters in 1983, the centenary of Keynes' birth, the *Cambridge Journal of Economics* organised a conference on methodological issues in Keynes' work. Such was the interest shown at this conference that it was decided that a selection of the papers presented should be extended and developed for publication. This volume is the outcome.

The following chapters, then, not only provide a general overview of aspects of Keynes' contribution to methodology, but are also concerned with clarifying, developing and criticising Keynes' work. Before providing a summary of what each particular chapter contributes, however, it seems worthwhile first to point out what this volume of papers does not achieve.

First of all it does not represent a unified whole, and many of the con-

1

tributions provide conflicting interpretations and criticisms of Keynes' work. For example, whilst Hodgson seems to interpret Keynes' position as both empiricist and rationalist, Carabelli interprets him as being anti-empiricist and anti-rationalist. Such differences in part reflect different uses of the same words and the reader is warned to beware of this. Differences in the use of words such as 'rationality', are, however, quite common in the literature, particularly in the philosophy of science; for this reason we have preferred authors to define their own particular use of these words within their papers. To give a further example of different interpretations of Keynes' contribution, whilst Lawson is sympathetic to Keynes' criticism of Tinbergen's work, believing it, in the main, to be well-founded, Klant finds such criticism 'presumptuous'.

Second, the volume does not provide a uniform interpretation of what is 'Keynes' or 'Keynesian'. Whilst many chapters reserve such terms for referring only to claims and theories actually put forward by Keynes, Wren-Lewis, for example, is explicit that he is not doing this; in his case the use of the term 'Keynesian' is reserved for models in which the 'primary role [is] given to effective demand in determining output, employment and unemployment'.

Finally, because the chapters concentrate on developing and criticising aspects of Keynes' views, the volume as a whole cannot represent a complete account of Keynes' methodological contribution. It is nevertheless a start. It is also to be hoped that this volume will stimulate a greater interest both in methodological issues to which Keynes contributed and in methodological issues generally.

The first chapter in the volume, by Hodgson, examines Keynes' views on expectations and the relationship between expectations and economic activity. Hodgson argues, perhaps contentiously, that Keynes failed to consider sufficiently the importance of institutions and 'the social culture and structures which give [expectations] colour and substance'. However, having emphasised the importance of institutions, Hodgson acknowledges the difficulties of producing the endogenous theory of institutions without which his own critique of Keynes is incomplete. Hodgson interprets Keynes as providing a 'psychologistic' and 'rationalist' conception of human action which is, however, highly qualified by the fact of uncertainty about the future. Within Keynes' analysis, however, Hodgson claims to find inconsistencies which stem from Keynes' implicit assumption that 'state personnel', in contrast to others, always 'act under the guidance of reason and persuasion'. The resolution of these inconsistencies, according to Hodgson, leads logically either to the rational expectations approach or to the ultra individualism of the Austrian School. The author's alternative strategy is to suggest that we reject Keynes' psychologistic and rationalist conceptions of human action and adopt instead a more institutionalist approach. Thus among the methodological conclusions drawn out by Hodgson are the desirability of interdisciplinary study and the need for resources to be devoted to the study of institutions and their historical development.

Central to Hodgson's analysis is Keynes' theory of expectations formation, and the essentially indeterminate nature of long-term expectations. This is a theme which is taken up and developed in the second chapter, by Alexander Dow and Sheila Dow. These authors examine the notion of animal spirits in Keynes' analysis and show how it is related to his earlier work on probability. Dow and Dow argue convincingly against those who interpret animal spirits as involving irrationality. (This theme is also taken up elsewhere in the volume by Carabelli.) In enquiring why the notion of animal spirits should have fallen into disfavour, the authors conclude that it is because there is no place for this notion in the methodological framework employed by the neoclassical orthodoxy. To emphasise the importance of incorporating animal spirits into the analysis, therefore, is to reject the current neoclassical orthodoxy and to adopt the methodology of Keynes. For Dow and Dow the notion of animal spirits epitomises the view that the process of expectations formation does not lend itself to the probability calculus. The position of these authors is more subjectivist than Hodgson's. Whilst the latter gives greater weight to the social and cultural factors and thus feels that studying the role and nature of institutions will provide important insights, Dow and Dow place greater emphasis on the impossibility of prediction in the social sciences and the need for economists, instead, to be 'alert to a change of mood in the economy'. A methodological implication that Dow and Dow draw from their analysis is the need 'to tackle each question from a variety of angles, with a variety of methods' or, in short, a return to the methodological framework employed, as they see it, by Keynes.

The theme of expectations formation is also taken up by Wren-Lewis, who focuses on how the process of expectations formation has been treated in practice in specific models of the UK economy. Wren-Lewis considers the responses of builders of large-scale 'Keynesian' models to the 'challenge' of the Rational Expectations Hypothesis (REH) and argues that the REH and the theoretical underpinnings of Keynesian models are not necessarily incompatible. In doing so the author is implicitly adopting a particular view of REH which emphasises *only* that expectations should be consistent with the underlying macro-economic model in question. However, like Hodgson, Wren-Lewis emphasises the importance of divergent expectations on the part of economic agents and thus would appear to cast doubt on the merits of assuming such consistency.

With their concentration on the role and nature of expectation the three chapters discussed above can be said to share a common theme. The same is also true of the next four chapters appearing in the volume, where Keynes' views on methods of analysis, and especially on induction and statistical inference, are assessed.

The first of these chapters, by Klant, examines how economists have failed in their attempts to reduce their subject to the explanatory ideal of Newton's mechanics, and considers Keynes' argument that such a reduction is impossible because economics is essentially different in nature to the 'natural sciences'. Klant, in fact, is highly critical of Keynes, both in the latter's failed attempt to solve Hume's induction problem and in his criticisms of Tinbergen's work on econometrics. However, the author does conclude that in emphasising the problems involved in the 'slippery transition' from description to inference in statistical work, Keynes' contribution is highly relevant. Ultimately the author agrees with Keynes that modelling cannot be mechanical but instead is highly judgemental; and he shares Keynes' conclusion that economics is essentially a moral science. The implication for statistical modelling drawn by Klant is not that quantitative models should be abandoned, but rather that they should be handled with 'care'.

The next chapter, by Pheby, attempts to provide clear insights into Keynes' methodology by examining explicit criticisms that Popper and his supporters have made of it. The author concludes that Keynes and Popper are not as far apart as is usually believed and, moreover, that on issues where their views do diverge it is Popper's position that seems untenable. Thus, for example, Pheby rejects Popperian criticisms of Keynes on the grounds that Popper himself needs to employ something like the principle of the 'uniformity of nature' adopted by Keynes. In fact the author proceeds to argue that Popper and Keynes, on some issues, are probably closer than, say, either of them is to Friedman, whose influential views are considered to be instrumentalist.

Lawson's chapter, which follows Pheby's, argues that contributions which focus on Keynes' comments dealing with 'technical issues' in econometrics risk missing what are really Keynes' more fundamental criticisms. These criticisms, according to Lawson, stem from theories and arguments developed by Keynes in his *Treatise on Probability*. In order both to illustrate significant aspects of this work and to pave the way for a discussion of Keynes' views on econometrics, Lawson finds it helpful to discuss Keynes' arguments concerning the value of prediction in the context of model or hypothesis evaluation. This facilitates a contrast between Keynes' inductive account and other, more prominent, falsificationist accounts. Focusing on Keynes' inductivist theory, Lawson argues that it is this which underlies Keynes' more fundamental criticisms of econometrics, and contends that if econometricians are to continue to refer to Keynes' comments as though they remain relevant then it is Keynes' inductivist criticisms that should be 'answered'. The remaining 'technical' criticisms, after all, can be found in a much more comprehensible and complete form in most modern econometric text-books.

Pesaran and Smith also focus on the 'debate' between Tinbergen and Keynes but, unlike the previous authors (and indeed unlike most authors who have written on this subject), spend some time examining Tinbergen's side of the debate. In going over the debate, the authors liken themselves to military historians, whose 'purpose in refighting this battle is not to change the result, but to learn its lessons'. The authors argue that Keynes, like many others at the time, chose in his criticism to concentrate exclusively on Tinbergen's work on testing economic theories and overlooked altogether the importance and novelty of Tinbergen's approach for practical policy analysis. As a result, they argue, Keynes held a one-sided view of the usefulness of econometrics and misjudged its potential for policy analysis — an area of special concern to Keynes himself. The authors conclude that econometric 'practice expanded not because Keynes was wrong in his technical and methodological criticisms of Tinbergen's work, but because Tinbergen's work happened to fill a vacuum that was created by the need to formulate and implement the type of interventionist policies that Keynes himself had advocated'. In this, therefore, Pesaran and Smith reach a similar conclusion to that of Klant.

The final four chapters in the volume each focuses on distinct aspects of Keynes' methodological contribution. The first of these, by Carabelli, explores the notions of 'cause', 'chance' and 'possibility' in Keynes' writings. Carabelli argues that in his use of the terms 'cause' and 'chance' Keynes was not concerned with the properties of objects but rather with reasons for knowing and believing. Thus, according to Carabelli, 'cause' (like probability) was treated by Keynes in a practical way, as in ordinary discourse, with constant reference, albeit implicit, to a limited body of knowledge. As with 'cause', Keynes used the term 'chance' in a subjective sense, reflecting a cognitive perspective. Thus, argues Carabelli, Keynes rejected any idea of objective chance. In fact, chance was interpreted by Keynes as a situation where there is complete ignorance — a situation in which there is no reason to believe one alternative in preference to any other. However, Keynes thought that such a situation would be particularly uncommon and therefore doubted the usefulness of the 'probability calculus' for characterising actual situations. Since he believed that social science is ultimately founded on belief rather than on material truth, for Keynes, as Carabelli notes, change can occur as a result of the process of persuasion. Thus Keynes arrived at the notion of 'possibility'. Such a notion, amongst other things, enabled Keynes to judge the past from the perspective that things could have been different, and this view lay behind his faith in attempts at public persuasion.

Boland's chapter examines the strategy adopted by Keynes in arguing against the Marshallian orthodoxy. Keynes' 'claimed assault', according to Boland, was to try and show that the classical Marshallian theory was a special case of a more general theory. Keynes' concept of generality, in Boland's view, 'rests . . . on the methodological position that considers a model with more exogenous givens to be more general', whilst, in the neoclassical orthodoxy, generality is measured by the number of endogenous variables. Therefore, although a short-run model that treats 'macro-variables' (such as the level of aggregate demand, the general level of prices and interest rates) as exogenously given is regarded as general in Keynes' methodological framework, the same model is interpreted by neoclassical theory as a special case of a long-run model where all variables, apart from the naturally-given psychological states of individuals, given technology and natural resources, are endogenously determined, including the macro-variables. As long as these are the only variables permitted to be exogenous, then the neoclassical interpretation of Keynes' general-*vs*-special case argument will 'always see Keynes' assault as a failure'. Instead, according to Boland, what is fundamental in Keynes' 'assault' is a notion of liquidity (which following Hicks is interpreted very generally by Boland as both financial and non-financial liquidity, the latter including spare productive capacity). Liquidity enters the analysis because of the existence of uncertainty. Accepting the necessity of the notion of liquidity as a short-run endogenous variable, then, argues Boland, any long-run model, such as neoclassical models, must be irrelevant. However, Boland concludes that, 'until mainstream neoclassical economics drops its dependence on narrow psychologistic individualism, Keynes' assault will not be much of a struggle for neoclassical economic theorists'.

In the next chapter Chick argues that in *The General Theory* Keynes finds it possible to present a static analysis of output, employment and prices whilst incorporating historical time, and that in achieving this Keynes' use of the device of the wage-unit for measuring 'real' output is fundamental. Chick considers it to be typical of a firm in an 'entrepreneur economy' that costs of production are set before actual demand is known. For a static analysis of production to proceed, therefore, something must be assumed not only about capital, as is usually the case, but also about costs including wages. Chick argues that for Keynes it is significant that the 'supply curve' need not enter into the determination of actual wages and employment. This does not mean, however, that wages are indeterminate, for this 'view ignores the role of history in determining wages'. However, Chick argues that by denoting demand and supply functions in terms of the wage unit — the wage of 'ordinary labour' — these functions become 'independent of the level of wages and hence independent of the historical component of their determination'. This permits a static analysis 'while allowing the historical element in wage determination to be preserved in the background'. Thus Chick maintains that while static analysis permits the determination of the value of output in wage-units, the nominal level of output cannot be found unless the nominal level of money wages is first determined.

The final chapter, by Backhaus, attempts to further our understanding of the rise and success of Keynesianism. This task is seen by the author as being especially difficult both because there is no undisputed interpretation of what is the central message of Keynes' *General Theory*, and, more importantly, because Keynesianism as a phenomenon in macro-economic policy did not originate with the publication of *The General Theory*. Backhaus thus believes it is necessary to disentangle Keynes' economics from Keynesianism, and argues that this is facilitated 'if we geographically remove an analysis of the roots of Keynesianism from Cambridge'. The author in fact concentrates on Germany where, he argues, 'the first full-scale application of [Keynes'] *General Theory* had taken place . . . well before the book was actually published'. Backhaus proceeds by raising the issue of the extent to which Keynes' main economic contributions were in fact anticipated within Germany. In this he acknowledges not only the problems associated with deciding what Keynes' main economic contributions are, but perhaps more importantly, the difficulty of interpreting what is meant by 'anticipated'. These questions have recently been addressed by Patinkin (1982) and Backhaus takes this work as his point of departure. However, Backhaus concludes that Patinkin's account is inadequate, pointing out that 'variations in the professional organisation of economics, across cultures and over time, are not captured by Patinkin's approach to studying applications of the General Theory'. In particular, Backhaus argues that Patinkin's account rules out the German economists W. Sombart and W. Launtenbach as possible anticipators of Keynesianism. He then provides convincing arguments based on case-studies, that these two economists should in fact be seen as anticipators of Keynesianism. Sombart, a professor at Berlin University, argued for Keynesian policy measures on the basis of historical theory and analysis, whilst according to Backhaus Lautenbach, a civil servant shaped the 'German economic policy for recovery during the crucial years of 1932-1935 . . . in a Keynesian mould almost singlehanded'. However it was Keynes who became influential. Keynes' writings and lectures had received significant attention in Germany well before the publication of *The General Theory*, and his contributions proved more quantifiable than the historical analysis of Sombart, whilst Lautenbach 'never claimed to be an original thinker but preferred to describe himself as Keynesian'. This study, as the author writes, may thus 'be seen as preparatory for a more precise understanding of the methodological basis of Keynesianism, including the reasons for its astonishing success'.

Although the chapters in this volume are limited in scope, they nevertheless reveal that Keynes' methodological contribution is extensive and that it remains highly pertinent, bearing as it does on issues that continue to be important and contentious in economics. Collectively, these chapters bring out strengths and weaknesses in Keynes' methodological position and emphasise aspects of Keynes' contribution — such as the role of institutions, the use of econometrics for testing theories, the value of prediction, the nature of animal spirits, and the importance of persuasion in the conduct of economic policy — that have, by and large, been ignored, especially by mainstream economics. They also suggest ways in which we might usefully proceed in reassessing economic theory and methods of analysis.

Finally, it remains for us to acknowledge gratefully the help of those who have contributed to the preparation of this volume, particularly Geoff Harcourt and the other participants at the conference on Keynes' methodology, and the editors of the *Cambridge Journal of Economics*. We wish especially to thank Ann Newton for her generous help both with organising the conference and with preparing the manuscript for publication.

References

Boland, L.A. (1982) *The Foundations of Economic Method,* George Allen and Unwin, London

Blaug, M. (1980) *The Methodology of Economics,* Cambridge University Press, Cambridge

Caldwell, B. (1982) *Beyond Positivism: Economic Methodology in the Twentieth Century*, George Allen and Unwin, London

Hollis, M., and Nell, E.J. (1975) *Rational Economic Man: a Philosophical Critique of Neo-Classical Economics,* Cambridge University Press, Cambridge

Katouzian, H. (1980) *Ideology and Method in Economics,* MacMillan, London

Pantinkin, D. (1982) *Anticipations of the General Theory? And other essays on Keynes*, University of Chicago Press, Chicago

2 PERSUASION, EXPECTATIONS AND THE LIMITS TO KEYNES

Geoff Hodgson

> For although Keynes had so much to say about the effects of expectations about the future on present economic behaviour, he seems to be not nearly so informative about the causation of these expectations. (Champernowne 1963, 192)

Uncertainty, limited knowledge and the nature of expectations are of increasing concern to economists today. After the long decades in which a complacent orthodoxy assumed these problems away, they have rapidly re-emerged with the rise of the rational expectations hypothesis and renewed interest in the Austrian School. Theoretical work from both these camps has been used in attempts to rebut Keynes and to justify a laissez-faire approach to economic policy. Yet for Keynes too the existence of uncertainty in economic life was a central theme in *The General Theory of Employment, Interest and Money*. He was, however, drawn to less conservative policy conclusions. His ideas inspired the reforming consensus of the post World War II period.

Joan Robinson and other left-wing Keynesians have frequently pointed out that Keynes' work is capable of even more radical interpretation; but the discussion of expectations is not central to this argument. Instead, attention is directed to the sparse and apparently contradictory notes in the final chapter of *The General Theory* where Keynes calls for an unspecified and unexplained 'comprehensive socialisation of investment' (CW, VII, 378) and other undetailed measures of collective or state guidance. Yet he moves on immediately to defend economic 'individualism', and the market system, from further socialisation (379).

It is the aim of this chapter to examine more closely Keynes' view of the relationship between expectation and economic activity emphasising some implications for economic policy. The first section contains a discussion of the role of expectations in *The General Theory* and related works of Keynes from that period. The main elements of a critique of this are contained in the second section, which proceeds from a

10

discussion of the concept of the expecting agent in the firm and elsewhere. It is suggested that Keynes had a psychologistic and rationalist conception of human action which was defective and led to a mistaken view of government policy and the state. Furthermore, it is argued that an alternative, institutionalist approach may be able to account for some of the problems with the application of Keynesian policies to capitalist economies in recent years.

The third section is directed at the alternative approaches of 'rational expectations' and the Austrian School. Although it is impossible to discuss them in detail, brief reference to these now fashionable theories is unavoidable. A fourth and final section draws together the argument with some conclusions for post-Keynesian theory and policy.

Expectations and Production in *The General Theory*

Expectations 'upon which business decisions depend', make their first full appearance in Chapter 5 of *The General Theory*. They are said to 'fall into two groups'. The first, called 'short-term expectation', is the price 'a manufacturer' expects to get from current commenced output. The second, called 'long-term expectation', is concerned with the expected future yield on investment in additional capital equipment (CW, VII, 46-7).

Keynes devotes considerable attention to the effects of the general state of expectations on the level of production and employment. Past expectations helped to determine previous levels of output and investment. Thus they remain 'embodied in to-day's capital equipment with reference to which the entrepreneur has to make to-day's decisions'. For this reason 'it will often be safe to omit express reference to short-term expectation, in view of the fact that in practice the process of revision of short-term expectation is a gradual and continuous one, carried on largely in the light of realised results' (CW, VII, 50). This argument enables Keynes to focus attention on 'The State of Long-Term Expectation' (Ch. 12). Much significance is attributed to this in the work of many modern post-Keynesians (e.g. Davidson, 1972; Loasby, 1976; Minsky, 1976; Robinson, 1973; Shackle, 1972, 1974).

In his 1937 lecture notes, Keynes himself seems to place even greater relative emphasis on the effects of shifting long-term expectations by suggestions that *The General Theory*, if rewritten, should assume at the outset that 'short-period expectations were always fulfilled; and then have a subsequent chapter showing what difference it makes when short-period expectations are disappointed.' (CW, XIV, 181; see also Kregel, 1976).

Long-term Expectations

As post-Keynesians have emphasised, long-term expectations are formed not merely in the context of risk, to which a definite probability can be attributed, but also in that of uncertainty regarding future events for which 'there is no scientific basis on which to form any calculable probability whatever.' (CW, XIV, 114). Long-term expectations are, in Keynes' view, guesses with minimal information regarding future economic and other related events. There is also, Keynes pointed out, the question of the confidence with which we make such forecasts (CW, VII, 148; see also Stohs, 1980). Typically, crucial information is lacking to make sound estimates of future investment yields. The confidence of any estimates will depend on the quantity and quality of the information that is available. Given that these estimates are usually little more than guesses, they are tentative and precarious by nature. Lacking firm evidence and sound calculation they can be revised with startling rapidity with any shift in the economic or political wind.

Keynes' theory of long-term investment is not ahistorical. Noting the 'separation between ownership and management which prevails today' and the 'development of organised investment markets', Keynes (CW, VII, 150) argues that decisions to invest in financial terms are no longer irrevocable, and are being constantly revalued on the stock market. This adds to the instability of the system. Keynes indicated that he regarded his theory as having greatest relevance to a capitalist system with large-scale enterprises and a developed and relatively autonomous financial sector.

Despite the precariousness of investment decisions in an uncertain world, 'the necessity for action and decision' compels the investor to act *as if* he or she had 'a good Benthamite calculation of a series of prospective advantages and disadvantages, each multiplied by its appropriate probability, waiting to be summed'. What guidelines are to be used for action in the face of such uncertainty?

> We assume that the present is a much more serviceable guide to the future than a candid examination of past experience would show it to have been hitherto . . . (and) that the *existing* state of opinion as expressed in prices and the character of existing output is based on a *correct* summing up of future prospects . . . Knowing that our own individual judgement is worthless, we endeavour to fall back on the

judgement of the rest of the world which is perhaps better informed. That is, we endeavour to conform with the behaviour of the majority or the average. (CW, XIV, 114)

In both *The General Theory* and the 1937 *Quarterly Journal of Economics* summary of its main points (from which the above is quoted) Keynes refers to the 'psychology' of a society of individuals, each trying to copy or anticipate the others. Decisions are then taken, he argues, on the basis of past convention. This, however, is not always stable:

> A conventional valuation which is established as the outcome of the mass psychology of a large number of ignorant individuals is liable to change violently as the result of a sudden fluctuation of opinion . . . the market will be subject to waves of optimistic and pessimistic sentiment, which are unreasoning and yet in a sense legitimate where no solid basis exists for a reasonable calculation. (CW, VII, 154)

According to Keynes, human beings are rational but they live and act in a world where widespread uncertainty places severe limits on the capacities of individuals to make detailed, rational calculations about the future. These constraints derive not from the limited rationality of individuals but from the ubiquitousness of uncertainty. Actions flow from judgements about the future (which often lack a firm, objective, empirical foundation) as well as from observation of 'the convention' that is formed by the action of others.

Keynes' Policy Conclusions

Keynes' above remarks form the basis for his famous critical judgement on stock market speculation: 'When the capital development of a country becomes a by-product of the activities of a casino, the job is likely to be ill-done.' (CW, VII, 159). The policy conclusions are well-known: government intervention to regulate the overall level of effective demand and the propensity to consume, and the forementioned 'socialisation of investment'. Government steps in, as it were, to change 'the convention' that currently dominates entrepreneurial activity, and to fix it at a level which would create and maintain full employment. In Keynes' view the market mechanism cannot achieve this on its own. The limits to rational calculation within the market system have to be overcome by the reason and action of state personnel.

Keynes is careful to note that the formation of economic conventions is not entirely chaotic and unstable. If it were, successful state intervention to maintain full employment would be unlikely for prolonged periods. He ends Chapter 12 of *The General Theory* with assurances of the possibility of stability:

> We should not conclude . . . that everything depends on waves of irrational psychology. On the contrary, the state of long-term expectation is often steady, and, even when it is not, the other factors exert their compensating effects. We are merely reminding ourselves that human decisions affecting the future, whether personal or political or economic, cannot depend on strict mathematical expectation, since the basis for making such calculations does not exist; and that it is our innate urge to activity which makes the wheels go round, our rational selves choosing between the alternatives as best we are able, calculating where we can, but often falling back for our motive on whim or sentiment or chance. (CW, VII, 162-3)

It would seem that the establishment of a firm convention by the state would make the influence of whim or chance less prominent; the level of effective demand would be backed and regulated by state action rather than 'mass psychology'. Then, Keynes suggests, the market will come into its own: 'I see no reason to suppose that the existing system seriously misemploys the factors of production which are in use . . . It is in determining the volume, not the direction, of actual employment that the existing system has broken down.' (CW, VII, 379)

Implicit in Keynes' theory is the idea that a sustained 'convention' corresponding to full employment cannot depend on state action alone. In addition 'average opinion' would have to identify 'correctly' economic indicators as being consistent with the preservation of full employment and buoyant effective demand, and the actions of economic agents would have to be 'rational' and consistent with this perception. Without this, government action would be unable to achieve any kind of full employment equilibrium; its objectives would be thwarted by 'irrational' behaviour on the part of investors and managers. To support its policy conclusions, therefore, Keynes' theory has to bring a qualified notion of economic stability and a conception of rational action once again to the fore.

Some Limitations of Keynes' Theory

Keynes' theory of the relationship between expectations and the level of production and employment is, of course, a major landmark in the history of economic thought. It is a clear break from the self-regulating equilibrium models of the still prominent neoclassical school, and it is in advance of the mechanistic approach that is found in some Marxist economic theory.[1] Both these traditions neglect the role of uncertainty and limited knowledge in the modern economy, mechanically relating the actions of economic agents to past and present stimuli alone, without giving due consideration to their (essentially indeterminate) expectations. [Pre-Keynesian economics finds its analogue in the classical mechanics of Newton; in contrast, Keynes' work has been compared to the physics of Einstein where information is no longer obtainable without cost (Leijonhufvud, 1968, p. 397).]

With his theory of investment and employment, Keynes is able to argue, even more clearly than Marx did before, that the capitalist system is potentially unstable, containing no automatic machinery of self-regulation which can always move it towards full employment and optimal output. This message remains poignant and relevant today, even if it is not universally accepted. However, without detracting from the enduring value of Keynes' analysis, on close inspection there are some gaps. It is the aim of this section to bring some of these into view. The object is not to destroy the whole Keynesian argument but to suggest a plan for restoration and extension.

The following discussion starts with the topic of the expecting agent ('the entrepreneur' in Keynes' work) and this is then related to firms and financial institutions. Next, a consideration of Keynes' methodological standpoint is followed by a critique of his view of government. Although these topics are diverse, it will be argued that they connect together as a whole, forming a qualified critique of Keynes which has important policy implications.

The Expecting Agent

It is notable how frequently Keynes' discussion of expectations is couched in the first person plural. 'We' calculate, 'we' reason and 'we' form our expectations. This understandable literary device raises a more serious question: Who is the expecting agent to which Keynes refs? Does he mean everyone involved in the economy, or a single group or class?

The agent that appears most frequently in his analysis is the entrepreneur. Is the discussion of expectations related primarily or even exclusively to this person? This would appear to be the case. Keynes adopts a distinction between 'entrepreneurs' and 'rentiers', redolent of his Marshallian background. However, these terms are not used with sufficient precision in *The General Theory*. In one passage 'the entrepreneur' is the owner-manager of the firm. In another he is an investor on the stock market. In yet another the separation of ownership and control is observed and the process of expectations-formation is split between the financier and the directors of the firm.

What is apparent from Chapters 11 and 12 of *The General Theory* is that the agent which Keynes has in mind has money capital to invest and is making comparisons between its expected yield if it is converted into means of production, and the expected rates of interest if this money is lent to financial institutions. However, this economic agent is not the Marshallian entrepreneur, nor one who is necessarily making the actual decisions concerning the scale of output, investment and employment in the firm. Joan Robinson (1971, 31-2) has pointed out that 'Keynes rather lost his grip on the distinction between the rentier and the entrepreneur. His discussion of "the state of long-term expectations" is devoted to the Stock Exchange rather than to the accumulation of means of production.'

A clear definition of 'the entrepreneur' and other crucial actors may have eluded Keynes because of an assumption that his account of expectations-formation applies more or less equally to all economic agents, or at least to those with ready money to invest or exchange. This would help to explain his frequent reference to 'psychology' in his discussion of the formation of expectations. Keynes' account, it appears was based on a view of human nature, rather than of institutional structures or social relations, despite its concrete references to the nature of modern capitalism.

The problem is not simply one of defining the expecting agent. In Keynes' work there is also a failure to consider the processes through which expectations are formed and the social culture and structures which give them colour and substance. This omission is not untypical of the overwhelming majority of economic theorists, but it is all the more acute for Keynes who made uncertainty and expectations central to his analysis. Instead, Keynes made use of favourite analogies to explain the 'mass psychology' of expectations-formation. Chapter 12 mentions the games of snap, old maid and musical chairs and a beauty contest, illustrating the process of 'anticipating what average opinion expects average opinion to be' (CW, VII, 156). Important possible distortions or limitations in the perception and cognition of 'average opinion', and the institutions through which such opinions are processed and refracted, are not considered.

Hicks has made his misgivings in this area clear. Three decades after his first reading of Keynes' major work he reflected in the following terms:

> When I reviewed the *General Theory,* the explicit introduction of expectations was one of the things which I praised; but I have since come to feel that what Keynes gave with one hand, he took away with the other. Expectations do appear in the *General Theory,* but (in the main) they appear as *data;* as autonomous influences that come in from outside, not as elements that are moulded in the course of the process that is being analyzed. Perhaps it is the famous (but now I think rather wicked) chapter on 'Long-term expectations' which is the root of the trouble (Hicks, 1969, 313)

Firms and Financiers

Taken literally, Keynes' theory would seem at first sight to apply to such institutions as the organised investment market where 'average opinion' is communicated more readily to all agents involved. But once matters are complicated by adding other institutions and more complex mechanisms then the general applicability of Keynes' account of expectations-formation is put into doubt. What if, for example, finance is provided through the banks, as well as or instead of through the sale of stock? Unless it is assumed that there is near-perfect financial market competition between the banks and the stock market (and it is not in the spirit of Keynes' work to assume this) then 'average opinion' and 'conventions' in the one will not be the same as in the other.

Some of the implications of this possible divergence are discussed further below. But the example should indicate that the nature and structure of economic institutions is at least as relevant as 'psychology' in the determination of expectations. This is illustrated most graphically with the firm itself. Keynes only partly came to terms with the fact that the Marshallian entrepreneur is a rare, if not extinct, species of capitalist. Thus the agency forming expectations within the firm is rarely a single, commanding individual. In any case, the firm should not be treated as a purely psychological entity. Decisions to invest and to expand the firm's output and employment are taken by a number of individuals in structured social interaction which psychology alone cannot explain.

Of course, 'the end of laissez-faire' and the growth of the large enterprise was recognised by Keynes himself and in the postwar literature on the theory of the firm. But the descriptive idea of the firm as an entrepreneur is still prominent. This is because economists have continued to believe that the firm has a set of consistent objectives which are the subject of rational calculation, or have assumed that the firm performed 'as if' this were the case. In this way the relevant expectations and objectives of a large and complex enterprise are reduced to those of a single individual. In this guise the ghost of the entrepreneur still haunts the economic theory of the firm.

Of course, important advances have been made since Baumol (1959) and Marris (1964) suggested that the firm did not maximise profits, but something else. For example, behavioural theorists such as Cyert and March (1963) reject the very idea that the firm is maximising at all: it is 'satisficing' instead. With Simon (1976) the very notion of rationality receives important qualification and amendment. But with none of these approaches is the ghost of the entrepreneur entirely exorcised; a kind of 'individual' rationality remains.

However, there is an increasing awareness of the importance of the organisation and internal structure of the firm. In some accounts it is no longer treated as a unitary being ('the entrepreneur'), but as a complex system. This innovation is apparent, in various forms, in the work of the behavioural economists and of management systems-theorists (Beer, 1972). Here the firm does not have a single objective. Its agents are motivated in a number of different and often conflicting ways. The enterprise contains a number of functional organisations (production, research, marketing, financing, etc.) which are part of an overall complex structure, but they may not be in harmony with each other. Thompson (1982, 235) has suggested that: 'Instead of conceiving of the enterprise or firm as a relatively homogeneous, organic, functioning *unity* typified by a universal calculating subject ("management")' it should be regarded as 'a heterogeneous, non-unitary, dispersed and fractured *entity* or social agency'.

Furthermore, there are a number of possible types of structured relationship between the management and the workforce of the firm and these are likely to influence productivity and performance in different ways (Kilpatrick and Lawson, 1980; Hodgson, 1982a) and thereby have a feedback effect on the motivations, objectives and expectations of management. Class conflict within the enterprise is likely to have a crucial effect on expectations and performance.

Consequently, the idea that the performance of the firm relates to a single set of individual expectations can no longer be readily accepted. This does not mean, however, that expectations and objectives within the firm can be disregarded. But these too are dispersed and non-unitary within the firm; their formation reflecting the structure and routine of the institution itself. We have left the unitary entrepreneur, pondering and acting in a uncertain world of atomistic individuals, a long way behind.

Similar considerations apply to the financier and financial institutions, although structures and motivations will be different. To some extent an earlier work by Thompson is relevant here. He notes that the gearing ratio of fixed interest capital to risk capital is over five times greater in Japan than in the UK. Thus the acceptance of risky investment projects by Japanese financial institutions is much greater. Is it 'psychologistic attitudes to "risk" which are supposed to underlie the determination of the most appropriate level of gearing for any company in given circumstances'? Given Keynes' predilection for psychological formulations, one would suspect that he would have sought an explanation largely in these terms. In contrast, Thompson answers in the following manner: 'In fact, it is precisely the structural relationships between the financial and industrial sector which "enables" a much higher level of gearing to be acceptable, not some psychologistic aversion or otherwise to risk.' (Thompson, 1977, 268)

Psychological issues cannot be entirely excluded from any complete explanation. But it is important, in contrast to a tendency in Keynes' work, to put adequate stress on the institutional frameworks which both influence and constrain economic action in the real world. Especially with international and inter-institutional comparisons of economic behaviour, the influence of structure and routine is much more plausible as an explanation than differences in individual psychology. As institutions and habitual practices are diverse, both between and within countries, then so too will divergences of expectations and objectives between economic agents be likely.

It is important to emphasise that the existence of non-unitary structures and institutions does not simply mean that expectations have to be related to a multiplicity of economic agents. It also means that the formation of expectations is affected by institutions and structures themselves. The very perceptions of economic agents are moulded by institutions, culture and routine.

It is not the intention here to propose a kind of 'structural determinism' in which the ideas and actions of economic agents are completely determined by the appropriate structures and institutions. Proper allowance should be made for insight, will, flair, accident, etc. A deterministic view is unacceptable. But so too is an outlook which assumes that the firm or the financial institution can be equated with a single subject, especially one that functions largely on the basis of rational calculation. Still inadequate is the view which recognises the plurality of agents within the institution, but sees the whole merely as the sum of its individual parts: an example of the 'fallacy of composition'. Neither conception appreciates the role of the structure or institution itself.

The point being stressed here is that culture, habits and institutions colour perception and judgement and play a very important part in the formation of expectations. In turn, they help to explain the persistence of apparently 'irrational' expectations which do not appear to be based on a sound assessment of existing information, or of divergent expectations between agents who may be placed in a different institutional setting. Whilst recognising supplementary (largely indeterminate) influences in the process of expectations-formation, expectations are not here treated as exogenous, as they are in the work of Keynes.

An alternative, endogenous treatment of expectations is, of course, found in the work of the 'rational expectations' school. This is discussed below. A further point to be made here, however, is that whilst the importance of institutions is a major theme of this essay, it is beyond its scope to discuss the ways in which organisations and routines are themselves formed, or how they may change. The determination of expectations may have been largely 'brought in' to the system by this treatment of institutions, but the chain of causality has only been hauled in by one (important) link. The processes of the formation and evolution of the institutions themselves still remain exogenous. To move the chain still further would require painstaking historical and comparative study which cannot be commenced here. It is a serious omission, but its recognition is a vital preliminary step towards its eventual rectification. In any case, what is urgently required to some extent already exists in a few of the more robust achievements of economic history and case study.[2]

Keynes' Rationalist Conception of Action

It has been argued above that Keynes' theory involves the assumption that the actions of economic agents are, as far as possible, governed by reason and calculation. His important qualification of this principle was the addition of the element of uncertainty about the future, which in many circumstances made rational calculation impossible. Despite this qualification, a rationalist conception of action remains. Reason and calculation are highlighted, to the neglect of the effects on action of institutional structure and routine.

These shortcomings are even more obvious, if not quintessential, in the work of the neoclassical school. Other writers have suggested ways in which Keynes remained ensnared in this paradigm (e.g. Robinson, 1971) but the common notion of the rational economic agent has not come under a great deal of scrutiny. Apart from the institutionalist school, few economists have questioned it. Shortly after the turn of the century Veblen (1909) had developed a critique of the view of human conduct 'as a rational response to the exigencies of the situation in which mankind is placed'. His follower, Mitchell (1937, 177) wrote:

> In the social sciences we are suffering from a curious mental derangement. We have become aware that the orthodox doctrines of economics, politics and law rest upon a tacit assumption that man's behaviour is dominated by rational calculation. We have learned further that this is an assumption contrary to fact. But we find it hard to avoid the old mistake, not to speak of using the new knowledge.

Economists still find it hard to avoid the 'old mistake', even if they have realised that the rationalist assumption is contrary to fact. But if we then turn to allegedly less regal social sciences, there are more consistent efforts to avoid the pitfalls of rationalism. Sociologists have long insisted that the parameters of human rationality are partly determined by culture and social structures.[3] Political scientists have long realised that the rational action paradigm is extremely limited, largely because it pays insufficient attention to the cognitive and other effects of organisations and routine processes.[4] But a combination of classic liberal ideology (reducing social behaviour to the choosing individual) and a voluminous neoclassical formalism (diverting attention from methodology and basic assumptions to mathematical manipulation) has long pulled the wool over economists' eyes. Keynes too was never led to challenge the rationalist conception.

It is important to note that the orthodox economists' belief that human action is based on rational calculation is allied to empiricist assumptions about the perception and cognition of the real world data upon which such calculations are based. There is a notion of 'evidence' out there, which can be appraised independently of concepts and theories, and which is the substance of individual processes of rational decision-making.

A similar methodological combination of empiricism with a rationalist conception of action is found in the work of Keynes. Arguably, he had strong empiricist leanings, albeit of a sort more sophisticated than those found in the writings of many other economists. Empiricist interpretations can be made of several passages from his earlier work *A Treatise on Probability*. For example:

> We start from things, of various classes, with which we have, what I choose to call without reference to other uses of the term, *direct acquaintance*. Acquaintance with such things does not in itself constitute knowledge, although knowledge arises out of acquaintance with them. The most important classes of things with which we have direct acquaintance are our own sensations, which we may be said to *experience*, the ideas or meanings, about which we have thoughts and which we may be said to *understand*, the facts or characteristics or relations of sense-data or meanings, which we may be said to *perceive*; — experience, understanding, and perception being three forms of direct acquaintance. (CW, VIII, 12; Keynes' emphasis)

The above passage supports the allegation of empiricism in various ways, such as its assumption that sense-data carry meaning for the subject, without any mention of the language, the symbolic order, or the conceptual framework through which they are perceived. The term 'direct acquaintance', although defined with some caution, is itself grounds for suspicion.[5]

In the same work Keynes criticises the 'Empiricist School', but only for their alleged assumption that 'the data of experience' are sufficient to derive 'judgements of probability without the aid either of intuition or of some further *a priori* principle.' (CW, VIII, 94) Such an assumption would be invalid. But it is made only by the most extreme and vulgar of empiricists, and not by other empiricist philosophers. Furthermore, contrary to Keynes' implication, 'the data of experience', even with the addition of appropriate intuition and *a priori* principles, are *not* sufficient. A conceptual or symbolic framework is required as well, otherwise cognition of the sense-data is not possible.

There is a third and related element in Keynes' methodology which should be mentioned here. His combination of a rationalist view of human action with an empiricist epistemology is closely related to an over estimation of the powers of reason and persuasion in affecting and changing economic policy. Moggridge, an editor of Keynes' collected writings, has pointed out: 'Keynes always believed that "a little clear thinking" or "more lucidity" could solve almost any problem . . . reform was achieved by the discussion of intelligent people . . . using the method of persuasion.' (Moggridge, 1976, 38-9) Similar criticisms of Keynes have been made by others with quite different views.[6]

Keynes' faith in reason and persuasion was fractured on two important occasions. The first was at the Versailles negotiations after the First World War (CW, II). The second was the response of the National Government to the deep slump of the early 1930s (CW, IX). These failures to 'face facts' and to bring reason to bear, are frequently discribed by Keynes as 'lunacy' or 'madness'. When clear thinking and persuasion failed to bring about the desired result, it seems that Keynes lost patience and was driven to suggest that his adversaries should be certified as incapable of rational appraisal and action. Keynes' equilibrium position was the optimism of a rationalist. Yet on occasions this was disturbed by frustration and doubt, especially, and to some extent understandably, in times of crisis.

It was late in his life that Keynes began to subject his earlier conception of human action to more critical scrutiny. Writing in 1938 he accused himself and his colleagues of misunderstanding

> human nature, including our own. The rationality which we attributed to it led to a superficiality, not only of judgement, but also of feeling. It was not only that intellectually we were pre-Freudian, but we had lost something which our predecessors had without replacing it. I still suffer incurably from attributing an unreal rationality to other people's feelings and behaviour (and doubtless my own too). . . . I behave as if there really existed some authority or standard to which I can successfully appeal if I shout loud enough — perhaps it is some hereditary vestige of a belief in the efficacy of prayer. (CW, X, 448)

This commendable self-criticism can be directed at some of the ideas in *The General Theory*, as well as at Keynes' own personality. Also, it is appropriate to ask why Keynes' affliction remained 'incurable' even when he himself was aware of it. Perhaps one reason for this can be found in his tendency to view the issue as primarily psychological and philosophical (note the reference to Freud above), rather than in his general under estimation of the force of vested interests and institutions in social life.

Government Action

Another related area where Keynes' work has been open to criticism is his treatment of government and the state. His neglect of the vested interests and influence of institutions led him to assume that government could always be persuaded to act in the common interest, even if more selfish motives such as the pursuit of profit and monetary reward prevailed throughout the rest of society. This rather elitist and somewhat unrealistic view has been criticised from both the New Right and the Marxist left. One does not necessarily have to accept either the view of the New Right that all social actors are entirely self-centred, or to assume, along with some Marxists, that the state exclusively represents the interests of the capitalist class, to see the serious limitations of Keynes' view of government. Like the classic liberals of old, he assumed a hermetic division between the state and civil society. Self-interest prevailed in the latter, but 'philosopher kings' guided by reason ruled the state. Such a view is clearly untenable, and has to be rejected.

In an early, perceptive and since neglected review of *The General Theory,* written from the point of view of a Labour Party socialist, Rowse criticised Keynes' trust in the potency of ideas and reason. Rowse went on to argue that in the political sphere 'it is the control of power . . . that matters; it is not what a party says or thinks that indicates what it will do: that depends almost entirely upon what it *is*, what is its social basis, what are the implications of its make-up' (Rowse, 1936, 56). From this point he goes on to criticise Keynes' now famous dictum that 'the power of vested interests is vastly exaggerated compared with the gradual encroachment of ideas' (CW, VII, 383). Rowse argues instead that

> ideas of action and policy do not operate *in vacuo;* they have to work in a field which is made up of pre-existing interests, group-interests and self-interests, economic, political, social and so on . . . But what makes these ideas effective in and for society, is, apart from their own internal tests, (coherence, clarity, consistency, etc.), the body of interests they express or elicit, themselves acting as the medium in which those interests communicate and struggle against each other. (Rowse, 1936, 60-1)

Rowse's background as a historian leads him to recognise and emphasise social relations, power and vested interests in economic behaviour. The 'rationalist fallacy' in Keynes' work led him not only to give an individualistic and inadequate picture of the process of expectations-formation in finance and industry. It also sustained a naive optimism concerning the influence of reason and persuasion on government policy. Both stem from the assumptions that behind the fog of uncertainty the facts are unambiguous and readily available, and that the overwhelming majority of political and economic agents are largely rational and calculating in response to the available information. Problems of divergent interpretations of given facts, of 'cognitive dissonance', of highly parcellised information, and the blind inertia of institutions, including the firm and the government department, are pushed to one side. Persuasion and reason were potentially supreme, Keynes thought, not only within the world, but in regard to theories about the world, including his own. The powers of vested interests and government could be tamed and controlled by reason.

It is suggested in this chapter that Keynes' empiricist epistemology, his rationalist conception of action and his faith in persuasion are connected in the following manner:

(a) From *A Treatise on Probability* to *The General Theory* there is an empiricist assumption of a more or less direct relationship between sense-data and the perception of 'facts' about the outside world.

(b) This directly-appraised factual knowledge is the substance of calculation and reason by economic agents, giving a common foundation for the formation of the 'convention' and 'average opinion'.

(c) Keynes' distinctive innovation is to recognise that rational calculation, whilst remaining central to individual action, is severely limited by the existence of uncertainty about the future. If uncertainty were to be removed (which can never happen completely) then the formation of expectations would be an objective and rational process, based on empirically given facts about the world.

(d) His faith in persuasion arises in areas where uncertainty is not apparent. Reason, and objective assessment of the evidence, would then lead intelligent people to reach shared conclusions about economic theory and policy, beyond the sway of mere intuition or personal whim.

(e) The power of reason applies to entrepreneurs in the sense that they will tend to form and conform to an 'average opinion' of the state of the economy on the basis of commonly-appraised facts.

(f) The power of reason and persuasion applies to the state for similar reasons and due to the assumption that narrow, and possibly conflicting, self or vested interests do not prevail in this arena.

Austrian and Rational Expectations Alternatives

It is neither necessary nor possible to give a full survey of the main approaches to expectations theory. However, two important alternatives to the work of Keynes are sketched in outline here, for they help to clarify the issues involved.

The Rational Expectations Hypothesis

The rational expectations hypothesis is frequently described by its proponents as being the assumption that economic agents make the best use of all the information they have. This 'weak' version of the hypothesis, as Gomes (1982) and others have pointed out, does not tell us very much. A wide variety of 'best' uses of information is conceivable for different agents. As we know from experience, much perplexing or ambiguous information may be best ignored, and the nature of a 'mistake', systematic or otherwise, is a matter of great potential controversy. In practice, advocates of 'rational expectations' follow Lucas (1972) and assume that the expectations of economic agents are formed on the basis of the complete economic model that is being proposed. It is this 'strong' version of the hypothesis that concerns us here.

Behind the 'strong' rational expectations hypothesis there are a number of assumptions. Consider the following:

(a) Tobin (1980), Begg (1982) and Wible (1982-3) have drawn attention to the almost universal assumption of market clearing in rational expectations models. Thus it is assumed what many of the theorists set out to demonstrate — that markets 'work' and that government intervention is not required.

(b) The idea of 'rational', optimising behaviour is usually explicit. Along with most neoclassical theorists, it is assumed that agents are optimising exclusively for their own gain (or that of their household), without even a tinge of autonomous altruism.

(c) As Buiter (1980), Handa (1982) and others have made clear, it is assumed that economic agents are virtually omniscient, in that they are assumed to know the basic elements of the 'objective underlying model' of the economy (which is usually presumed to be a neoclassical and monetarist one). Even in less cavalier versions of the hypothesis it is assumed that all economic agents are aware of, and implicitly agreed upon, the essential, 'reduced form' of the model.

Each one of these assumptions is open to doubt. It has been argued by Marx (1969, 501-5), Keynes, and Keynesians of all varieties (e.g. Leijonhufvud, 1968), that markets will not necessarily clear in a monetary economy. In an uncertain world people may wish to hold on to money, creating an excess demand for that commodity, and a corresponding glut of unsold non-money commodities. As Keynes emphasised in *The General Theory,* this excess demand will not in general lead to greater output and employment to satisfy that demand.

However, there is some common ground between Keynes' views and assumptions (b) and (c). As we have seen, the idea of the rational agent is central to his work. The key difference is that for Keynes, rational, calculating action is severely limited by considerable uncertainty regarding the future. Thus Keynes does not regard economic agents as 'optimisers' in the strict neoclassical, or 'substantive' (Simon, 1976), sense. Thus after some common concessions to the rationalist conception there is a significant divergence between Keynes and the rational expectations theorists.

Recent work has underlined the significance of introducing time and uncertainty in rational choice models. Simon (1976) echoes Keynes by arguing that 'rules of thumb' or 'heuristics' are appropriate with uncertainty and limited information. Behavioural experiments indicate that people do not make full use of all the information that is available, and they react to new information often by making only small changes in their routine. As Garner (1982) points out, this evidence contradicts the rational expectations hypothesis and is more in tune with the work of Keynes and some of his followers, such as Shackle. Davidson (1982-3) has argued that agents who wish to avoid making persistent errors through real time will *not* use all the information that is available to them. Bausor (1983) rejects rational expectations thinking after consideration of the epistemics of time. True uncertainty about the future in the sense of Keynes, rather than mere risk to which a calculable probability can be attributed, is not compatible with the rational expectations hypothesis.

Turning to assumption (c), the problem of uncertainty and limited information is still relevant. Shiller (1978) and others have argued that, contrary to the rational expectations theorists, most individuals do not have sufficient knowledge to form coherent economic models of the real world. Keynes' work contradicts (c) in the sense that he clearly believed that the economic system can work in ways which are counter to intuition and popular assumption. In particular, some recognition is given to the 'fallacy of composition'; the whole does not always correspond to the sum of the parts. Keynes sees relationships in macroeconomics which can be the reverse of those to which they correspond at the microeconomic level. Examples include the 'paradox of saving' (CW, VII, 358-71) and Keynes' (rather elliptical) suggestion that an inverse relationship between wages and employment 'for particular industries' does not apply 'to industry as a whole unless . . . aggregate effective demand is fixed.' (CW, VII, 259) Rational expectations theorists and many neoclassical economists fail to see the 'fallacy of composition' and assume that microeconomic relationships pertain automatically to the entire system. Common sense in one becomes 'sound economics' in the other.

However, in at least two ways, Keynes makes unwitting concessions to assumption (c). His empiricist epistemology has parallels in rational expectations theory, where great stress is put on the process of 'learning' the correct economic model simply through the acquisition of empirical information. 'Both Keynes and the [rational expectations] exponents see "true" knowledge as that which can be inductively assured and probable knowledge as that which can be confirmed by utilizing an inductive probability logic of some kind' (Rutherford, 1984, 383).

With his over estimation of the powers of reason and persuasion, Keynes suggests that there is an objective economic model which can be reached by clear thinking and successfully proselytised to others. If he did not hold this view then it would be impossible to persuade people as to the 'true' relationship between the economic variables. Thus, to a limited extent, Keynes shares the 'self-confidence' of the rational expectations theorists who believe that with sufficient reason and empirical research we can construct a 'true' and almost universally accepted model of the economic system.

A crucial weakness of *The General Theory* in comparison with the rational expectations hypothesis is Keynes' treatment of long-term expectations as exogenous to the model. In fact, his theory divides the economic world into two parts; determinate relationships between investment, output, employment, income, saving, etc., on the one hand, and indeterminate long-term expectations, governed by uncertainty, on the other. Keynes constructs a model which is part determinate, part indeterminate. As Shackle puts it:

> The *General Theory of Employment, Interest and Money* proceeds in terms of functions, and regards variables as in some sense 'dependent' on each other. But this dependence of many variables upon each other, in a web of mutual determination, is vain for the defence of the traditional standpoint. For *one* variable is left unchained. Investment . . . is at the mercy, not of the other variables, firmly clasping its shoulder in a function-grip, but of the ever-dissolving and re-appearing will-o-the-wisp of expectation . . . Investment is the maverick variable not fully harnessed into the team. (Shackle, 1972, 233)

For at least two decades after World War II, the very treatment of expectations and investment as the undetermined variables in the Keynesian system created the theoretical possibility of constructive government intervention, and prevented the resurgence of the 'self-adjusting' ideas of laissez-faire. However, since Shackle's words above were written the popularity of Keynesianism has been on the wane. Eventually, Keynes' failure to consider the processes through which expectations were actually formed and investment determined, became a weakness rather than a strength. Rational expectations theorists, alarmed by the apparent schizophrenia in the Keynesian system, bridged the division by ignoring real uncertainty and hauling expectations into the determinate camp, possibly with the addition of an element of probabalistic variation or risk. With this closed and complete model, the rational expectations theorists stormed through the gap in the Keynesian system, claiming to have an adequate theory to explain expectations where Keynes did not.

It has become typical of rational expectations theorists to associate Keynes with the adaptive expectations hypothesis, which was prominent in postwar macroeconomic modelling before the rational expectations 'revolution'. However, as Lawson (1981) has shown, the adaptive expectations hypothesis is not consistent with the work of Keynes himself, who argued that 'it is in the nature of long-term expectations that they cannot be checked at short intervals in the light of realised results.' (CW, VII, 51) This shows that Keynes' long-term expectations are *not* adaptive, but it fails to explain how such expectations *are* formed. The gap is not filled in Keynes' work, and it is this void which has now made the Keynesian system vulnerable; when in the past the same gap served to vindicate the Keynesian policy position.

'Austrian' Subjectivism

Keynes split the theoretical system into two parts, one determined, the other indeterminate. Rational expectations theorists attempt to construct a system which, apart from random shocks, is completely determined. The approach of the 'Austrian School' differs profoundly from both. The system is dis-aggregated and regarded as the sum of its atomised, individual parts, bonded by the regular communication of individual information through the market mechanism. For post-Keynesians the Austrian approach is not without its insights, particularly in its critique of the concept of economic equilibrium and of general equilibrium analysis, and its stress on the importance of information and knowledge in the economic system (e.g. Hayek, 1948). However, despite widespread misconception, it should be stressed that it is very different from the rational expectations framework, within which the notion of equilibrium is supreme.

A hallmark of the Austrian approach is its 'methodological individualism': its adoption of the purposeful, subjective individual as the theoretical building block. Given that we do not know the preferences of other individuals, and other relevant information is parcellised in the system, perceptions and expectations are regarded as being fundamentally subjective and individual in character. Thus there is an important difference here from the views of both of Keynes and the rational expectations theorists. Expectations are divergent *from individual to individual*. They are not generated according to a common model (as with the rational expectations hypothesis) nor a stable, social 'convention' (as in the work of Keynes).

Furthermore, contrary to Keynes' views on persuasion, and the rational expectations theorists' conception of a determined, objective model of the economy, some Austrian economists regard concept-formation as partially subjective in character; economic agents 'create' the reality in which they operate (Hayek, 1955). There is a strong anti-empiricist quality to Austrian theory, with its 'serious reservations about the general validity and importance of a good deal of the empirical work being carried on in the economics profession today' (Kirzner, 1976, 40). This is in clear contrast to the extensive use of econometrics by the rational expectations theorists in recent years.

In the rational expectations hypotheses it is the unalterable objectivity of the expectations-forming process which, in their view, helps to make economic intervention by government counter-productive. In the Austrian School it is the subjectivity and indeterminacy of perceptions and expectations which makes economic intervention by any 'collective' institution pointless and ineffective. They regard the market as the only institution which can coordinate the decisions based on the parcellised knowledge of individuals.

However, some serious deficiences in the Austrian position undermine their case. The first is their treatment of key economic categories such as value and property. These cannot be constructed simply in subjective and individual terms (Hodgson, 1982b, 1984). Property, for example, is not simply a relationship between a person and an object, it is also a relationship between persons, maintained in law by the state, and expressed in socially recognised 'rights' to ownership. Hence there is an objective dimension to economic concepts, despite the parcellisation of knowledge.

Secondly, whilst the Austrian argument that it is impossible to centralise all information is valid, it is wrong to assume that all knowledge is individual in character. Some information (often information about the location of other information) is necessarily centralised and institutionalised (e.g. in a telephone directory). It is doubtful that the market can provide an effective signalling device for all information and all activities in a complex economic system (Kornai, 1971).

The third deficiency concerns the Austrian treatment of the firm and the sphere of production. A stylised picture of 'the entrepreneur' is present throughout the analysis. As in the work of Keynes, this enables the Austrian School to put great emphasis on entrepreneurial expectations. Similarly, little attention is given to the nature and functions of the large and complex firm. The expectations of non-entrepreneurial agents within production are not considered as of great importance: the active agent is not the worker but the entrepreneur. As with Keynes, the 'road to freedom' bypasses the shop floor. There is silence about the real processes of production. This error is compounded in the work of Hayek (1955) who chooses to relegate the concept of the 'division of labour' in favour of the 'division of knowledge'.

Fourthly, as Carvalho (1983-4) points out, neither the Austrian School nor its derivatives can explain the existence of regularity and order in economic life. The Austrians

take the 'freedom' of the agent to its ultimate consequences. The individual mind is the ultimate source of all action and this makes the future completely unpredictable. . . . If, however, there is no order beyond the individual, decision is empty and powerless. The future then cannot be 'created' except as a result of accidental interactions of otherwise unrelated individuals. Shackle's approach to some extent shares this limitation of the Austrian approach; it over-emphasises the freedom of the agent and under-estimates the influence of conditions other than his own imagination. In this context, orderliness becomes an external necessity or constraint, something that cannot be explained within Shackle's theory. (Carvalho, 1983-4, 270)

In Keynes' theory the sphere of indeterminacy corresponds to the process of investment. In the Austrian scheme indeterminacy governs all market relations. In the intersection of the two lies the common ground. Shackle (1972, 1974) is the most important explorer of this intellectual territory, attempting a synthesis of the work of Keynes with that of the Austrian School. But to this synthesis the above objections still remain.

There have been recent, illuminating, developments following Shackle in his synthesis of Keynes' work with some aspects of the Austrian School, and in some cases with that of the behaviourists as well (Loasby, 1976; Earl, 1983). These choice-theoretic approaches are still largely future-orientated, emphasising the effects of uncertainty about the future on current imagination and choice. The past is a bygone. Its marks on human behaviour, transmitted through institutions, are unexplained. Instead, social behaviour is explained ahistorically on the basis of the datum of individual psychology.

Such individualistic and psychologistic conceptions pay insufficient attention to the work of sociologists and others, who have argued at great length that through social routine and the medium of institutions the past has a tremendous effect, not only on the constraints of choice and action, but on perception and reason itself. This point was made, with some poetic exaggeration, by Duesenberry (1960) when he suggested that economics is all about why people make choices, while sociology is all about why they do not have any choices to make. The one-sidedness that is present in both disciplines should be superceded.

Without the insertion of adequate defences against methodological individualism, Keynes' theory of expectations is liable to further decomposition into Austrian, atomistic terms. This is especially true because Keynes sets out this theory of expectations with frequent reference to psychology. To be fair, this latter defect is typical of mainstream economics as a whole, and it is not confined to Keynes. (See Boland, 1982, 28-43). However, this does not prevent an effective takeover of Keynesian expectations theory by the more consistent individualism of the Austrian School, especially since the latter provides an alternative to the mechanical determinism of much of neoclassical economics.

In addition there are insufficient defences against an Austrian critique of the role of persuasion in proselytising a consensus view of the world. If it is accepted that a great amount of information must remain decentralised, and for that reason, at least, conceptions of the world are likely to vary from person to person, then persuasion will no longer be paramount. Furthermore, expectations of economic agents, even with similar information, can diverge, making government manipulation of 'the convention' or 'average opinion' concerning the future more difficult than Keynes would admit.

Lessons for Post-Keynesian Theory and Policy

On the grounds of scientific improvement, as well as in self-defence, a number of modifications are necessary to the Keynesian theory of expectations and investment. These are related, in the main, to giving greater weight to the role of institutions in the economic system. An alternative to Austrian subjectivism, and to the uniformity of expectations-formation with the rational expectations hypothesis, is to use the building block of the social institution rather than the individual.

In some ways the two rival approaches, of the rational expectations theorists and the Austrian School, are more consistent than that of Keynes. The first erects a kind of holistic determinism, the second the indeterminacy of a mass of colliding individuals. In comparison, Keynes' uneasy juxtaposition of the determinism of his post-Marshallian model of the economy with the indeterminacy of expectations is unlikely to endure. For its apparent inconsistency on these crucial issues it is likely to be steadily eroded by Austrians and rational expectations theorists from both sides.

The argument in this chapter is that the ability of Keynesian theory to survive may well depend on its ability to abandon its individualistic and psychologistic precepts, and incorporate a theory of expectations based on a functional and historical study of political and economic institutions. Such an alternative framework for Keynesianism is not yet worked out in detail, although important elements are already present in the work of several Keynesians. It is far beyond the scope of this paper to attempt to complete such a massive task, but a few notes and suggestions for further inquiry follow.

Institutions and Social Relations

One of the most forceful critics of the individualistic standpoint was Marx. In his analysis, society cannot be broken down simply into its individual elements: 'Society does not consist of individuals, but expresses the sum of interrelations, the relations within which these individuals stand.' (Marx, 1973, 265) It is a system, comprising a set of social structures. There is no fallacy of composition here. Following Hegel, the whole is regarded as being greater than the sum of its parts. On close inspection, Marx's work implies a critique of what is now called 'methodological individualism'. A more recent refutation is provided by Lukes (1968).

Marx's economic theory breaks away from individualism, partly through an insistence that productive activity in a society necessarily involves social relations between persons as well as a relationship with nature:

> In production, men not only act on nature but on one another. . . . In order to produce, they enter into definite connections and relations with one another and only within these social connections and relations does their action on nature, does production, take place. (Marx and Engels, 1977, 211)

It is through an understanding of institutions and social relations that the weight of the past on current and purposeful activity, and on expectations of the future, is recognised. Action and expectation are formed in a social context. Recognition of the weight of the past on current action does not rule out the possibility of 'free' choice and purpose. In the words of Marx: 'Men make their own history, but they do not make it just as they please; they do not make it under circumstances chosen by themselves, but under circumstances directly encountered, given and transmitted from the past.' (Marx and Engels, 1979, 103)

However, Marx's work, whilst being relevant, is not adequate for our purposes. It has to be recognised that in Marx's theory there is an underestimation of the importance of knowledge, the consequences of uncertainty, the variability of expectations, and even the social weight of traditional institutions such as parliament, or the family. (For a discussion of some of these points see Hodgson, 1984.) But it is Marx's lead in developing a systems approach that has to be followed, even if his account is faulty in some respects.

Boland (1979) adds an important critical discussion of the treatment of institutions in orthodox economic theory. He points out that in neoclassical theory institutions are regarded as tacit or given constraints, under which the rational, calculating individual maximises utility. The problem with this, as Lazonick (1981) and Boland suggest, is that it puts to one side the problem of explaining the evolution of institutions themselves, and fails to incorporate the behaviour of those that may act to change other institutions and shift constraints, rather than taking them as given. The effects of the past are treated principally as constraints, but in the present the individual is 'free'. Consequently, the neoclassical paradigm cannot conceive of the present as history.

More specifically, Boland raises the question of the acquisition of the knowledge required for the supposed optimisation to take place. He notes that

the critical issues of the adequacy of the knowledge available to the decision maker and the methodological role of institutions are not independent. The reason is simple. One of the roles that institutions play is to create knowledge and information for the individual decision maker. In particular, institutions provide social knowledge which may be needed for *interaction* with other individual decision makers. (Boland, 1979, 963)

He points out that the equilibrium system and the laws governing trade, taxes and advertising are examples of such knowledge-purveying institutions. Remarkably, an almost identical point was made by Marx when he wrote in his 'chapter on money' in the *Grundrisse:* 'institutions emerge whereby each individual can acquire information about the activity of all others and attempt to adjust his own accordingly, e.g. lists of current prices, rates of exchange, interconnections between those active in commerce through the mails, telegraphs etc.' (Marx, 1973, 161) It is unfortunate that this stress on the importance of institutions in providing information is not sustained through Marx's work. It is a point which is central to the argument of this chapter.

Its relevance to Keynesian economics is immediate. Take, for example, the treatment of wages in Chapter 17 of *The General Theory*. Keynes discusses (CW, VII, 232-7) the 'stickiness' of money wages, noting that if this were not so their fall might disrupt expectations regarding future costs and other related variables. Keynes' main point here has been widely misinterpreted as an assertion that, given the real world as it is, wages happen to be sticky. Thus 'Keynesian economics' is interpreted as being a theory that is applicable to a market economy with unfortunate 'imperfections'. Keynes' *General Theory* is thus rendered a 'special case' of a more general, and therefore more attractive, (neoclassical) theory which allows an unbounded range of variable flexibility in the wage and price mechanisms. The validity of Keynes' approach becomes simply a matter of empirical tests of the real-world inflexibility of wages and prices. Furthermore, even if wage and price rigidity is observed, the policy conclusion could equally be that we should attempt to remove all these 'imperfections' and move towards a 'free' and completely flexible real-world market, rather than adopt Keynesian policies. The 'imperfectionist' version of Keynesianism can easily lead to economic policies far removed from those of Keynes himself.

A much stronger version of Keynesian theory involves the adoption of the 'institutionalist' perspective sketched above. Keynes' point in Chapter 17 could be interpreted in institutionalist terms. Not only are institutions necessary to provide information, but also rigidity and routine are to some extent required to reduce uncertainty and to make meaningful decision-making possible. In general, non-market institutions and 'imperfections' play a necessary role in enabling the market system to operate.

Keynes did not reach this conclusion explicitly, and his emphasis is on individual psychology rather than institutions. For example, trade unions are mentioned only once in the chapter on 'Changes in Money-Wages' and three times in *The General Theory* as a whole. However, the treatment of expectations and uncertainty in Keynes' work suggests a possible institutionalist interpretation.

An example of a bridge between institutionalism and Keynesian indeterminacy is found in the work of Richardson (1959, 1960). He argues that the system of perfect competition as envisaged by the textbooks is unworkable. Not only does it not exist: it could not exist. Central to his analysis is a consideration of expectations and information with regard to the investment decision. Richardson argues that if there were no market restrictions, and entrepreneurs had perfect knowledge, then no-one would be willing to invest.

A profit opportunity which is known by and available to everybody is available to nobody in particular. A situation of general profit potential can be tapped by one entrepreneur only if similar action is not intended by too many others; otherwise excess supply and general losses would result. In other words, a general opportunity of this kind will create a reliable profit expectation for a single entrepreneur only if there is some limitation upon the competitive supply to be expected from other producers. (1959, 233-4)

This turns the conventional, neoclassical view inside out. Richardson argues that' "perfect knowledge" . . . would have been no use to the members of the system even if they could ever be assumed to possess it . . . the conditions necessary for adequate information are incompatible with perfect competition' (1959, 233). He suggests that producers obtain information about the prospective activities of those to whom they are inter-related in a number of possible ways. First, there is explicit collusion or agreement. Second there is 'implicit collusion: a general understanding that no-one will alter what they are doing'. And third, there are 'frictions', 'imperfections' and 'restraints', which, although they appear to stand in the way of 'free competition', are actually necessary to make the market system function at all.

This third point moves the argument to the stage of accepting the role of institutions in transmitting the necessary information, without actually putting explicit emphasis on it. This slight deficiency in Richardson's account leads Earl to the mistaken interpretation that Richardson is writing mainly about 'imperfections of knowledge' (Earl, 1983, 7) rather than, in addition, social relations of implicit and explicit collusion, and, by implication, institutions *per se*. Earl's highly important and still valuable work falls back onto psychologism, after reaching the very point of its transcendence.

In Kregel (1980) more adequate emphasis is given to the epistemic role of institutions. Because of uncertainty regarding the future:

the information required for rational decision-making does not exist; the market mechanism cannot provide it. But, just as nature abhors a vacuum, the economic system abhors uncertainty. The system reacts to the absence of the information the market cannot provide by creating uncertainty-reducing institutions: wage contracts, debt contracts, supply agreements, administered prices, trading agreements. Since all are meant to reduce uncertainty over time, it is natural that their value be denominated in the unit whose value is most stable over time — money — or . . . in terms of a durable whose own rate of return declines least rapidly with an increase in demand. (Kregel, 1980, 46)

Kregel's presentation of the argument has strong functionalist over-
tones (e.g. 'the system reacts . . . by creating . . . '), but his point is
still well made and it can survive their removal. Clearly, it is an
institutionalist extension of the discussion of wages and money in
Chapter 17 of *The General Theory*, reaching the strong conclusion that
without rigidities and institutional constraints the market system could
not operate.

It would be wrong to conceive of these rigidities as simply resulting
from high 'transactions costs', in the tradition of Williamson (1975)
and others. The 'transactions costs' approach implies that the system
would function as a more or less 'pure' market if the 'transaction costs'
were sufficiently low. The contention here, however, is that there is no
way that the 'imperfections' and 'transactions costs' can be conceived
in theory or measured in practice. There is no effective choice between
a 'pure' and 'impure' market system. Thus there are no opportunities
forgone, and therefore no 'costs'.

To summarise, the observed (partial) rigidity of wages and prices
should not be treated in economic theory as a restrictive assumption to
be imposed upon a 'more general' model. Rigidities are not a 'special
case'. These so-called 'imperfections' help to impose coherence and
order on the market system. Markets function coherently *because of*
these imperfections, not *despite them* as mainstream theorists
presume.

It should now be sufficiently clear that there exists a foundation for an
extension of post-Keynesian theory along institutionalist lines. Unfortunately, this alternative approach is underdeveloped. Further progress
is likely to involve the use of the work of a wide range of theorists: from
that of Marx and some later Marxists, through Veblen, Polanyi (1944)
and other institutionalists in the American tradition, and Schumpeter
(1943), to modern post-Keynesians. We do not have to start from
scratch, but a start has to be made. For without major renovation and
extension, particularly in the area of expectations-formation, the
Keynesian theoretical system is likely to continue to decline in
terms of credibility.

Directions for Economic Policy

A number of policy directions may be inferred, in general terms rather
than in detail, from the argument in this chapter. The first main point to
note is that, paradoxically, the idea of a strict non-interventionist
economic policy is misconceived. The market functions through a web
of institutions. From the legal, and other, points of view these are

inevitably entwined with government and the state. As in the Britain of the nineteenth century (see Polanyi, 1944), and under contemporary Western governments of the 'laissez-faire' New Right, the attempt to create a 'free' market system involves continuous juridical, political and institutional meddling by the state. Note, for example, the cases of wage and working-day legislation in the nineteenth century, and the frequent amendments to trade union law and corporate competition policy in Britain under the government of Margaret Thatcher in the 1980s.

Consequently, the main argument is not really between intervention and non-intervention, but which type of intervention is to be carried out, and for which ends. Intervention is necessarily institutional in character. To some extent this contrasts with the kind of Keynesian perspective which prevailed for three decades after World War II, and which focused impractically and almost exclusively on overall, aggregate measures (e.g. taxes, public expenditure, economic growth) to the neglect of structural and institutional considerations.

Demand management is necessary but not sufficient. In addition, both the nature and result of adjustments to effective demand are never uniform. Given that institutions that are varied in structure and composition encourage divergent expectations and practices throughout the economy, institutional intervention at both the 'macro' and 'micro' level is required. This could include the radical restructuring of the institutions involved. It is far beyond the scope of this chapter to discuss this in detail, but structural changes in the banking system and industrial organisation all have to be considered. Structural and institutional intervention on this scale is likely to take place in the context of national planning which is partly indicative, partly regulatory, and partly directive in character. The task is to apply the wide literature on, and experience of, planning, industrial organisation, financial structures, and the management of production in a way that is appropriate for economic and social objectives. Commitment to a sole regulator such as 'the market', or 'national planning' or 'effective demand' is neither feasible nor effective. The complexity and variety within the expectations-formation process requires a multiplicity of regulatory mechanisms. As Scitovsky argues, capitalist economies are 'too fragmented for the broad-gauged, diffused action of Keynesian policies to do much good' (Scitovsky, 1980).

These are broad outlines, nothing more. But the arguments in this chapter suggest that this is the direction in which post-Keynesian policy thinking has to proceed. However, at the theoretical level, such an institutionalist approach requires interdisciplinary study which is neither fashionable nor encouraged by the structure of academia. It requires the lateral thinking and sweep of mind that is often frowned upon by the burrowing, mole-like specialists. The concrete application of institutionalist, post-Keynesian theory to practical problems requires detailed and painstaking study of institutions and their development. This may be a formidable and arduous task, often lacking in glamour for economists. But for those concerned about the retreat of Keynesian theory in the face of advancing laissez-faire ideas, it may well prove to be the only relevant radical alternative.

Summary of Main Conclusions

(a) Underlying Keynes' account of expectations in *The General Theory* is a psychologistic view of social behaviour, combined with a rationalist conception of action that is qualified by uncertainty about the future.

(b) His theory divides the economy into two halves, first a (largely Marshallian and deterministic) analysis of functional relationships between key economic variables, and second a non-deterministic account of expectations-formation and investment.

(c) Keynes assumes that state personnel act under the guidance of reason and persuasion, and, unlike the population at large, are not motivated by their own vested interests. This enables him to suggest economic policies involving state manipulation of the 'convention' that governs the expectations of 'the entrepreneur'.

(d) Resolution of the inconsistencies in (b) and (c) above, without the rejection of the psychologistic or rationalist conceptions, would require something like a rational expectations approach, or the adoption of the ultra-individualism of the Austrian School. Without attention to the issues involved in (a), Keynesian economics is likely to become increasingly vulnerable to attack from these adversaries.

(e) A way out of these problems for Keynesians is to adopt a far more 'institutionalist' approach, and to reject psychologistic or rationalist conceptions of human action. Institutions are not to be regarded merely as constraints, but as having epistemic consequences for economic actors, including in the formation of their expectations.

(f) One consequence of such a transformation of Keynesian economics would have to be a recognition of the likelihood of divergent expectations, based on a non-uniformity of institutional structure and routine. (see also Boltho, 1983; Peel and Metcalfe, 1979).

(g) This systematic divergence leads to the policy conclusion that global demand management is not enough. The Keynesian policy has to be supplemented by intricate institutional intervention, involving the restructuring of industrial and financial institutions, to make their pattern of operation more conducive to the achievement of the desired economic and social goals. These additions are in practice necessary, even in the least radical, 'hands off' versions of Keynesianism.

(h) Neoclassical economists treat market rigidities and imperfections as an unfortunate deviation from the 'ideal type' of the 'perfect' market. On the contrary, an institutionalist-Keynesian perspective regards them as entirely necessary to reduce uncertainty and to make decision-making possible. The 'perfect' market of the neoclassical textbooks is not only unrealistic; it could not function even if it were to exist. The market system functions *because of* its 'imperfections', not *despite them* as mainstream theorists presume.

(i) Thus the treatment of Keynes' work as the assertion of imperfections in the market system not only leads to the possible interpretation of *The General Theory* as a special case, it can easily lead to economic policies opposed to those of Keynes. Instead of government action to compensate for wage rigidities and other 'imperfections' it can lead to the conclusion that what is required is the very removal of those imperfections themselves. Without the institutionalist-Keynesian perspective outlined above, even *The General Theory* is vulnerable to this inversion of its policy conclusions. This is especially a problem with the 'Keynesian' economics of the postwar period, but it is also a matter of concern for the economics of Keynes.

Acknowledgements
I am grateful to Dick Bailey, Daniel Seidman, Brian Snowdon, David Welsh, Jim Tomlinson, Peter Wynarczyck, the editors of this volume, an anonymous referee, and the participants at the *Cambridge Journal of Economics* Keynes Centenary Conference for helpful comments on earlier drafts of this chapter.

Notes
1. Examples of mechanistic economic modelling in the Marxian tradition are well known. From this standpoint some Marxists (e.g. Sutcliffe, 1977, 173) completely exclude expectations as partial determinants of the level of economic activity, because of their allegedly 'subjective' nature. Not only is this view misconceived in its exclusion of expectations; as will be argued below, it is wrong to regard them as purely subjective in character. Sutcliffe sees the Keynesian explanation of booms and slumps, based as it is on expectations, as being 'methodically' equivalent to the sunspots theory of Jevons and worthy of similar disdain. This 'Marxist' zeal for a completely 'objective' (i.e. determinis-

tic) explanation of the workings of the economic system is shared by the rational expectations theorists.

2. Perhaps two of the best recent examples are Dore (1973) and Chandler and Daems (1980).

3. For recent, highly explicit statements in this vein see Giddens (1976) and Hindess (1977).

4. See, for example, the classic article on the political analysis of international conflict by Allison (1969) or the critique of Lukacs by Stedman Jones (1971).

5. Of course, Keynes had contact with Wittgenstein, who was far from being an empiricist. Keynes (CW, IX, 338) wrote of him and his follower Ramsey as reducing formal logic 'more and more to mere dry bones, until finally it seemed to exclude not only all experience, but most of the principles, usually reckoned logical, of reasonable thought'.

6. Hayek reported that Keynes 'was really supremely confident of his powers of persuasion and believed that he could play on public opinion as a virtuoso plays on his instrument'. When Hayek saw Keynes for the last time, in 1946, Keynes explained that if his theories 'should ever become harmful, [Hayek] could be assured that [Keynes] would quickly bring about a change in public opinion' (Hayek, 1972, 103-4).

7. See, for example, Buchanan, Wagner and Burton (1978), and Sweezy's (1946, 303) portrayal of 'Keynes habit of treating the state as a *deus ex machina* to be invoked whenever his human actors, behaving according to the rules of the capitalist game, get themselves in a dilemma from which there is apparently no escape'.

8. This is contrary to the work of Elster (1982) and Roemer (1982) who try to erect a 'Marxist' version of methodological individualism based on game theory. This is faulted, not only by its individualist assumptions (see Lukes, 1968) but also by Shackle's (1972, ch. 36) critique of game theory in individualist terms. In any case, methodological individualism can have little, if anything, to do with Marx.

References

Allison, G. T. (1969) 'Conceptual Models and the Cuban Missile Crisis', *The American Political Science Review, 63,* 689-718

Baumol, W. J. (1959) *Business Behaviour, Value and Growth*, Macmillan, New York

Bausor, R. (1983) 'The Rational-Expectations Hypothesis and the Epistemics of Time', *Cambridge Journal of Economics, 7,* 1-10

Beer, S. (1972) *Brain of the Firm*, Allen Lane, London

Begg, D. K. H. (1982) *The Rational Expectations Revolution in Macroeconomics: Theories and Evidence*, Phillip Allen, Oxford

Boland, L. A. (1979) 'Knowledge and the Role of Institutions in Economic Theory', *Journal of Economic Issues, 13,* 957-72

— — (1982) *The Foundations of Economic Method*, George Allen and Unwin, London

Boltho, A. (1983) 'Is Western Europe Caught in an Expectations Trap?', *Lloyds Bank Review*, April, 1-13

Buchanan, J. M., Wagner, R. E. and Burton, J. (1978) *The Consequences of Mr. Keynes,* Institute of Economic Affairs, London

Buiter, W. H. (1980) 'The Macroeconomics of Dr Pangloss: A Critical Survey of the New Classical Macroeconomics', *The Economic Journal, 90,* 34-50

Carvalho, F. (1983-4) 'On the Concept of Time in Shacklean and Sraffian Economics', *Journal of Post Keynesian Economics, 6,* 265-80

Champernowne, D. G. (1963) 'Expectations and the Links between the Economic Future and the Present', in R. Leckachman (ed.), *Keynes' General Theory: Reports of Three Decades*, Macmillan, London (pub. 1964), 174-202

Chandler, A. D. Jr., and Daems, H., (eds.) (1980) *Managerial Hierarchies: Comparative Perspectives on the Rise of the Modern Industrial Enterprises*, Harvard University Press, Cambridge MA.

Coddington, A. (1983) *Keynesian Economics: The Search for First Principles*, George Allen and Unwin, London

Cyert, R. M. and March, J. G. (1963) *A Behavioral Theory of the Firm*, Prentice-Hall, Englewood Cliffs, N.J.

Davidson, P. (1972) *Money and the Real World*, Macmillan, London

— — (1982-3) 'Rational Expectations: A Fallacious Foundation for Studying Crucial Decision-Making Processes', *Journal of Post Keynesian Economics, 5*, 182-98

Dore, R. (1973) *British Factory — Japanese Factory*, University of California Press, Berkeley and Los Angeles

Duesenberry, J. (1960) Comment on 'An Economic Analysis of Fertility' by G. S. Becker, in *Demographic and Economic Change in Developed Countries*, Universities-National Bureau Conference Series, No. 11, Princeton N. J.

Earl, P. E. (1983) *The Economic Imagination*, Wheatsheaf, Brighton

Elster, J. (1982) 'Marxism, Functionalism and Game Theory: The Case for Methodological Individualism', *Theory and Society, 11*, 453-82

Garner, C. A. (1982) 'Uncertainty, Human Judgement, and Economic Decisions', *Journal of Post Keynesian Economics, 4*, 413-24

Giddens, A. (1976) *New Rules of Sociological Method*, Hutchinson, London

Gomes, G. M. (1982) 'Irrationality of "Rational Expectations"' *Journal of Post Keynesian Economics, 5*, 51-65

Handa, J. (1982) 'Rational Expectations: What Do They Mean? — Another View', *Journal of Post Keynesian Economics, 4*, 558-64

Hayek, F. A. (1948) *Individualism and Economic Order*, University of Chicago Press, Chicago

— — (1955) *The Counter-Revolution in Science*, Free Press, Glencoe Ill.

— — (1972) *A Tiger by the Tail: The Keynesian Legacy of Inflation*, Institute of Economic Affairs, London

Hicks, J. R. (1969) 'Automatists, Hawtreyans and Keynesians', *Journal of Money, Credit and Banking, 1*, 307-17

Hindess, B. (1977) *Philosophy and Methodology in the Social Sciences*, Harvester, Brighton

Hodgson, G. (1982a) 'Theoretical and Policy Implications of Variable Productivity', *Cambridge Journal of Economics, 6*, 213-6

— — (1982b) *Capitalism, Value and Exploitation*, Martin Robertson, Oxford

— — (1984) *The Democratic Economy*, Pelican, Harmondsworth

Keynes, J. M. CW, II, VII, VIII, IX, X, XIV

Kilpatrick, A. and Lawson, T. (1980) 'On the Nature of the Industrial Decline in the UK', *Cambridge Journal of Economics, 4*, 85-102

Kirzner, I. (1976) 'On the Method of Austrian Economics', in E. G. Dolan (ed.), *The Foundations of Modern Austrian Economics,* Sheed and Ward, Kansas City, 40-51

Kornai, J. (1971) *Anti-Equilibrium*, North-Holland, Amsterdam

Kregel, J. A. (1976) 'Economic Methodology in the Face of Uncertainty', *The Economic Journal, 86*, 209-25

— — (1980) 'Markets and Institutions as Features of a Capitalistic Production System', *Journal of Post Keynesian Economics, 3*, 32-48

Lawson, T. (1981) 'Keynesian Model Building and the Rational Expectations Critique', *Cambridge Journal of Economics, 5*, 311-26

Lazonick, W. (1981) 'Factor Costs and the Diffusion of Ring Spinning in Britain Prior to World War I', *Quarterly Journal of Economics*, 89-109

Leijonhufvud, A. (1968) *On Keynesian Economics and the Economics of Keynes*, Oxford University Press, London

Loasby, B. J. (1976) *Choice, Complexity and Ignorance*, Cambridge University Press, Cambridge

Lucas, R. E. (1972) 'Expectations and the Neutrality of Money', *Journal of Economic Theory, 4*, 102-24

Lukes, S. (1968) 'Methodological Individualism Reconsidered', *The British Journal of Sociology, 19*, 119-29: Reprinted in D. Emmet and A. MacIntyre (eds.), *Sociological Theory and Philosophical Analysis*, Macmillan, London, 1970, 76-88

Marris, R. (1964) *The Economic theory of 'Managerial' Capitalism*, Macmillan, London

Marx, K. (1969) *Theories of Surplus Value*, Part II, Lawrence and Wishart, London

— — (1973) *Grundrisse*, Pelican, Harmondsworth

— — (1976) *Capital*, Vol. I, Pelican, Harmondsworth

Marx, K. and Engels, F. (1977) *Karl Marx and Frederick Engels, Collected Works*, Vol. 9, Lawrence and Wishart, London

— — (1979) *Karl Marx and Frederick Engels, Collected Works*, Vol. 11, Lawrence and Wishart, London

Minsky, H. P. (1976) *John Maynard Keynes*, Macmillan, London

Mitchell, W. C. (1937) 'Bentham's Felicific Calculus', in J. Dorfman (ed.), *The Backward Art of Spending Money and Other Essays*, McGraw-Hill, New York

Moggridge, D. E. (1976) *Keynes*, Fontana, London

Peel, D. A. and Metcalfe, J. S. (1979) 'Divergent Expectations and the Dynamic Stability of Some Simple Macro Economic Models', *The Economic Journal, 89*, 789-98

Polanyi, K. (1944) *The Great Transformation*, Rinehart, New York

Richardson, G. B. (1959) 'Equilibrium, Expectations and Information', *The Economic Journal, 69*, 223-37

— — (1960) *Information and Investment*, Oxford University Press, Oxford

Robinson, J. (1971) *Economic Heresies*, Macmillan, London

— — (1973) 'What Has Become of the Keynesian Revolution?' in J. Robinson (ed.) *After Keynes*, Basil Blackwell, Oxford, 1-11

Roemer, J. E. (1982) 'Methodological Individualism and Deductive Marxism', *Theory and Society, 11*, 513-20

Rowse, A. L. (1936) *Mr Keynes and the Labour Movement*, Macmillan, London

Rutherford, M. (1984) 'Rational Expectations and Keynesian Uncertainty: A Critique', *Journal of Post Keynesian Economics, 6*, 377-87

Scitovsky, T. (1980) 'Can Capitalism Survive? — An Old Question in a New Setting', *American Economic Review (Papers and Proceedings), 70*, 1-9

Schumpeter, J. A. (1943) *Capitalism, Socialism and Democracy*, George Allen and Unwin, London

Shackle, G. L. S. (1972) *Epistemics and Economics*, Cambridge University Press, Cambridge

— — (1974) *Keynesian Kaleidics*, Edinburgh Univesity Press, Edinburgh

Shiller, R. J. (1978) 'Rational Expectations and the Dynamic Structure of Macroeconomic Models', *Journal of Monetary Economics, 4*, 1-44

Simon, H. A. (1976) 'From Substantive to Procedural Rationality', in S. Latsis (ed.), *Method and Appraisal in Economics*, Cambridge University Press, Cambridge

Stedman Jones, G. (1971) 'The Marxism of the Early Lukacs: An Evaluation', *New Left Review*, No. 70, November-December

Stohs, M. (1980) '"Uncertainty" in Keynes' *General Theory*: A Rejoinder', *History of Political Economy, 15*, 87-91

Sutcliffe, R. (1977) 'Keynesianism and the Stabilisation of Capitalist Economies', in F.

Green and P. Nore (eds.), *Economics: An Anti-Text*, Macmillan, London, 163-81

Sweezy, P. M. (1946) 'John Maynard Keynes', *Science and Society, 10*, reprinted in R. Lekachman (ed.), *Keynes' General Theory: Reports of Three Decades,* Macmillan, London, 1964, 297-314

Thompson, G. (1977) 'The Relationship Between the Financial and Industrial Sectors in the United Kingdom Economy', *Economy and Society, 6*, 235-83

— — (1982) 'The Firm as a "Dispersed" Social Agency', *Economy and Society, 11*, 233-50

Tobin, J. (1980) 'Are New Classical Models Plausible Enough to Guide Policy?', *Journal of Money, Credit and Banking, 12*, 788-99

Veblen, T. (1909) 'The Limitations of Marginal Utility', *Journal of Political Economy, 17*, 235-45

Wible, J. R. (1982-3) 'The Rational Expectations Tautologies', *Journal of Post Keynesian Economics, 5*, 199-207

Williamson, O. E. (1975) *Markets and Hierarchies: Analysis and Anti-Trust Implications: A Study in the Economics of Internal Organization*, Free Press, New York

3 ANIMAL SPIRITS AND RATIONALITY

Alexander Dow and Sheila Dow

Introduction

The notion that 'animal spirits' govern investment decisions can be viewed as being central to Keynes' theory of aggregate demand and, at the same time, as being its weakest point. An autonomous shift in long-run expectations among entrepreneurs can drive a wedge between effective demand and full employment output, requiring government stabilisation policy if full employment is to be achieved. That shifts in long-run expectations may occur autonomously is, however, regarded by many as cause for concern. If Keynes' theory can neither explain nor predict these shifts, then it appears to be lacking a crucial element.

If individual entrepreneurs are viewed as acting according to reason, i.e. they are rational in the broadest sense of the term, then 'in principle' it may be possible to capture that reasoning in a complete theory of long-run expectations, endogenising animal spirits. Some have advocated that Keynesians attempt to develop Keynes' theory of long-run expectations in this way (Tarshis, 1980, and Kenyon, 1980, for example). Animal spirits would then lose their special status. Coddington (1982) pushes the argument further. If long-run expectations formation by entrepreneurs *cannot* be explained by rational behaviour which can be modelled, he argues, then this must be true for all the expectations of agents in all sectors. But then if all decision-making is subject to the exogenous influence of expectations shifts, economists must retreat into nihilism.

The purpose of this chapter is to re-examine the concept of animal spirits in the light of these charges. The first task is to go back to the origins of the concept of animal spirits in Keynes' early work on probability theory and its development in his theory of entrepreneurial behaviour. This textual analysis allows us to assess Keynes' own views as to the significance of animal spirits as an influence on expectations formation. The third section is devoted to considering why the concept of animal spirits should subsequently have fallen into such disfavour. Our conclusion is that the orthodox critique of animal spirits is the natural outcome of attempting to understand it within the orthodox framework. In particular, the narrow use of the rationality concept employed within the orthodoxy rules out the possibility of the type of indeterminacy implied by animal spirits. Indeterminacy in the formation of expectations does however make sense within the method which Keynes employed. This method is outlined in the fourth section. Indeterminancy still poses problems, particularly for empirical work. But within the Keynesian framework, the solution lies in being alert to a change of mood within an economy, and understanding its significance, rather than in ruling it out of order in academic debate.

Keynes on Uncertainty and Confidence

A textual analysis of Keynes' own writings clarifies his notion of animal spirits, and confirms the importance he attached to confidence factors in determining the level of investment, and so of aggregate demand. Keynes' definition of animal spirits is in his discussion of long-term expectations in Chapter 12 of *The General Theory,* although the ideas on uncertainty and confidence denoted by the term had surfaced much earlier in Keynes' career in his *Treatise on Probability* (CW, VIII).

In *The General Theory* Keynes draws a fundamental distinction between speculation, or the buying and selling of assets (real or financial) in anticipation of changed asset prices, and enterprise, a synonym for new investment in real assets. Keynes asserted:

Even apart from the instability due to speculation, there is the instability due to the characteristic of human nature that a large proportion of our positive activities depend on spontaneous optimism rather than on a mathematical expectation, whether moral or hedonistic or economic. Most, probably, of our decisions to do something positive, the full consequences of which will be drawn out over many days to come, can only be taken as a result of animal spirits — of a spontaneous urge to action rather than inaction, and not as the outcome of a weighted average of quantitative benefits multiplied by quantitative probabilities. Enterprise only pretends to itself to be mainly actuated by the statements in its own prospectus, however candid and sincere. Only a little more than an expedition to the South Pole, is it based on an exact calculation of benefits to come. Thus if the animal spirits are dimmed and the spontaneous optimism falters, leaving us to depend on nothing but a mathematical expectation, enterprise will fade and die; — though fears of loss may have a basis no more reasonable than hopes of profit had before. (CW, VII, 161-2)

The implications of this psychological factor are introduced a few paragraphs later:

> We should not conclude from this that everything depends on waves of irrational psychology. On the contrary, the state of long-term expectation is often steady, and, when it is not, the other factors exert their compensating effects. We are merely reminding ourselves that human decisions affecting the future, whether personal or political or economic, cannot depend on strict mathematical expectation, since the basis for making such calculations does not exist; and that it is our innate urge to activity which makes the wheels go round, our rational selves choosing between the alternatives as best we are able, calculating where we can, but often falling back for our motive on whim or sentiment or chance. (CW, VII, 162-3)

A very few scholars have insisted that Keynes' ideas on uncertainty were central to his vision (Davidson, 1978; Shackle, 1974, 35-45; Minsky, 1975, 64-8). For the most part economists have regarded them as peripheral, as do, for instance, Patinkin and Eatwell in recent reviews (Patinkin, 1982, 61; Eatwell, 1979, 39-41). Though doctrinal matters are not our main concern in this chapter, we contend here, not only that Keynes viewed expectations under uncertainty as vital, but also that entrepreneurs' expectations, a prime determinant of the level of investment, were of particular importance to his theory.

The evidence that Keynes thought animal spirits to be an important part of his contribution comes from his discussion of long-term expectations in *The General Theory,* the emphasis taken in the article (a sort of 'reply to the critics') published in the *Quarterly Journal of Economics* in 1937, and from observations by his contemporary, Bertil Ohlin (Patinkin and Leith, 1977). Furthermore, the criterion adopted by Patinkin (1982) for such doctrinal judgements, that those themes which are important in a scholar's work resurface like themes in an orchestral work, is seen to support the centrality of uncertainty to Keynes.

In *The General Theory* it is obvious that Keynes placed enterprise in an important social role. As Keynes re-drafted the 'pre-first proof index version', little in Chapter 12 changed. However, later versions substituted the term 'enterprise' for 'investment' (CW, XIV, 468). In writing of enterprise Keynes sought to distinguish investment in real assets from the alternative meaning of purchasing financial, or other, liquid assets. (Investment in the latter sense plays an equally important role in the theory of aggregate demand, but is not our concern here.)

The following passage also appeared in the 'pre-first proof index version', and was rearranged and expanded subsequently:

There is much of great importance which can be said, quite independently of the rate of interest, concerning the state of long-run expectation and the methods by which the prospective yield of investment is estimated by the market, as distinct from the methods by which this prospective yield is capitalised or converted into present value. It is a subject to which practical men always pay the closest and most anxious attention under the name of the *state of confidence*. But economists have not analysed it carefully and have been content, as a rule, to treat it in general terms. (CW, XIV, 464-5, emphasis in original)

A comparison of the above with the final version (CW, VII, 148-9) shows little change of sense, and we conclude that clarity in drafting rather than modification of meaning motivated the revision. The earlier version had the virtue in retrospect of emphasising concisely Keynes' opinion that long-run expectations, and the state of confidence they dwelt on, were important both to transactions of a speculative sort and to investment decisions involving real assets, or more precisely in the latter case to assets whose value to the enterprise is given by converting the prospective yield into a present value.

Further evidence of the importance Keynes placed on this matter comes from his article in the *Quarterly Journal of Economics* in 1937, which Joan Robinson (1973, 3) describes as a summing-up of *The General Theory*. Keynes himself presented this article as 'a discussion as to certain definite points where I seem to myself to be most clearly departing from previous theories' (1937, 212). Keynes goes on to discuss at length the economic implications of our having 'only the vaguest idea of any but the most direct consequences of our acts' (1937, 213).

Defending *The General Theory* in this article Keynes asserted with respect to investment:

This does not mean, of course, that the rate of interest is the only fluctuating influence on [the] prices [of capital assets]. Opinions as to their prospective yield are themselves subject to sharp fluctuations, precisely for the reason already given, namely, the flimsiness of the basis of knowledge on which they depend. It is these opinions taken in conjunction with the rate of interest which fix their price. (1937, 217)

It is hard not to conclude that Keynes, in the 1937 article, nailed his colours firmly to the mast.

A final piece of evidence in this brief attempt to demonstrate the central importance of confidence and animal spirits in Keynes' eyes comes from Bertil Ohlin. Writing in 1977, he remarks:

> I now turn to other important aspects of Keynes' theory. In the *General Theory* he emphasises *the uncertainty of the future* and the importance of opinions about the future as a basis for action by businessmen and consumers. When he came to Stockholm in the autumn of 1936 and gave a lecture to our little Political Economy Club he — to our surprise — emphasised the analysis of this aspect of the *General Theory*. His opinion was that its vital importance had been underestimated. (Patinkin and Leith, 1977, 159-60, emphasis in original)

There can be no doubt that Keynes saw his treatment of uncertainty and confidence as central to his new approach.[1] However, he acknowledged that his discussion had an inductive basis of 'actual observation of markets and business psychology' which placed it on a different level of abstraction from the rest of *The General Theory* (CW, VII, 149). The impact of Keynes' approach to uncertainty was to make suspect mathematical calculations of an exact sort respecting real asset values.

Keynes argued that a precise value for real assets cannot be ascertained because of the uncertainties involved. No probability statistic can be derived as to the likely returns, as no adequate information exists on certain possible events. Yet these possibilities are often of substantial importance to the decision-maker. The valuation of capital assets is affected in two ways:

(a) Liquidity preference alters as confidence in the future waxes and wanes. An optimistic outlook leads portfolio holders to value liquidity less, making the interest rate fall as bonds and other long-term securities are substituted for money balances. The falling interest rate directly increases the present value of investment goods.

(b) Future revenues and costs are anticipated values. Not only is there a risk, quantifiable in probability terms, that estimates will be in error, but there is also uncertainty of a non-quantifiable type. For instance there is no sensible information in the statement that the price of copper will be between £1 and £1,000 in ten years' time.[2] Thus present value is undefined over a very wide range in many realistic investment situations.

Animal spirits relate to the latter set of decisions, judgements concerning revenues and costs in the future as well as the scrap value of the asset through time. Because uncertainties cannot always be reduced to probability statements (not even to a mean expected value, far less other moments), the rational investor, by which Keynes means the entrepreneur, will resort to alternative sources of guidance. Hope, perusal of the general opinion, or satisfaction in the enterprise for its own sake can replace, or supplement, detached assessments of present values.

Thus in Keynes' thought animal spirits play their part in determining investment, along with the rate of interest, technological advance, and other variables. Changes in confidence, by altering investment levels, expand or contract investment, and with it aggregate demand, and the level of income and employment. The individual is subject to the emotions of the herd. Nor is this wholly undesirable; without such psychologically-determined motives for investment there would probably be inadequate private entrepreneurship as individuals recognised the significance of the uncertain hazards on which their judgements were exercised.

How did Keynes come to these views? The great work of the early part of Keynes' scholarly life was the *Treatise on Probability*, published in 1921 after fifteen years of study and revision. Braithwaite explains Keynes' concern there as

> to explain how a degree of belief could be rational, and thus not merely a matter of the believer's psychological make-up but one which all rational men under similar circumstances would share. (CW, VIII, xxi)

That such a task should have preceded the development of Keynes' views on uncertainty in economics gives pause for thought to those who interpret Keynes' views on animal spirits as involving irrationality on the part of entrepreneurs.

His study of probability, Keynes acknowledged, was encouraged by the moral philosophy of G. E. Moore, and by Bertrand Russell's work in *Principia Mathematica* (CW, X, 445). Keynes maintained that certain rational belief arises only from knowledge, which (apart from the direct knowledge obtained, for instance, by sensation) takes the form of propositions. However, some propositions, in which rational belief is possible, are those which, given the evidence, are probable rather than certain (CW, VIII, 12-16). Probability then was defined by Keynes as being 'concerned with degrees of rational belief' (CW, VIII, 21).

Keynes concluded that the probability underlying a rational belief, deriving from the evidence, differed from the weight to be attached to that belief. Only the accretion of evidence could increase the weight of the belief, though such an accretion might increase or decrease the probability involved (CW, VIII, 77-85). Keynes makes explicit reference to this distinction in order to clarify his meaning when he asserts in *The General Theory* that it is foolish 'to attach great weight to matters which are very uncertain' (CW, VII, 148).

If evidence is scant for the propositions put to business decision-makers, then they may legitimately weigh them lightly as offering little in the way of prescience. This behaviour is wholly rational, as is the use of direct knowledge (such as business intuition) in such circumstances. Knowledge of the present, or of the past, may be quite a poor guide to the future, but if such is the only available knowledge then an enterprise must use it. Even if enough evidence exists to make some probabilistic statements about the future, if widespread uncertainty is still extant (that is to say the evidence is seriously incomplete), then once again experience, habit and other modes of decision irreducible to a calculus must be relied upon for guidance.

Just as in a symphony, the theme of decision-making in the face of an unknowable future resurfaces in *The General Theory* after its introduction in the *Treatise on Probability* composed some two decades earlier. Once again, according to Patinkin's criterion, these ideas are central to Keynes' vision.

What Became of Animal Spirits?

It is revealing to trace subsequent thought on Keynes' concept of animal spirits. The term itself is now rarely used, even by Keynesians. At an early stage in the development of the neoclassical synthesis, much of the source of investment variability was believed to have been captured by the accelerator principle; what remained of animal spirits was absorbed into the residual term of investment equations (see Cuthbertson, 1979, 15). One is left with the inescapable conclusion that 'animal spirits' have been regarded simply as another slightly embarrassing example of Keynes' purple passages, to be excluded from scientific enquiry.[3]

While the orthodox neoclassical representation of investment behaviour left scope for non-random changes in long-run expectations to shift the autonomous component of investment demand (see Hicks, 1980-1, 140), attention was focused on those conventional variables which could explain at least some investment demand. Indeed, the main thrust of investment theory was to explain as much investment demand as possible by quantifiable variables such as interest rates and income levels. The remnants of Keynes' theory which were preserved in the orthodox framework built on IS-LM analysis took the form of behavioural assumptions, of inelastic expectations, rigid money wages, etc. Lacking any explanation within this framework, it is no wonder that these assumptions smacked of ad hocery and irrationality (see Loasby, 1976, 14-15).

These behavioural assumptions further posed the problem that successful empirical testing was predicated on the stability of institutional parameters. If a model failed to predict, it was not possible to say whether the failure resulted from the model itself or from a change in behavioural parameters. The next step was thus to endogenise as many behavioural parameters as possible, first with adaptive expectations, then with rational expectations which were more directly derived from neoclassical microfoundations.[4]

Lucas (1980) is quite explicit in claiming to have progressed beyond Keynes by developing a framework within which animal spirits could 'play a well-defined role' (Lucas, 1980, 708; see also Begg, 1982a). Within this rational expectations framework, long-run expectations are based on an assessment of all available information, using the 'true' predictive model of the economy. Expectations only shift when new information becomes available which could not have been anticipated. The response to new information pushes the economy onto another path, but one which leads to the same long-run equilibrium as before. In contrast, shifts in long-run expectations were, in Keynes' theory, themselves capable of changing the long-run outcome.

Before considering directly whether these developments in expectations theory actually do constitute a progression from the animal spirits concept, it is worthwhile considering further what lies behind the urge to endogenise long-term expectations in the first place, an urge common to economists across the spectrum. First, why does the treatment of animal spirits as exogenous constitute a problem? It is the business of economists, certainly, to explain or predict economic events, so that it is natural to try to extend that capacity to a major determinant of investment demand. But the explanation must go further. It must lie in what is *conventionally* acceptable as exogenous. Thus, while attempts are made to endogenise technological change, for example, the difficulties in doing so have encouraged the convention of treating it as, at least in part, exogenous.

Among those concerned with endogenising long-term expectations there is a contrasting lack of concern to endogenise the money supply process. Indeed, the parallel between the roles of these two potentially exogenous variables was explicitly drawn in the Friedman-Meiselman (1963) controversy. Just as general equilibrium theorists charge Keynesians with neglecting to endogenise the crucial long-run expectations variable, so Keynesians charge Walrasian general equilibrium theorists with neglecting to endogenise the crucial money supply variable. The two concepts are also similar in involving problems of definition and thus of measurement. Particular money supply aggregates can be measured, as can surveyed business attitudes and intentions, but there must be doubt as to whether any one measure of either variable is what *actually* influences expenditure.

There is nevertheless one significant difference between the two variables: the money supply by some definitions is partially under the control of the central monetary authority and is thus potentially exogenous to private sector behavioural relationships.[5] Long-run expectations on the other hand are the product of entrepreneurs' or managers' minds, and as such are subject to indeterminate influences, given the uncertainty surrounding the future. Herein lies the root of much of the anxiety expressed by Coddington (1982). If long-run expectations are generated by a conventional optimising procedure, using 'rational' criteria, then it is simply a question of finding the appropriate technique with which to model them. The only other possibility considered is that the process is irrational. But irrational in this context can only mean not susceptible to modelling; rationality in general requires the application of reason, which may nevertheless elude modelling.

Joan Robinson (1973, 3) is using the narrow concept of rationality when she explains, '. . . the [Keynesian] revolution lay in the change from the principles of rational choice to the problems of decisions based on guesswork and convention'. The need to rely on guesswork and convention stems from the uncertainty with which any view is held about reality, but particularly views about the future. Coddington suggests that, since expectations in all sectors must similarly reflect resort to guesswork and convention in the face of similar uncertainty, economists therefore must relinquish the capacity to model any behaviour, not just that of investors. With such a prospect in view, it is not surprising that the alternative of presuming animal spirits to be 'rationally' based and thus potentially predictable is chosen.

It must be emphasised further, however, that the standard economist's definition of 'rationality' is a very particular one. The definition of consumer rationality employed is that consumers have 'consistent preferences' and know their current and future budget constraints (see, for example, Laidler, 1974, 140). For producers, the equivalent requirement is that the cost and revenue functions are known for production of all different amounts and using any of the entire range of different production processes.

The existence, far less the ordering, of consumer preferences and information on production processes requires a degree of knowledge which commonsense tells us is impossible. Even if our lack of knowledge about existing commodities and processes could be explained by information costs, we have no means of knowing about commodities and processes to be developed in the future. Herein lies an important distinction between consumption and investment (where consumer durables are included in the latter category), and thus between short-run consumers' expectations and animal spirits. Current consumption is not generally profoundly affected by surprises such as the emergence of new products (if only because the scope for such surprises is limited within the short run) whereas investment and the estimation of its rate of return *are* profoundly affected: new processes may render the planned process obsolete, as may the design of new products by rival producers. The decision-making process under uncertainty is the same for the consumer as for the producer (see Earl, 1983, 65-7, 134) but the scope for surprise is so much greater for the latter that it is quite appropriate for expectations formation to be analysed separately.

Using the orthodox definition of rationality, investors do not have access to the information which would allow them to be rational. This definition of rationality is clearly too restrictive to cope with the unknowable future, and thus with any decision-making involving expectations, as all decision-making must.

As long as it was apparent that investors' behaviour necessarily contained 'irrational' elements (by the orthodox definition), there was still a role for animal spirits as an exogenous variable within general equilibrium models. But this role was eroded by the introduction of rational expectations. The general proposition of rational expectations is that all *available* information is brought to bear on decisions, so that expectations are arrived at 'reasonably'. This proposition is consistent with the broad definition of rationality. At this level of generality, Keynes and the rational expectations theorists have something in common in their view of expectations-formation (see Colander and Guthrie, 1980-1).[6]

By further defining expectations to be rational if their probability distribution is the same as the probability distribution of the forecast variable (see Muth, 1961, and Lucas and Prescott, 1971), the rational expectations theorists part company with Keynes and the broad definition of rationality. Keynes' own work on probability and Shackle's work (see, for example, Shackle, 1955, and Bausor, 1983), have shown the limitations of probability theory in generating predictions among economists, let alone the general population. It is indeed widely acknowledged that the rational expectations model does not reflect actual behaviour. But lack of realism is freely admitted by Lucas (1980, 696-7) on grounds similar to those used by Machlup (1967) to justify 'as if' models of individual behaviour.[7] If deterministic models are to represent individual behaviour then unrealistic assumptions must be made. The question now to be addressed, then, is whether this 'as if' method of endogenising long-run expectations constitutes progress relative to Keynes' use of animal spirits. While not reflecting actual investment behaviour, does it capture the essence of the situation for either predictive or explanatory purposes?

The answer lies in Colander and Guthrie's (1980-1, 230) observation that, within general equilibrium theory, 'the model determines expectations', while the reverse was true for Keynes. In other words, once the general equilibrium framework is adopted, the way in which expectations may be incorporated is severely constrained. Hahn (1952) at an early date anticipated the necessity for general equilibrium models, when attempting to deal with time, to specify the procedure of expectations-formation. He then spelled out the limits to be imposed on that specification if a stable equilibrium were to be maintained. Hahn (1973) later limited the relevance of Walrasian general equilibrium theory to those commodities with futures markets, since only in these cases could actual expectations conform at all closely to the limitations imposed by the general equilibrium framework. In general, the acceptability of any form of expectations modelling (whether rational or adaptive expectations), depends on the acceptability of the framework in which it is incorporated.[8].

A general equilibrium model cannot incorporate surprises in the form of new products or processes other than as exogenous shocks. The economic system, as modelled by general equilibrium principles, must be either dynamically stable or dynamically unstable. The observed general absence of chaos has encouraged the presumption that economies are dynamically stable, that there is an automatic tendency for economies to approach an equilibrium position. The only reason for the economy to depart from such a position in the first place is a shock from a variable exogenous to the model.

But it is unacceptable for entrepreneurs' long-term expectations to consititute such an exogenous variable since the behaviour represented by the 'as if' model is put forward as being *uniformly* motivated. It has been regarded as one of the achievements of the marginalist revolution that it allowed economists to abstract from groupings of individuals by function, class, location of residence, etc., and concentrate on the universal principles governing individual behaviour itself. It is from this standpoint that Coddington (1982), for example, insists that if entre-preneurial expectations cannot be explained within the model in ques-tion, then on grounds of consistency within a universal theory of human behaviour, neither can any other form of expectations. If rational expectations are imposed with respect to the price level, investors' expectations must be treated likewise.

In summary then, once a Walrasian general equilibrium framework is chosen, and decision-making is included which refers (as it must) to the future, then expectations must be endogenised in such a way as to drive the economy along an adjustment path which leads to the long-run equilibrium position. Within such a framework it is logically difficult, as well as antithetical, to leave one set of expectations outside the model. Indeed it is an inherent property of closed, deterministic models, which are designed to represent a complete system, to enforce a strict dualism (between endogeneity and exogeneity, as between rationality and irrationality) which is consistently upheld throughout the system. Either a variable can be explained by other variables or it cannot. It is within this particular framework, rather than in Keynes' framework, that classifying a variable as exogenous constitutes a throwing in of the explanatory towel.

Animal Spirits in their Spiritual Home

Animal spirits, insofar as they survived the neoclassical synthesis, have taken on a meaning quite different from that intended by Keynes. It is the difference in methodological framework which is crucial.[9]

But then how should animal spirits be dealt with in the Keynesian framework? It is significant that concern over reliance on animal spirits has been expressed among Keynesian sympathisers as well as by critics. Is it sufficient to regard animal spirits simply as an exogenous variable? In terms of empirical modelling, there appears to be no alternative, although the difficulty of identifying a quantifiable proxy for expectations is of no small importance for predictive work. As long as it is accepted that some sets of expectations, such as price-level expectations, can be captured reasonably well by other variables while others, like animal spirits, cannot, then the former can be treated as endogenous and the latter as exogenous, on operational rather than logical grounds (see Lawson, 1981). That need not prevent judgements being formed as to trends in animal spirits, on the basis of detailed observation of the economy, and of business attitudes in particular. For example, any receptive observer of Western economies in the early 1980s could detect a pervasive air of pessimism (except in a few readily identifiable industries). By allowing that factor to be incorporated exogenously into predictive models, the effect of animal spirits could be captured. Rational expectations models can only incorporate expectations in the form of the model's own predictions.

At the theoretical level, also, there is a range of approaches to analysing confidence shifts: these include Shackle's (1955) concept of surprise, Leijonhufvud's (1981, ch. 6) corridor theory or Harris' (1979) use of catastrophe theory. Such theoretical work can be justified by the fact that, while animal spirits cannot easily be quantified *ex ante*, evidence can be interpreted as measuring the effect of animal spirits *ex post*. Thus, for example, Andrews' (1982) study demonstrates the degree to which conventional economic variables failed to explain the cutback in private sector investment in the United States prior to and during the Great Depression. The results are consistent with the explanation that a wave of pessimism (a collapse of animal spirits) initiated the contraction in the capital goods sector which played such a significant role in the general contraction in aggregate demand during the Depression.

It is unfortunate, however, that in econometric work animal spirits of necessity fall within the residual term. This fact encourages the view of animal spirits as being of residual importance, or as something which should if possible be brought into the body of the equation. Furthermore, it encourages the conceptual separation between the past values of variables and expectations as to their future values.[10] In its turn, the residual, being stochastic, gives every appearance of being irrational according to the narrow definition of rationality, equated with 'ability to be modelled'. These implications are not a logical consequence of stochastic formulations, nor necessarily the intention of the econometrician, but they are of considerable rhetorical significance, i.e. they influence intrepretation, communication, and future channels of thought and investigation.[11]

In contrast, 'Chapter 12 Keynesians' view animal spirits as being of central significance, and the epistemological problems associated with long-term expectations as being a more serious version of those facing all decision-makers (see Loasby, 1976, ch. 9). Indeed, from this view of decision-making stems the explanation for money's (non-neutral) role in the economy as the refuge of uncertainty, and, more generally, the necessity to conduct analysis within the context of historical time and thus to eschew any focus on general equilibrium. In short, this view of expectations is integral to the entire Keynesian theoretical framework.

It is possible to take this analysis further, however, by looking at the epistemological basis both of the view of expectations and of the theoretical framework. Perceptions of how expectations are formed are themselves not objective, but the product of a particular way of looking at the world. Indeed it is at this level that we must look for the difference in methodological framework which underlies differences in analysing expectations. The mode of perception and analysis on which Keynesian theory is built is quite different from the all-encompassing closed system derived deductively from a set of axioms which is the basis for orthodox theory. This latter approach has been dominant or perhaps, more significantly, aspired to in Western thought since the ancient Greeks (see Dow, 1980). Given the difficulties of identifying appropriate universal axioms, an alternative theoretical structure can be built using a variety of logical chains (expressed with varying degrees of formality depending on the content) with different starting points, and taking different parts of the system as exogenous. As a result, the duality of endogeneity and exogenity loses its universal application and becomes specific to the particular chain of reasoning at hand. Stohs (1983) categorises Keynesian methodology as Babylonian, relying on 'several, parallel, intertwined and mutually reinforcing' chains of reasoning.[12]

Keynes himself was in his early years influenced by G.E. Moore to aspire to the orthodox, axiomatic mode of thought, although he later rejected it (CW, X, 433-50). It is clear from the style of Keynes' writings, as much as from their content, that in practice he conformed more to what, for want of a better term, we may call the 'Babylonian' mode. In line with this view, the 'purple passages' in *The General Theory*, including the term 'animal spirits', were an integral part of his attempt to communicate and persuade. Thus it was in a sense from the traditional Western mode of scientific thought that he had his 'long struggle to escape'.

One implication of the non-dualistic Keynesian approach is that, while there are objective facts, perceptions of these facts are not objective. Information is thus not always an absolute of which one has knowledge, or absence of knowledge.[13] On this epistemological basis, rationality takes on a different hue. Decision-makers organise their perceptions and their expectations around world views, or paradigms. Such behaviour is rational in the sense of reasoned, according to the theories adopted by each decision-maker.

Indeed, long-run expectations can be viewed as 'theories' about how the future will unfold. What will shake one investor's theory poses questions as complex as those which arise in discussions of what constitutes an effective falsification of an economic theory, i.e. one which will persuade an economist to switch theories. Further, since members of a group (of consumers, or investors, say) tend to share ways of perceiving and analysing the world, they can also be expected to share expectations to a considerable degree. Again it seems legitimate to consider expectations by group: for example, the animal spirits of investors, the short-term expectations of consumers of non-durable goods, and those of purchasers of financial assets.

Finally, the notion of what is 'central' to a theory is inherent in the theory's own methodological framework. The dualism of orthodox theory requires certain variables to be exogenous to explain change other than movement along a steady-state path. What these variables are is then of central importance. Thus isolated, these variables become the subject of uncomfortable scrutiny; only the caprices of government have survived this scrutiny, remaining exogenous (and, by implication, irrational according to their narrow definition of rationality) in the rational expectations framework.

Within a non-dualistic Keynesian framework, the centrality of the animal spirits concept takes on a different significance. It does not make sense to say that, if only investors were rational in the narrow orthodox sense, there would be no unemployment. Rather, implicit in the choice of a framework designed for studying economies in historical time is the judgement that this framework allows analysis of the most important features of the economy. The framework requires that attention be paid to decision-making under uncertainty. The area of decision-making where that uncertainty impinges most, with the most widespread implications for employment and incomes, is in the purchase of new capital goods. This accounts for the importance of the animal spirits concept. It epitomises the methodological framework from which it arises; ultimately it is that methodological framework which determines the content of Keynesian theory.

Conclusion

We have attempted to show that the animal spirits concept was significant within Keynes' own thought and considered why it should have become so peripheral to the subsequent development of macroeconomics. The formation of expectations in conditions of uncertainty, as something beyond probability analysis, was a theme which recurred in Keynes' work throughout his life. The scope for those expectations to be volatile and to affect profoundly the level of investment, and thus of income and employment, was for Keynes a serious concern.

We suggest that this feature of Keynes' theory failed to hold the attention of later macroeconomists for methodological reasons. The prevailing orthodox mode of thought in macroeconomics seeks a uniform behaviour pattern in all economic agents, which is rational in the narrow sense of 'capable of being modelled', and which is consistent with a modelling system which is not dynamically unstable. Entrepreneurs' long-run expectations must thus be treated consistently with other forms of expectations. Thus endogenised, there is no scope for sudden shifts in these entrepreneurial expectations other than those resulting from the emergence of unanticipated objective information; long-run expectations lose their capacity to have any independent effect on the economy. The only alternative, that they be exogenous, renders them unsatisfactorily arbitrary.

Within Keynes' methodological framework, however, animal spirits are no longer arbitrary, but follow logically from his epistemological stance. Keynes' method reflected the judgement that no one method can satisfactorily explain or predict within a social science such as economics. Rather the preferred approach was to tackle each question from a variety of angles, with a variety of methods, in fact just as an entrepreneur in reality forms long-run expectations in the face of uncertainty. Thus, what is exogenous within one approach, or line of reasoning, is endogenous within another. For example, long-term expectations must be exogenous to predictive econometric models, but can be explained by a questionnaire method combined with historical analysis of the economy in question.[17] Indeed this methodology was adopted by Keynes following his work on probability theory which indicated the limited ability of the probability calculus to deal with economic decision-making.

In conclusion, then, the question of whether or not animal spirits should be singled out for special theoretical treatment must first refer to the methodological framework to be employed. Within the orthodox framework, it makes no sense to single out animal spirits. Within a Keynesian methodological framework, however, the behaviour of different groups, as groups, is the focus of attention. The means are available for analysing the behaviour of the entrepreneurial group, with the particular epistemological problems involved. Any judgement as to the value of the animal spirits concept thus requires a judgement as to the relative value of the two available methodological frameworks.

Notes

1. Further evidence is found in a letter from Keynes to Hugh Townshend dated 7 December 1938 (CW, XXIX, 294). Keynes remarks there: 'Generally speaking, in making a decision we have before us a large number of alternatives, none of which is demonstrably more "rational" than the others, in the sense that we can arrange in order of merit the sum aggregate of the benefits obtainable from the complete consequences of each . . . we fall back, therefore, and necessarily so, on motives of another kind, which are not "rational" in the sense of being concerned with the evaluation of consequences, but are decided by habit, interest, preference, desire, will etc.'

2. This point was missed completely by Coddington (1976). Keynes explained his meaning clearly in the QJE article of 1937: 'The sense in which I am using the term [uncertain] is that in which the prospect of a European war is uncertain, or the price of copper and the rate of interest twenty years hence, or the obsolescence of a new invention, or the position of private wealth owners in the social system in 1970. About these matters there is no scientific basis on which to form any calculable probability whatever' (Keynes, 1937, 213).

3. Meltzer (1981) has however attempted to revive interest in the marginal efficiency of capital as a major innovation of *The General Theory*.

4. See Begg (1982b) for an account of these developments in expectations theory.

5. The degree of potential control is more limited the more open the economy.

6. Simon's (1955) concept of bounded rationality which refers to decision-making with incomplete information is also consistent with this definition. His concept of procedural rationality is used to explore the process by which decisions are arrived at when

information is incomplete, contrasted with substantive rationality when complete information is available (see Simon, 1976; Garner, 1982).

7. By no means all general equilibrium theorists accept that their microfoundations are unrealistic (see Hahn, 1973).

8. Boland (1981) makes the similar argument that a model such as that based on the neoclassical maximisation hypothesis ultimately can only be judged on the grounds of its own 'metaphysics'.

9. Rational expectations have been the subject of a range of critiques from the Keynesian perspective; these critiques have demonstrated the inability of rational expectations to deal with historical time (Bausor, 1983), with crucial experiments (Davidson, 1982-3), with conflicts between individual and collective rationality (Evans, 1984) and with observed facts (Pesaran, 1982).

10. As Keynes put it: 'There are not two separate factors affecting the rate of investment, namely, the schedule of the marginal efficiency of capital and the state of confidence. The state of confidence is relevant because it is one of the major factors determining the former, which is the same thing as the investment demand schedule' (CW, VII, 149).

11. McCloskey (1983) makes the case that language (including mathematical and statistical language) is of fundamental significance to the development of economic thought.

12. See Dow (1985) for a detailed discussion of the origins, character and significance of these differences in modes of thought.

13. Coddington (1976) identifies this subjectivist view of knowledge as being an identifying characteristic of fundamentalist Keynesians. It is at least a feature of what might be called Keynesian microfoundations, as developed for example by Earl (1983).

14. The wider use by economists of the questionnaire method is advocated by McCloskey (1983).

References

Andrews, P. (1982) 'Manufacturing fixed investment and the Great Depression', Unpublished PhD dissertation, University of California, Berkeley

Bausor, R. (1983) 'The Rational-Expectations Hypothesis and the Epistemics of Time', *Cambridge Journal of Economics, 7*, 1-10

Begg, D. K. H. (1982) 'Rational Expectations, Wage Rigidity and Involuntary Unemployment', *Oxford Economic Papers, 34*, 23-47

— — *The Rational Expectations Revolution in Macroeconomics: Theories and Evidence*, Philip Allan , Oxford

Boland, L. (1981) 'On the Futility of Criticizing the Neoclassical Maximization Hypothesis', *American Economic Review, 71*, 1031-6

Coddington, A. (1976) 'Keynesian Economics: The Search for First Principles', *Journal of Economic Literature, 14*, 1258-73

— — (1982) 'Deficient Foresight: A Troublesome Theme in Keynesian Economics', *American Economic Review, 72*, 480-7

Colander, D. C. and Guthrie, R. S. (1980/81) 'Great Expectations: What the Dickens do "Rational Expectations" Mean?', *Journal of Post Keynesian Economics, 3*, 219-34

Cuthbertson, K. (1979) *Macroeconomic Policy: The New Cambridge, Keynesian and Monetarist Policies*, London, Macmillan

Davidson, P. (1978) *Money and the Real World*, second edition, Macmillan, London

— — (1982/3) 'Rational Expectations: A Fallacious Foundation for Studying Crucial Decision Making', *Journal of Post Keynesian Economics, 5*, 182-98

Dow, S. C. (1980) 'Methodological Morality in the Cambridge Controversies', *Journal of Post Keynesian Economics, 2*, 368-80
— — (1985) *Macroeconomic Thought: A Methodological Approach,* Basil Blackwell, Oxford
Earl, P. E. (1983) *The Economic Imagination: Towards a Behavioural Theory of Choice,* Brighton, Wheatsheaf
Eatwell, J. (1979) 'Theories of Value and Employment', *Thames Papers in Political Economy,* Summer
Evans, G. (1983) 'The Stability of Rational Expectations in Macroeconomic Models', in R. Frydman and E. Phelps (eds.), *Individual Forecasting and Aggregate Outcomes: Rational Expectations Examined,* Cambridge University Press, Cambridge
Friedman, M. and Meiselman, D. (1963) 'The Relative Stability of Monetary Velocity and the Investment Multiplier in the United States, 1897-1958', in E. C. Brown *et al., Stabilization Policies,* Prentice-Hall, Englewood Cliffs, N. J
Garner, C. (1982) 'Uncertainty, Human Judgement, and Economic Decisions', *Journal of Post Keynesian Economics, 14*, 413-24
Hahn, F. H. (1952) 'Expectations and Equilibrium in Economics', *Economic Journal, 72*, 802-19
— — (1973) *On the Nature of Equilibrium in Economics,* Cambridge University Press, Cambridge
Harris, L. (1979) 'Catastrophe Theory, Utility Theory and Animal Spirit Expectations', *Australian Economic Papers, 18*, 268-82
Hicks, J. (1980/81) 'IS-LM: An Explanation', *Journal of Post Keynesian Economics, 3*, 139-54
Kenyon, P. (1980) 'Discussion' of Tarshis (1980), *American Economic Review Proceedings, 70*, 25-6
Keynes, J. M. (1937) 'The General Theory of Employment', *Quarterly Journal of Economics, 51*, 209-13
— — CW VII, VIII, X, XIV, XXIX
Laidler, D. (1974) *Introduction to Microeconomics,* Philip Allan, Oxford
Lawson, T. (1981) 'Keynesian Model Building and the Rational Expectations Critique', *Cambridge Journal of Economics, 5*, 311-26
Leijonhufvud, A. (1981) *Information and Coordination: Essays in Macroeconomic Theory,* Oxford University Press, Oxford
Loasby, B. J. (1976) *Choice, Complexity and Ignorance,* Cambridge University Press, Cambridge
Lucas, R. E. Jr. (1980) 'Methods and Problems in Business Cycle Theory', *Journal of Money, Credit and Banking, 12*, 696-715
— — and Prescott, E. C. (1971) 'Investment under Uncertainty', *Econometrica, 39*, 659-81
Machlup, F. (1967) 'Theories of the Firm: Marginalist, Behavioural, Managerial', *American Economic Review, 57*, 1-33
McCloskey, D. N. (1983) 'The Rhetoric of Economics', *Journal of Economic Literature, 21*, 481-517
Meltzer, A. H. (1981) 'On Keynes's *General Theory:* A Different Perspective', *Journal of Economic Literature, 19*, 34-64
Minsky, H. P. (1976) *John Maynard Keynes,* Macmillan, London
Muth, J. F. (1961) 'Rational Expectations and the Theory of Price Movement', *Econometrica, 29*, 315-35
Patinkin, D. (1982) *Anticipations of the General Theory,* Basil Blackwell, Oxford
— — and Leith, J. C. (eds.) (1977), *Keynes, Cambridge and the General Theory,* Macmillan, London
Pesaran, M. H. (1982) 'A Critique of the Proposed Tests of the Natural Rate —Rational Expectations Hypothesis', *Economic Journal, 92*, 529-54
Robinson, J. (1973) *After Keynes,* Basil Blackwell, Oxford

Shackle, G. L. S. (1955) *Uncertainty and Economics*, Cambridge University Press, Cambridge

— — (1974) *Keynesian Kaleidics*, Edinburgh University Press, Edinburgh

Simon, H. A. (1955) 'A Behavioural Theory of Rational Choice, *Quarterly Journal of Economics, 69,* 99-118

— — (1976) 'From Substantive to Procedural Rationality', in *Method and Appraisal in Economics* (ed. S. J. Latsis), Cambridge University Press, Cambridge

Stohs, M. (1983) '"Uncertainty" in Keynes' *General Theory:* A Rejoinder', *History of Political Economy, 15,* 87-91

Tarshis, L. (1980) 'Post-Keynesian Economics: A Promise that Bounced?' *American Economic Review, Papers and Proceedings, 70,* 10-14

4 EXPECTATIONS IN KEYNESIAN ECONOMETRIC MODELS

Simon Wren-Lewis

Introduction

A discussion of the treatment of expectations in Keynesian econometric models is almost bound to be conducted in terms of responses to
the Rational Expectations Hypothesis (REH). In this chapter I want to
examine how the proprietors of large-scale Keynesian econometric
models have or could respond to the challenge presented by the REH.
My main theme is that this response should involve exploration rather
than confrontation, with Keynesian modellers experimenting with
some, but not necessarily all, of the ideas embodied in the REH.

I shall first try and illustrate why there is no necessary incompatibility between the REH and the theoretical underpinnings of
Keynesian models. Nevertheless, the dominant treatment of expectations in Keynesian econometric models is far from ideal. In examining
alternative approaches to modelling expectations in the remaining sections of this chapter, I distinguish between the theoretical model of
expectations formation used, and the method by which this model is
estimated. In both cases there appears to be a wide spectrum of
possibilities between the traditional Keynesian approach and the
rational expectations framework which could be tried by modellers,
without necessarily adopting some of the REH's more questionable
methodological precepts. A conclusion summarises the main issues
and choices involved.

The emphasis on Keynesian models is in keeping with the theme of
this volume, as well as my own knowledge and interest. I should state at
the outset that by labelling a model 'Keynesian', I do *not* wish to imply
that Keynes himself would have approved of its main characteristics.
Partly as a result, I shall not restrict the term Keynesian to models
developed in Cambridge, as in Lawson (1981) for example. The defining characteristic of Keynesian models as far as I am concerned here is
the primary role given to effective demand in determining output,
employment and unemployment. Under this heading come the models
of the National Institute and HM Treasury as well as those of the Cam-

bridge Growth Project and the Cambridge Economic Policy Group.[1] One other reason for focusing on Keynesian models is that the REH was seen, by both sides, as a direct attack on this class of model, and it is to this issue that I turn first.

Are Keynesian Econometric Models and the REH Compatible?

The familiar applications of the REH are almost all to models whose theoretical basis is fundamentally neoclassical. Furthermore, the initial popularisation of the REH owed much to its use in attacking the 'prevailing Keynesian orthodoxy'. It is hardly surprising that many assume that there is a fundamental incompatibility between the axioms of the REH and the theoretical foundations of Keynesian models.[2] I believe this is an important misconception, which may have prevented many Keynesians from exploring some of the ideas associated with the REH.

The genesis of this misconception might be summarised, in a somewhat cavalier fashion, as follows. If ouput is determined by (effective) demand and not supply, trade must be taking place in at least some markets at prices that differ from those of Walrasian equilibrium. These 'sticky' prices may be confined to the labour market (as in Buiter and Lorie, 1977, for example), extend also the goods market (as in Barro and Grossman, 1976), or may reflect 'incorrect' asset prices (Leijonhufvud, 1968). One common justification for agents trading at non-Walrasian equilibrium prices is that, in the absence of an auctioneer or re-contracting, agents cannot be expected to process efficiently the vast amount of information required to compute equilibrium prices. The REH, on the other hand, appears to require agents to utilise efficiently all available information. The informational assumptions of each theory therefore appear to differ substantially.

Of course it is possible to use rational expectations in fixed price models, and in these circumstances Keynesian results may in fact be enhanced (Neary and Stiglitz, 1981). The question posed here (following, for example, Lucas, 1981) is whether the basic assumption of fixed prices presupposes some form of irrationality behind the scenes. If it did, it could be argued by Keynesians and followers of the REH alike that such models involved a logical inconsistency.

This inconsistency argument appeared to gain some support when some macroeconomic modellers attempted to allow for flexible wages by including within Keynesian econometric models an expectations-augmented Phillips curve. Although perhaps more popular in the US, a Phillips curve was imposed for a period up to 1980/1 in the Treasury model (see HM Treasury, 1982, for example) and used optionally in versions of the National Institute and Cambridge Growth Project models (see National Institute, 1981; Barker *et al.*, 1980). In these UK examples the Phillips curve was part of a system which included the Keynesian features of mark-up pricing and employment as a function of output (rather than real wages). As long as inflation expectations in the Phillips curve were adaptive in form, so that agents might make persistent errors, output could remain demand determined and unemployment could deviate from its 'natural rate' for some time.[3] If, however, inflation expectations were rational, and the coefficient on expected inflation unity, then in these models both unemployment *and* output could not deviate systematically from their 'natural rates'.

Now it may be possible to defend some form of the adaptive expectations hypothesis on the grounds that the costs involved in avoiding persistent errors are too great. The importance of costs in utilising information is a basic issue underlying many of the choices considered in the other sections of this chapter. The point I wish to make here is not whether or not this defence is justified, but that it is not a *necessary* condition for the construction of a Keynesian model. One can believe that agents in the labour market or elsewhere form their expectations about prices rationally, and also that an unemployment equilibrium may exist. Models with Keynesian properties can be derived by considering market 'imperfections' or externalities of various kinds where agents nevertheless use available information optimally. The implicit contract literature provides familiar examples, although only in certain circumstances is it found that contracts lead to involuntary unemployment. These circumstances will be enhanced, however, if we allow for plausible informational imperfections and asymmetries (Hahn, 1984). Following Keynes, consideration of workers' concern over wage relativities, coupled with fixed training costs for the firm, is likely to have Keynesian consequences (Hahn, 1982). Another example can be found in current research into the nature and effect of price adjustment costs on macroeconomic behaviour (e.g. Woglom, 1982, or Rotemberg, 1983 — following an idea by Stiglitz).

One interesting development, following the ideas of Kallečki rather than Keynes (Sawyer, 1982), has been the exploration of some of the macroeconomic consequences of imperfect competition. In both Weitzman (1982) and Hart (1982) a 'long-run' Keynesian unemployment equilibrium exists which does not rely on incorrect expectations.

Indeed, the existence of an unemployment equilibrium in these cases does not depend on informational problems of any kind.

These models suggest that it is possible to follow the REH in our treatment of information and yet still construct essentially Keynesian macroeconomic models.[4] But why should Keynesian modellers wish to do such a thing in the first place? Let me answer this first by outlining briefly the main problem associated with the traditional treatment of expectations in Keynesian models.

Macroeconomic modellers have recognised for a long time the importance of expectations in behavioural relationships of various kinds. For example, consumption plans depend on future expectations of (or permanent) labour income, and firms' investment plans depend on future levels of output. Many theories therefore relate some variable X to expectations about Y, where these expectations may involve short-term, medium-term and long-term anticipations. Typically, however, estimated versions of these theories relate X to some lags on X and Y. These are often termed autoregressive distributed lag (ADL) models. This transition involves two difficulties. The first concerns the implicit theory of expectations formation, which relates expected Y only to lags in Y itself (and possibly lagged X as well). This theory is in one sense simplistic in excluding the possibility that other variables might influence expected Y, but it is also potentially complex in the lag structures that could relate expected Y to current and past values. It is not obvious that such a combination is plausible.

The second difficulty is that we normally do not know just how complex or otherwise the relationship between expected and past Y is, because the expectations model cannot be identified in the reduced form. Reduced-form estimation inevitably involves problems, such as an inability to impose theoretical priors involving structural relationships on the reduced-form parameter estimates. In this respect it is interesting to note some recent literature that has attempted to formulate possible restrictions for ADL equations (e.g. Currie, 1982, or Salmon, 1982), although even here the structure of expectations models is generally neglected.

The contrasts provided by the REH are stark. The assumed relationship between expectations and actual out-turns enables the parameters of the expectations model to be estimated explicitly. The complexity of this expectations model involves the same dimensions as the model as a whole. In the remainder of this chapter I shall discuss some of the advantages and disadvantages of each approach and mention, using some specific examples, a few of the possibilities that lie between these two 'extremes'.

Theories of Expectations Formation

The REH is often described as 'merely' assuming that agents make the best use of available information. This may be a meaningful description of the process of, say, finding out whether a coin is fair. In building a model of macroeconomic behaviour, on the other hand, it begs one key question: what theory do agents use in processing this data? The laws of probability associated with tossing a coin are fairly simple, well known and hardly contentious. The way the economy works is complex, mysterious and highly controversial.The econometrician must first decide how firms or consumers think the economy works before he estimates his model of expectations. In this section I discuss alternative views and methodological approaches to modelling agents' 'interpretative schemes' (Giddens, 1979), reserving problems of estimation until later.

As I suggested above, the standard assumption in most large models is that $Y^e = A(L)Y$, where $A(L)$ is a polynomial in the lag operator (or possibly the ratio of two polynomials). Its parameters need not be fixed (see Lawson, 1981, in relation to the Cambridge Growth Project model, or Harvey, 1981) but they are normally independant of other model, or Harvey, 1981) but they are normally independent of other is both sufficient for modelling purposes and realistic. Indeed exponents of the REH have often used this model themselves for variables taken as exogenous (e.g. real wages in Sargent, 1978). Simple models may be most robust in environments that are complex and uncertain in structure (Heiner, 1983).

In other cases this model of expectations formation may be too simplistic in ignoring other variables. Take the example of firms' output expectations. Surely it is likely that firms take some systematic account of the level of their international competitiveness, or the stance of fiscal policy, when they try and guess future levels of demand. It seems unlikely that, at the end of 1979, firms did not realise some of the implications of the high real exchange rate and a restrictive budget for their own future output.

Once we admit the possibility that Y^e may depend on other variables besides Y, we have to decide what variables these might be. The issue can be subdivided into two questions: how sophisticated are agents in forming expectations, and how close are their theories to the modeller's own? Research currently in progress at the National Institute represents a point somewhere in the middle of the range of possibilities defined by these two questions. In Wren-Lewis (1984) a model of manufacturing employment is developed which depends in part on expectations about future output, and these expectations are generated by a vector autoregression in output, fiscal policy, the real exchange rate and (post 1972) real oil prices. This expectations model is obviously more complex than $Y^e=A(L)Y$, but it remains far simpler than the full National Institute model itself. The choice of variables determining expected output reflects the Keynesian character of the full model, but that is as far as any theoretical consistency between the two goes.

We can illustrate some of the implications of this approach by returning to the decisions of firms at the end of 1979. In traditional Keynesian models of manufacturing employment, in which $Y^e=A(L)Y$, the 1980 recession comes as a complete surprise. Equations of this type also underpredict the extent to which manufacturing employment fell in 1980. In the more complex output expectations model, on the other hand, by the end of 1979 firms had already revised down their output expectations and were therefore planning larger reductions in their workforces. This Keynesian model of output expectations may therefore help to explain at least in part the severity of the 1980 recession. It also has important implications for the speed at which an expansionary fiscal policy might begin to reduce unemployment.

There is no reason why agents' expectations models should be based on Keynesian theory agents'. Similarly, there is no reason why a Keynesian model should not embody expectations based on, say, monetarism. Different agents may hold different views about how the economy works. A good example of a 'mixed' model of this kind is provided by the 1982 version of the Treasury model. This model contains two different variables measuring expected price inflation. In the consumer durables equation we have a familiar, though explicit, model of the $Y^e=A(L)Y$ type, where $A(L)$ represent the ratio of two polynomials. The other variable, which influences the exchange rate, has expected inflation depending partly on changes in unit costs, and partly on changes in sterling M3. These two variables are unlikely to produce the same forecasts of inflation, and neither will be identical to the model's own inflation forecast. While I do not think we should be worried about this divergence (for reasons discussed below), it is important in these 'mixed' models to justify the assumption that one group's expectations model might differ from another's. Unfortunately the model manual in question (HM Treasury 1982) does not attempt to do so.

Although developments along the lines of the National Institute work or the Treasury model involve more complicated expectations models than the traditional approach, they can be viewed as sharing the same methodological perspective. Agents in the economy are seen as formulating their expectations models within a social context in which there are various, *alternative* world views, paradigms or ideologies about how the economic system works. To the extent that these theories conflict there may be a tendency for agents to fall back on relatively simple but perhaps more robust models of the traditional type. If on the other hand theories enjoy more of a consensus (and this consensus may be confined to a particular group, e.g. monetarism and the City) and/or fit in with the agent's own experience, they may form the basis of agents' own views about how the economy behaves.

Proponents of the REH often seem to take a rather different methodological standpoint, in which agents are said to know the true model of the economy. Now whatever 'true model' might mean in this context, one clear implication is that agents are taken to be at least as knowledgeable as the econometric modeller. While this may have some justification when it involves relationships specific to the agent (e.g. the firm's own demand curve), it seems less defensible in the context of general macroeconomic relationships. Within this perspective it is also rather difficult to account for the diversity of economic theories that in practice exist.

It would be unfair to suggest that all advocates of complete theoretical consistency would adopt this methodological view. Another argument often used is that although agents may not currently use the same model as the modeller, if this model is seen to be a comparatively successful representation of reality there will be an incentive for agents to adopt it themselves. Although this idea does not depend on the concept of a 'true model', it does seem to be based on a Popperian view that theories can be easily compared, evaluated and rejected by using past data or the estimated model's predictions. Unfortunately anyone concerned with large-scale econometric models will know the difficulties involved in formulating generally accepted methods of model comparison, let alone testing 'core' theories. If we define a model's 'long-run equilibrium' as one in which all agents hold exactly the same view as to how the economic system works, then this is a 'long run' to which Keynes' famous remark would apply. Advocates of complete theoretical consistency in expectations models might also appeal to simplicity. The argument would be that, as we know so little about the different interpretative schemes used by agents, we would not sacrifice much by abstracting from possible divergencies and instead assuming consistency with the modeller's own theory. Now whether it is true or not that we know little about how economic agents perceive the world, it does not follow that theoretical consistency is the only simplifying assumption available. The assumption that everyone forms expectations adaptively would be another. In the context of econometric models it also turns out that assuming theoretical consistency involves severe complications when it comes to estimation (see below).

Another argument frequently used to support consistency between the modeller's own theory and the theory used by agents to form expectations is that this assumption avoids the Lucas critique. Although the importance of regime changes should not be overstated (see Sims, 1982, for example), major changes of this type do occasionally occur, the most notable recent UK example being the move to floating exchange rates around 1972. The Lucas critique points out that without a *structural* model of expectations formation, where in particular expectations about policy are modelled explicitly, the model cannot simulate satisfactorily the effects of perceived discrete changes in policy regime. However, these explicit models of expectations formation do not have to have the same 'degree' of structure as the host model to cope with this problem. Nor is there any need for these expectations to be theoretically consistent with the modeller's theory. In the model of output expectations described above, for example, the inclusion of fiscal policy as a dependent variable allows us to examine the effects of an announced and believed move to a type of permanent balanced budget fiscal policy. This model could not cope with a perceived policy of fixed exchange rates, although it could examine the effects of a policy designed to fix the real exchange rate. The possibility of regime changes should clearly be considered when designing the structure of a theoretical model of expectations formation.

One final theoretical approach, which as far as I know has not been incorporated in any large model to date, is to use published forecasts as proxies for expectations. If these published forecasts are the modeller's own, then this idea appears at first sight to be close to the REH concept of theoretical consistency. As it provides proxy data for expectations, it also seems to avoid the econometric difficulties involved in implementing the REH. However, on closer inspection the idea reveals some of the basic methodological difficulties noted earlier. A time series of, say, National Institute forecasts would not be based on their current model, but on various versions of their model as it developed through time. If these forecasts represent agents' expectations, then agents cannot be using the true model. Furthermore there seems little justification for using the forecasts of one group alone, as agents have had over the last ten years or so a number of different forecasts to choose from, which in turn illustrates the range of different views about how the economy works.

It might be more realistic to use some weighted average of past forecasts as proxies for expectations, although it is not clear how the weights should be chosen. A further problem would then arise as to how to forecast with this model, as to predict expectations we seem to need to be able to forecast the forecasts of other forecasters! We could solve the model 'rationally', using the model's own predictions as representing agents' expectations (as in Holly and Zarrop, 1983, for example), but this would involve the heroic assumption that from now onwards agents ignored all other forecasts, or that these other forecasts were identical to the model's own. An alternative would be to use these proxy series for expectations as dependent as well as independent variables in the model, i.e. to use them to estimate expectations models. In doing this we should have the advantage that we had some idea of the theoretical models that were used to produce these series. The usefulness of this method depends crucially of course on the extent to which these forecasts did in fact influence agents' expectations.

Estimating Expectations Models

We should need to decide on our theoretical approach to modelling expectations even if we had actual data on these expectations, or if we intended to stick to reduced forms. In that sense decisions concerning theory and estimation are potentially independent. However, as we have already noted, practical considerations do link the two issues.

The major practical consideration is of course the lack of data on expectations. However, there are some data. In particular, in the UK, the CBI *Industrial Trends* survey provides a useful source of information, going back some way, about the expectations of manufacturing firms. There are serious problems involved in translating this qualitative information (i.e. proportions of firms saying output, for instance, will go up, stay the same or fall) into quantitative expectations series, but these difficulties are not insoluble.[5] Data of this kind have been used in some studies, mainly related to inflation expectations, but as far as I know they are not used in any Keynesian econometric models. This is surprising, particularly given the importance of output expectations in

Keynesian theory.

One reason why so little use has been made of survey data may be that they tend to be confined to the very short term (i.e. expectations about the next four months). Most theoretical models suggest that expectations ranging over a much longer time horizon are likely to be important. However, we can still use the short-term expectations data derived from surveys to produce estimates of longer-term expectations if we are willing to make the following assumption: that the model agents use to generate their short-term and longer-term expectations is the same. (This assumption is of course implicit in the REH.) Using this assumption we can estimate our expectations model with the transformed survey data as the dependent variable, and then solve the estimated equation(s) forward to generate longer-term expectations.[6] The assumption remains strong, however, and Keynes himself made much of a qualitative distinction between short-term and long-term expectations.

In the absence of expectations data it is natural to substitute out the unobserved variable and estimate a reduced form. (Whatever estimation method is adopted, the reduced form should be estimated if possible for testing purposes.) When the theoretical model of expectations formation is fairly simple, i.e. $Y^e = A(L)Y$, there is much to be said for going no further. However, this traditional approach involves two difficulties.

The first involves identification. In many cases it will be impossible to establish the structural model, of employment and output expectations for example, from the reduced form relating employment to output. This is by no means always true, particularly if the theoretical model is tightly specified. To take the employment example, the lagged dependent variables implied by costs of adjustment dictate the relative importance of short-term, medium-term or long-term expectations (see Sargent, 1978, for example). Given the reduced-form parameters estimated on lagged employment and output, we could in principle work backwards using the lagged dependent variable coefficients to derive the implicit expectations equation. Even when this is possible it is rarely attempted. But why should it matter that the structural model is identified? The reasons are similar to those used to justify structural modelling in general. We have already noted the advantages of explicit expectations variables/equations in the context of the Lucas critique. To take another example, suppose legislation is introduced which changes in a quantifiable way the adjustment costs of changing employment. Without identifying the structural model, how can we analyse its effects?

The second problem with reduced-form estimation involves the psychology of modellers themselves, and links estimation with theory. Reduced-form estimation involving a relatively complex expectations model will, because no restrictions are placed on the expectations model, involve relatively few degrees of freedom and therefore relatively inefficient parameter estimates. As modellers typically wish to estimate equations which contain parameters that are individually statistically significant, they will be tempted to adopt simpler expectations models than might be appropriate.

The alternative to reduced-form estimation provided by the REH is to use actual data as a guide to expectations. In the example based on National Institute work on employment cited above, the parameters of the expected output model were estimated by, in effect, estimating a model of output over the same data period as the employment equation was estimated. There are two separate assumptions involved here. The first, which is akin to 'agents making the best use of available data', is that agents use regression techniques to derive their expectations-generating models. The second, which is more dubious from a methodological point of view, is that the structure which agents are trying to estimate is *perceived* to have remained stable over time. This second assumption justifies using data of time $t+i$, $i > 0$ to construct an expectations model which agents are assumed to have at time t.

One assumption that is *not* necessarily involved in this use of actual data is consistency between the agent's and modeller's theoretical views. In a Keynesian model, for example, we could still assume that $Y^e = A(L)Y$ and yet estimate the parameters of $A(L)$ by estimating a univariate time series model for output. This distinction between complete theoretical consistency and the use of actual data in estimating expectations models is I believe important, yet it is rarely made. This may be because the two ideas do naturally go together if we adopt the methodological position that agents know the true model.[7]

The problem with assuming a constant perceived structure is partly that we know that the 'underlying parameters' of the economic system do change, but also because it is likely that agents' models change through learning. As a result it is possible to take the methodological view that all attempts to model expectations are doomed to failure; one may, however, make some allowance for learning in a number of ways, In principle, for example, we could extend our data set backwards and estimate a different output expectations model at each point in time using only past data. A computationally less demanding procedure would be to re-estimate the expectations model whenever it failed some kind of prediction test. A similar effect could be achieved by using Kalman filtering techniques. The only one of our Keynesian econometric models to include learning of this kind is the Cambridge Growth Project model (Barker *et al*, 1980).

Conclusion

The modelling of expectations presents formidable problems. This is partly because of a (relative) lack of data on these expectations, and partly because our own theories about how expectations are formed are weak. In this chapter I have discussed some of the ways in which these problems might be tackled. I have suggested that in some circumstances alternatives to the traditional Keynesian approach, i.e. the reduced-form estimation of relatively simple (in variables) expectations processes, may be at least worth exploring. The fact that these alternatives all owe something to the REH should not concern us, as there is no inevitable contradiction between this hypothesis and the theoretical foundations of Keynesian models and it is possible to use elements of the REH without adopting the methodological standpoint of some of its advocates.

The choices open to modellers involve both the theory of expectations formation employed, and the means by which the model is estimated. In terms of theory, a wide range of possibilities have been and could be tried, including expectations models for at least some agents that are theoretically inconsistent with the rest of the model. In estimation, it seems sensible to make the maximum possible use of survey data. When survey data are not available, modellers have to weigh up the advantages of attempting to identify expectations processes explicitly, by for example using actual data or published forecasts as a guide to these expectations, against the strong assumptions required to achieve identification.

Acknowledgements

This is a substantially revised version of the paper given at the September 1983 C.J.E. Conference. I would like to thank Charlie Bean, Keith Cuthbertson, David Grubb, Stephen Hall, Brian Henry, Gerald Kennally, Hashem Pesaran, Tony Lawson and other conference participants for helpful comments, without in any way attributing to them opinions or errors in the paper.

Notes

1. I have not examined non-UK models simply through lack of knowledge. The theoretical position of versions of the London Business School model is less clear, although most of what I have to say in the main part of this chapter is applicable to this and other models besides those cited above.

2. At the risk of repetition, I should stress that this is quite different from the question of what Keynes might have thought of the REH.

3. The particular assumption of adaptive expectations is not necessary here, although it helps. Any 'non-rational' expectations scheme will generate persistent errors following a sustained change in some well-chosen exogenous variable. This example is also problematic because these particular models with a Phillips curve are not Keynesian in long-run equilibrium (involving constant inflation), because unemployment always tends to its natural rate. I should prefer a model that treated involuntary unemployment as an equilibrium rather than disequilibrium phenomenon, but this is really a separate issue.

4. Sims (1980) has questioned the very possibility of estimating structural models of any kind satisfactorily, because of the lack of identifying exclusion restrictions once the REH is allowed for. Instead he advocates reduced-form estimation in the form of vector autoregressions. Whether the problems of omitted variable bias and spurious correlation inevitably involved in 'estimation without theory' are less serious remains an open question.

5. What these difficulties do imply is that, in using these derived series, we cannot avoid the issue of measurement error (see Pesaran, 1984).

6. Difficulties arise, unfortunately, when solving these equations forward if survey data on any independent variables do not exist. An alternative already noted is to use published forecasts as a proxy for expectations.

7. If theoretical consistency is assumed, then efficient estimation of large models may be extremely difficult (see Wallis, 1980, or Wickens, 1982, for a discussion of the econometric methodology involved). In practice modellers may have to fall back on Instrumental Variable methods of the type discussed by McCallum (1976) which are only consistent. The output expectations model mentioned above could be interpreted in this way, although it need not be. Interpretation is important when it comes to forecasting. Identification may also be a problem in RE models that are theoretically consistent (Pesaran, 1981).

References

Barker, T.S., Borooah, V., van der Ploeg, R. and Winters, A. (1980) 'The Cambridge Multi-sectoral Dynamic Model', *Journal of Policy Modelling, 2*

Barro, R. and Grossman, H. (1976) *Money, Employment and Inflation,* Cambridge University Press, Cambridge

Buiter, W.H. and Lorie, H.R. (1977) 'Some unfamiliar properties of a familiar macroeconomic model', *Economic Journal, 87,* 743-54

Currie, D. (1981) 'Some long-run properties of dynamic time series models,' *Economic Journal, 91,* 704-15

Giddens A. (1979) *Central Problems in Social Theory,* Macmillan, London

Hahn, F. (1982) *Money and inflation,* Blackwell, Oxford

— — (1984) 'Implicit contracts and involuntary unemployment,' mimeo, Cambridge

Hart, O (1982) 'A model of imperfect competition with Keynesian features,' *Quarterly Journal of Economics, 386,* 109-38

Harvey, A.C. (1981) *Time Series Models,* Phillip Allan, Deddington

Heiner, R. A. (1983) 'The origins of predictable behaviour', *American Economic Review, 83,* 560-95

HM Treasury (1982) *Macroeconomic Model Technical Manual,* HM Treasury, London

Holly, S. and Zarrop, M.B. (1983) 'On optimality and time consistency when expectations are rational,' *European Economic Review,* February

Lawson, T. (1981) 'Keynesian model building and the rational expectations critique,' *Cambridge Journal of Economics, 5,* 311-26

Leijonhufvud, A. (1968) *On Keynesian Economics and the Economics of Keynes,* Oxford University Press, New York

Lucas, R.E. (1981) 'Tobin and monetarism: a review article,' *Journal of Economic Literature, 19,* 558-67

McCallum, B. (1976) 'The rational expectations hypothesis: some consistent estimates,' *Econometrica,* 43-52

National Institute (1981) 'The British economy in the medium term,' *National Institute Economic Review, 98*

Neary, J.P. and Stiglitz, J.E. (1981) 'Towards a reconstruction of Keynesian economics,' *Quarterly Journal of Economics, 96*

Pesaran, M.H. (1981) 'Identification of rational expectations models' *Journal of Econometrics, 10,* 375-98

— — (1984) 'Formation of inflation expectations in British manufacturing industries,' mimeo, Faculty of Economics, University of Cambridge

Rotemberg, J.J. (1983) 'Monetary policy and costs of price adjustment,' *Journal of Economic Dynamics and Control, 5* 267-88

Salmon, M. (1982) 'Error correction mechanisms,' *Economic Journal, 92,* 615-29

Sargent, T. (1978) 'Estimation of dynamic labour demand schedules under rational expectations,' *Journal of Political Economy, 86,* 1009-44

Sawyer, M.C. (1982) 'Towards a post-Kaleckian macroeconomics,' *Thames Papers in Political Economy,* Thames Polytechnic

Sims, C. (1980) 'Macroeconomics and reality,' *Econometrica, 98,* 1-48

— — (1982) 'Testing economic theories,' *Brookings Papers,* 1

Wallis, K.F. (1980) 'Econometric implications of the Rational Expectations Hypothesis,' *Econometrica, 48,* 49-74

Wickens, M. (1982) 'The efficient estimation of econometric models with rational expectations', *Review of Economic Studies, 49,* 55-67

Weitzman, M. (1982) 'Increasing returns and the foundations of unemployment theory', *Economic Journal, 92,* 787-804

Woglom, G. (1982) 'Unemployment equilibrium with rational expectations', *Quarterly Journal of Economics, 386,* 89-108

Wren-Lewis, S. (1984) 'The roles of output expectations and liquidity in explaining recent productivity movements', *National Institute Economic Review, 108*

5 THE SLIPPERY TRANSITION
Johannes J. Klant

The Mechanistic Ideal

In his *Theory of Moral Sentiments* Adam Smith wrote that 'Human society, when we contemplate it in a certain abstract and philosophical light, appears like a great, an immense machine, whose regular and harmonious movements produce a thousand agreeable effects' (1976, 316). These words give expression to an explanatory ideal adhered to by economists to this day. René Descartes, Christiaan Huygens and Isaac Newton had taught mankind to see nature as a mechanism. Moral laws, John Locke had explained, are not essentially different from natural laws. The natural order of human society could thus be viewed as a system of stable relations.

Newton's method of discovery was dominated by his mechanistic ideal and it entailed mathematical treatment. He described nature as a *structure,* a composite of relations specified in terms of variables and constants. The variables are spatiotemporal magnitudes. The constants are either universal numerical coefficients (such as the gravitational constant) or can be calculated from them (such as the constants in the analysis of motions under constraint). Some constants have different values for different bodies or materials and must be ascertained independently (such as the mass of a body) (Nagel, 1968, 169-70). The descriptions of such structures, called *theories,* satisfy the requirement of empirical proof. They enable us to make conditional predictions. They are 'concrete' descriptions.

David Hume was quite explicit, right from the subtitle of his *Treatise of Human Understanding*, that he was attempting 'to introduce the experimental method of reasoning into moral subjects'. He was aware of the peculiar disadvantage of moral philosophy that precludes the possibility of controlled experiments, but, he contended, we must put our trust in 'cautious observation of human life', which included introspection. 'Where experiments of this kind are judiciously collected and compared, we may hope to establish on them a science, which will not be inferior in certainty, and will be much superior to any other of human comprehension' (1975, xviii-xix).

Most economists have optimistically followed his counsel, but it took almost two centuries before they claimed to have rendered the Newtonian mechanisation of their world picture in mathematical language (Dijksterhuis, 1961). The picture was not complete, however. In 1968 Gerhard Tintner had to 'concede that economics had not yet derived universal laws and constants like physics', but unperturbed by this deficiency he could state that mathematical economics and econometrics did exist, the latter being 'defined as the utilization of mathematics, economics, and statistics in an effort to evaluate economic models empirically with the help of concrete data and to investigate the empirical support of certain economic theories'. Its ultimate goal is to achieve reliable predictions. (1968, 16, vii, 83)

The development of econometrics has been considered 'one contributory stream to the Keynesian revolution' (Roll, 1973, 499). What is Keynesian about it, however, is not necessarily Keynes'. Keynes was of the opinion that economics cannot be cultivated in the manner of physics. 'Economics is essentially a moral science and not a natural science', he wrote to Harrod. It employs introspection and judgements of value (CW, XIV, 297). It deals with motives, expectations and psychological uncertainties (CW, XIV, 300). Yet he did not tell us *why* in moral science, contrary to what the Scottish moralists had claimed, the method of natural science was not applicable. Harrod did not seem convinced. Keynes virtually confined himself to remarking that economists should do it differently. He wrote that 'to convert a model into a quantitative formula is to destroy its usefulness as an instrument of thought' (CW, XIV, 299), but he did not explain this. In his introduction to the *Cambridge Economic Handbooks* he described economic theory as what seems to boil down to a form of applied logic. 'It is a method rather than a doctrine, an apparatus of the mind, a technique of thinking, which helps its possessor to draw correct conclusions.' To Harrod he wrote (my italics): 'It seems to me that economics is a *branch of logic,* a way of thinking' (CW, XIV, 296). If we take these words literally, they convey that economics is merely applied logic, some kind of formal system such as geometry or decision theory, thus without empirical content.

Marshallian Instrumentalism

Keynes' introductory text to the *Cambridge Economic Handbooks* is in letter and spirit similar to Alfred Marshall's characterisation when he called economic theory 'not a body of concrete truth, but an engine for the discovery of concrete truth' (1966, 159). Keynes quoted these words and a large part of their context in his biographical essay on Marshall, presenting them as the 'view that the bare bones of economic theory are not worth much in themselves and do not carry on far in the direction of useful practical conclusions' (CW, X, 196). In the same Cantabrigian tradition Joan Robinson labelled her contribution to price theory as 'a box of tools' (1948, 3).

Marshall favoured a method which, he thought, had also been applied by Adam Smith, but had been neglected by Ricardo and his followers. Economists are dealing with a world which is incessantly changing. They study facts, which 'by themselves are silent' (1966, 166) and 'are so complex that they generally teach nothing directly; they must be interpreted by careful reasoning and analysis' (1961, 1, 759 n). He realised, however, that even an interpretation which takes account of variety and complexity cannot produce a concrete description of economic relations. The world is kept in constant motion by forces which have not been examined by economists. 'In this world . . . every plain and simple doctrine as to the relations between cost of production, demand and value is necessarily false, and the greater the appearance of lucidity which is given to it by skilful exposition the more mischievous it is. A man is likely to be a better economist if he trusts to his common senses, and practical instincts, than if he professes to study the theory of value and is resolved to find it easy' (1961, 1, 368).

Keynes refrained from formalising his theories. In *A Treatise on Money* he plays extensively with identities and in *The General Theory* he uses mathematics to make shorthand notes. Nowhere does he apply formal mathematical analysis. This also seemed to be the Marshallian way of theorising. Mathematics in Marshall's view illicitly simplifies what is too complex and too varied for formulae. The world is not so simple as to be amenable to representation in a mathematical model. He used mathematics mainly as a device for *framing* a theory, only to be preserved in appendices and footnotes (1961, 1, x-xi). He also wanted to avoid esoteric argument accessible only to specialists. Economics has a social function. 'A missionary he remained all his life' (CW, X, 167). Economics is meant to better the world and must, therefore, be comprehensible to anybody, businessmen in particular. 'Economics', Marshall wrote when discussing the curriculum in which it should be taught, 'is a science of human motives . . . it could not be better grouped than with the other Moral Sciences' (1966, 171). In his inaugural lecture on 'The Present Position of Economics' he faced the ideas of the historical school and struggled with what Walter Eucken later called 'the great antinomy' between ideographic and nomothetic description, but notwithstanding his consequential view on the bare bones of economic theory he does not see a methodological difference between mechanics and economics. Mechanics too 'supplies a universal engine', he thought (1966, 159). Keynes view thus differed on this point from his teacher's. Marshall's scrappy methodology, scattered in his inaugural address and a number of places in his *Principles of Economics* leaves some essential questions on this matter unanswered, as does Keynes' philosophy.

Marshall rejected the idea of 'political economy' as an art, preferring to cultivate 'economics', a positive science. His particular kind of instrumentalism and his appeal to common sense and practical instincts, however, testify to a concept of economics which in the last resort seems to be an art. The analysis is in his opinion not undertaken in an effort to produce a model which lends itself to making predictions, but to serve as a device for men with practical instincts who know the world to interpret a multiplicity of facts and choose good policies. There is something odd in economics which makes one distrust economists, even when they are philosophising about their trade. In my opinion this oddity results from a particular logical feature of economic theory, one which provides the missing explanation for Keynes' apodictic statements in his letters to Harrod. In order to arrive at it, we must first consider Keynes' methodology a little more closely.

The Induction Problem

A Treatise on Probability (1921) is Keynes' purest theoretical work and his most elaborate. It is not about economics, but about logic. Its inspiration does not come from Marshall, but from W.E. Johnson, G.E. Moore and Bertrand Russell. He digested more literature in writing that book than he is likely to have ever read about economics. His intention was to solve the induction problem that had been set by David Hume.

Newton thought that he derived laws from facts through a process of 'analysis' that is induction. He thought that empirical generalisations were 'deduced from the phaenomena' (Noxon, 1975, 95). Hume showed that laws, which are generalisations about relations between events, cannot be logical conclusions from observations of facts. They rest on assumptions about regularities. They are not the outcome of a purely rational process. They are anticipations rooted in habit, convention, convenience, instinct or passion. 'Reason is, and ought only to be the slave of the passions' (1975, 415).

John Stuart Mill, however, tried to save the idea that induction is a form of logic. He tried to justify inductive argumentation by providing the missing premisses in a syllogistic form of reasoning. Applying this deductive-enthymematic approach he arrived at the conclusion that eliminative induction rests upon an assumption concerning the general constitution of nature. His Law of Universal Causation, in keeping with the Principle of Uniformity, was, however, no more than a Humean maxim subservient to habit, convention, convenience, instinct or passion.

Mill's four canons of eliminative induction, which he offered as reliable means of inference producing new knowledge, were merely experimental methods. They cannot bring about verification, but only refutation or confirmation of hypotheses. His canons do not warrant any certainty that a right choice of hypotheses to be tested has been made. His justification of induction, based on assumptions about the constitution of nature, leads to an infinite regression. As Popper has rightly observed, Hume never accepted the full force of his own logical analysis (1965, 45). The ideas of causality and repetition are not the only maxims rooted in passion. No hypothesis, as Mill willy-nilly makes us realise, can be deduced from phenomena. They are selected. Concealing the problem of choice he leaves the process of discovery hidden in the clouds of passion.

The syllogism of the Method of Difference, for example, can be rendered as follows:

(1) All events have a cause,

(2) $A_1, A_2 \ldots A_n$ are the only events eligible to be causes of E,

(3) In a number of cases has been observed that E takes place without the occurrence of $A_2 \ldots A_n$, but never without that of A_1.

(4) A_1 is the cause of E_1.

Whereas the universal proposition (1) seems to be a respectable premiss because of its lawlike nature, it is impossible to pin one's faith on (2). It does not define a principle of eligibility which could make the syllogism an acceptable model of sound argument justifying induction in general as a rational procedure.

John Maynard Keynes tried to supply that general principle. He replaced (2) by the 'inductive hypothesis', that is to say, 'the absolute assertion of the finiteness of the system under consideration' (CW, VIII, 289) and he rejected the Baconian belief, shared by Mill, that induction is capable of establishing a conclusion which is absolutely certain. Generalisations can be demonstrated *more or less* conclusively.

Following Jacobus Bernouilli (1713), Laplace 1814) and J.J. Fries (1842), he assumed that universal statements are more or less certain, that is, that they are *probable*, as formalised in the probability relation $a/h = P$. The inductive 'hypothesis' h is a set of 'premisses', from which the inductive 'conclusion' a is drawn, and P is the degree of rational belief or probability (CW, VIII, 43). In other words, the probability of the general statement a supported by the set of statements h is P. If the relation between a and h is a tautology, $a/h = 1$ and if it is contradictory $a/h = 0$. Induction, on which 'almost all empirical science rests' (CW, VIII, 241), determines the degree of probability, which in general is not measurable but must lie between both extremes.

'An inductive argument affirms, not that a certain matter of fact *is* so but that *relative to certain evidence* there is a probability in its favour' (CW, VIII, 245). According to Keynes this implies that 'the validity of the inductive method does not depend on the success of its predictions'. Repeated failure may supply us with new evidence, 'But the force *relative to the old evidence* is untouched' (CW, VIII, 245) 'It is a matter of logic and not of experience, what rational conclusions can be drawn from given evidence' (CW, VIII, 246).

Keynes referred here to the (supposed) validity of the inductive method, but not to the reasons for constructing theories. Theories are formulated to solve problems. New theories to predict new events. He seemed to ignore that. He wrote: 'The peculiar virtue of prediction or predesignation is altogether imaginary. The number of instances examined and the analogy between them are the essential points, and the question as to whether a particular "hypothesis" happens to be propounded before or after their examination is quite irrelevant' (CW, VIII, 337).

Popper took him seriously to task for it, but rather out of context. He wrote that 'if the value of a theory would be merely in its relation to its evidential basis, then it would be logically irrelevant whether the supporting evidence precedes or follows in time the invention of the theory' (1965, 247). That, however, is not so. A good theory should be successful in its predictions. The standpoint of inductive logic, Popper contends, makes scientific activities quite incomprehensible (1959, 272). In my opinion this does not invalidate Keynes' argument. Keynes did not deal with the value of a theory. He was not reasoning in a Marshallian manner either and did not have economics in mind at all. He only tried to show that induction is a rational procedure. When he mentioned predictions, it was in relation to the question whether a hypothesis should be proposed before or after the event. It does not matter, he says.

From Keynes to Popper

The Principle of Limited Independent Variety, as Keynes called his inductive hypothesis, implies that nature is not infinitely complex. Keynes sees in the success of modern science a strong indication of the likelihood of this premiss and of the additional principle of atomism. At the end of the book, when drawing his conclusions as to the rationality and the progress of knowledge, he writes that the practical usefulness of induction 'can only exist if the universe of phenomena does in fact present those peculiar characteristics of atomism and limited variety which appear more and more clearly as the ultimate result to which material science is tending' (CW, VIII, 468).

The number of eligible hypotheses is limited and we have a rational method to search for the best one. The eligible hypotheses have positive *a priori* probabilities dependent upon the intension of the statements they contain. The smaller the intension of the condition Px, and the larger the intension of the conclusion Qx, the greater *a priori* probability do we attribute to the generalisation (x) $(Px \rightarrow Qx)$. The *a priori* probability of 'swans are white' is smaller than that of 'swans are non-white'. The *a priori* probability of the latter generalisation is smaller than that of 'birds are non-white'. The *a priori* probability of 'swans are non-swans' is nil.[1].

Some generalisations stand initially in a stronger position than others. They need different amounts of favourable evidence to support them (CW, VIII, 250). The testing of hypotheses under different conditions decides whether their probability can be increased beyond their *a priori* probability or not. Progress in science, it follows from Keynes' analysis, is brought about by testing more and more hypotheses under as great a variety of conditions as possible. The probability of non-refuted hypotheses is then increased. Because there is a finite number of hypotheses we move in the direction of the best one. By pursuing the highest likelihood we improve our theories.

'Logic, like lyrical poetry, being no employment for the middle-aged' (CW, X, 336), Keynes left it at that and turned into an economist. Before the publication of *A Treatise on Probability* he had written about problems of statistics (CW, XI, 49-237). A short review of Frank Ramsay's book in 1931 is his only further publication connected with his probability theory of induction. Its essence, Richard Braithwaite assured us, was kept alive in the work of Harold Jeffreys and Rudolf Carnap, but the details have not survived (CW, VIII, xvi). Bayesian statistics has been the most fruitful result. The concept of psycho-subjective probability developed by L.J. Savage and Bruno de Finetti is a distant relative of Keynes' logico-subjective probability.

The inductivist logicians have tried to reinforce one of his weakest spots. Keynes had introduced 'probability' as a primitive concept and did not attempt to show that 'degree of belief' satisfies the laws of probability calculus. 'On Keynes's theory', Braithwaite wrote, 'it is something of a mystery why the probability relations should be governed by probability calculus' (CW, X, xx). Ramsay suggested, therefore, what Richard C. Jeffrey called, 'a pragmatic analysis of belief'. 'The kind of measurement of belief with which probability is concerned is', Ramsay wrote, 'a measurement of belief *qua* basis of action' (Jeffrey, 1968, 166).

Braithwaite and Carnap considered the degree of belief along this line as a fair betting coefficient. According to Carnap it depends upon the degree of confirmation $c(h,e)$, which measures the reliability of hypotheses h on the basis of the evidence e that supports it. The values of the c-function are probabilities, measurable in a simple language. 'The sociologically booming industry' of inductive logic, displaying a degenerating research programme, as Lakatos saw it (1974, 259), has not produced that language yet. A formal inductive logic, free from assumptions about the constitution of nature, has not been constructed so far.

Karl Popper, who dropped the deductive-enthymematic approach, suggested, however, how we can evade the (unsolvable) problems of probabilistic logic. Universal statements cannot be verified, but a principle of induction is superfluous. Popper replaces 'degree of belief' and 'degree of confirmation' by 'degree of corroboration', but the latter cannot be equated with mathematical probability. A theory is corroborated so long as it stands up to tests. The 'degree' thereof is an appraisal of the severity of these tests under various conditions. Popper holds 'that science has no certainty, no rational reliability, no validity, no authority. The best we can say about it is that although it consists of our own guesses, of our own conjectures, we are doing our very best to test them; that is to say, to criticize them and refute them' (1983, 222).

According to Popper, scientists do not aim at the highest probability.

He uses the concept of 'logical probability', which is complementary to 'degree of falsifiability' and identical to Keynes' *'a priori* probability' (1959, 119, 271). Popper argues that scientists do not start from hypotheses with the highest *a priori* probability and do not go for hypotheses with the highest *a posteriori* probability; 'they have so far always chosen high informative content in preference to high probability, provided that the theory stood up well to its tests' (1959, 363). A higher degree of falsifiability implies a greater empirical content. 'Unemployment rises to 12%' is more falsifiable than 'unemployment changes' and, therefore, contains more information. Scientists like entrepreneurs take risks. They do not make hypotheses as *certain* as possible. 'Always choose the hypothesis which is most *ad hoc!*' is an unacceptable rule (1959, 272).

Hypotheses, in Popper's view, are indeed subservient to the passions but not only to these. The process of criticism to which hypotheses are subjected warrants the rationality and progressiveness of science. Efforts by Hanson, Kuhn, Toulmin, Lakatos, Laudan and others to specify the ideals which scientists set themselves and to describe how they did their research, led to a weakening of Popper's conditions in modern philosophy of science. It seems, however, that where the road of the travelling philosophers bends, it is into the direction of augmented Humean maxims and not of Keynesian logical probabilism.

Keynes' theory of universal induction can at worst be interpreted as bad advice to strive for tautologies and *ad hoc* explanations. It does not take us far, anyhow, if we are trying to find out what scientists do or ought to do. It does not offer a clue as to the difference between physics and moral science either, and does not contain a justification of Marshallian instrumentalism. But *A Treatise on Probability* also includes a theory of statistical induction, which has been at least a stepping stone to Keynes' standpoint on econometrics.

Statistical Induction

Statistics deals with quantities, long-run frequencies of events, that is, chances which satisfy the Kolmogorov axioms for probability (Hacking, 1976). Universal induction consists, as implicitly shown by Mill, in testing alternative *universal* hypotheses. 'The generalisations which they assert . . . claim universality, and are upset if a single exception to them can be discovered (CW, VIII, 244). Statistical induction or inductive correlation similarly consists in testing alternative *statistical* hypotheses. Keynes assumes that 'only in the more exact sciences . . . do we aim at establishing universal inductions' (CW, VIII, 244). 'If we base upon the data this and those swans are white and that swan is black, the conclusion that *most* swans are white, or that the probability of a swan's being white is such and such, then we are establishing an inductive correlation' (CW, VII, 244-5). If one takes into consideration that so-called induction actually consists of testing hypotheses, the field of statistical inference is even larger than Keynes assumed. When universal hypotheses are being tested, inaccuracies in observation attributable to the influence of the investigator, his instruments and his environment have usually to be taken into account. Significance tests are also required then. According to Wald they rest upon the use of decision functions under conditions of uncertainty. To reject or not to reject, that is the question to decide upon.

The last part of *A Treatise on Probability* deals with the foundations of statistical inference. Statistics, Keynes ascertained, has a descriptive and an inductive function. This union is the occasion of a great deal of confusion. 'The statistician, who is mainly interested in the technical methods of his science, is less concerned to discover the precise conditions in which a description can be legitimately extended by induction. He slips somewhat easily from one to the other, and having found a complete and satisfactory mode of description he may take less pains over the transitional argument, which is to permit him to use this description for the purpose of generalisation' (CW, VIII, 359-60).

Keynes looked askance at statisticians. From their comprehensive descriptions no general conclusions can be drawn without extraneous knowledge regarding their samples and without knowledge of the mode and the conditions of the observations themselves. 'The truth of this is obvious; yet, not unnaturally, the more complicated and technical the preliminary statistical investigations become, the more prone inquirers are to mistake the statistical description for an inductive generalisation' (CW, VIII, 361).

He devoted a separate chapter to 'the inductive use of statistical frequencies for the determination of probability *a posteriori*', (CW, VIII, 427), which can be translated into Popperian terminology as 'the use of statistical frequencies to corroborate hypotheses'. He shows himself to be mainly interested in the problem of the stability of correlation coefficients. Statisticians ought to limit their business, in his view, to preparing the numerical aspects of the collected data in an intelligible form. If the investigators wish to try inductive correlation, the statisticians can render them a useful service by 'breaking up a statistical series, according to appropriate principles, into a number of sub-series, with a view to analysing and measuring, not merely the frequency of a given character over the aggregate series, but the *stability* of this frequency amongst the sub-series' (CW, VIII, 428).

In this connection Keynes discussed the dispersion theory of Wilhelm Lexis and its development by Ladislaus von Bortkiewicz. 'Though an admirer', he criticises them, Bortkiewicz in particular, whom he calls, 'like many other students of probability an eccentric, preferring algebra to earth' (CW, VIII, 441). Keynes stressed the point that a statistical analysis is inconclusive without a hypothesis about a causal connection between the quantities. 'The argument can only strengthen a pre-existing presumption; it cannot create one' (CW, VIII, 406). However, 'if we have a considerable body of pre-existing knowledge relevant to the particular inquiry, the calculation of a small number of correlation coefficients may be crucial' (CW, VIII, 467).

Professor Tinbergen's Method
Preferring earth to algebra and being aware of the dangers of slipping from description into induction, Keynes published in *The Economic Journal* of September, 1939 a rather presumptuous criticism of Jan Tinbergen's pioneering work in econometrics, 'Professor Tinbergen's Method' (CW, XIV, 306-12). The publication of this review had been preceded by an epistolary discussion from which I quoted above.

It started in the summer of 1938, when Keynes replied to R. Tyler of the League of Nations, who had sent him proof copies of Tinbergen's *A Method and its Application to Investment Activity* and *Business Cycles in the United States of America.* Tinbergen was temporarily attached to the Financial Section and Economic Intelligence Service (of which A. Loveday was the director) of the Secretariat of the League of Nations. His task was 'to submit to statistical test some of the theories which have been put forward regarding the character and causes of cyclical fluctuation in business activity' (Tinbergen, 1968, 11).

Lawrence Klein has called Keynes' review 'one of his sorriest professional performances' (1951, 450). Even Keynes himself had his misgivings. To Tyler he wrote that he had the utmost difficulty in making head or tail of the two books and in a note to Richard Kahn he called their content 'a mess of unintelligible figurings' and thought it all 'hocus' (CW, XIV, 289). But this time he must have felt himself walking on slippery ground for to Tinbergen he wrote 'I hope you will continue your investigations' (CW, XIV, 293). When submitting his review to his assistant editor, Austin Robinson, he was, as Donald Moggridge reports, uneasy that the review might be 'probably a waste of time' and 'not within my competence' (Moggridge, 1974, 60). 'The probable is the hypothesis on which it is rational for us to act' (CW, VIII, 339), but the probability of the waste of time was apparently too small this time to induce rational conduct.

Keynes displayed much ignorance and misunderstanding of what Tinbergen had done. Richard Stone blamed Keynes' character, bad health and rusty mathematics for it (Stone, 1978). Keynes' criticism was indeed rather awkward and embarrassing. On the one hand he claimed to be an authority, preferring 'the mazes of logic' to those of arithmetic, being one whose tastes in statistical theory had their beginning many years ago. On the other hand he showed himself unfamiliar with the logic of Tinbergen's simple arithmetic. His remarks on the 'ridiculousness' of linear relations, the 'devastating inconsistencies' in the fact that regression coefficients are widely different in various countries (relating to differently defined magnitudes, as he had failed to notice) are beside the point.

The first efforts to test business cycle theory by making use of multiple regression analysis provoked Keynes to indulge his suspicion of statisticians and to apply indiscriminately what he had written on statistical inference and in particular on his favourite subject of stable correlation coefficients.

Thirty years ago I used to be occupied in examining the slippery problem of passing from statistical description to inductive generalisation in the case of simple correlation; and today in the era of multiple correlation I do not find that in this respect practice is much inproved. In case Mr. Loveday or others may nurse inductive hopes, it is worth pointing out that Professor Tinbergen makes the least possible preparations for the inductive transition. (CW, XIV, 315-16).

Keynes' review, all the same, contained a valuable core which Klein apparently failed to notice and which left Tinbergen rather at a loss in his otherwise trenchant reply (1940, 141-54). Keynes wrote that econometrics must necessarily fail as a method of induction. He uses a Popperian argument *avant la lettre* (in Britain, in any case) in stating that multiple correlation analysis is no proper method of testing, because the incorrectness of an economic theory cannot be demonstrated by it:

the method is only applicable where the economist is able to provide beforehand a correct and indubitably complete analysis of the significant factors.

The method is one neither of discovery nor of criticism. It is a means of giving quantitative precision to what, in qualitative terms, we know already as the result of a complete theoretical analysis (CW, XIV, 308).

In other words, in Keynes' judgement Tinbergen did not test but estimated.

Keynes believed that statistical analysis as a means of induction must fail in economics because the condition of a constant environment is not met; 'the environment in all relevant respects, other than the fluctuations in those factors of which we take particular account, should be uniform and homogeneous over a period of time' (CW, XIV, 316). This condition not being met, the curves discovered by the statisticians are a historical presentation but a dubious means of predicting the future.

The Falsifiability of Economic Theories

Economic theories describing a complex world which is liable to unpredictable 'structural' changes cannot be falsified. Keynes' philosophical remarks are perfectly apt. They are not merely applicable to testing by means of econometrics but to all attempts to corroborate economic theories, Falsifiability as a demarcation criterion is a logical affair (Popper, 1983, xx). An analysis of the logical structure of economic theories. Falsifiability as a demarcation criterion is a logical economics describe what Andreas Papandreou (1958) called 'generic structures', that is sets of structures. They do not contain universal numerical constants as in theories which describe unique structures.

In economics, the structural parameters of a theory are often assumed to be liable to change, dependent upon unexplained changes in the environment. Suppose we have the following miniature theory describing an equilibrium (I assume linearity for simplicity's sake):

$$Y = C + I \tag{1}$$
$$C = (1-s)Y,\ 0 < s < 1 \tag{2}$$

This is an idealisation, because we have abstracted from many other relations needed to explain the concrete events, but that is not a methodological deficiency. Physics also deals with idealisations. Concrete physical events can be explained through a synthetic combination of relevant hypotheses. The resultant of the combined hypotheses can be computed, because each hypothesis contains numerical parameters. A hypothesis can only be tested jointly with other hypotheses.

The real problem in economics is that idealisations describe generic structures which permit an unlimited class of interpretations. The miniature theory implies:

$$dI \rightarrow \frac{dY}{dI} = \frac{1}{s} > 0 \tag{3}$$

This is a qualitative prediction, under the condition, however, that s is a constant. If we assume, as Samuelson did (1948, 276-83), that s is a freely-changing variable (according to place and time) and if we do not have at our disposal a theory which enables us to predict changes in s, the theory does not contain meaningful theorems. This is contrary to what Samuelson inferred. The theory now implies:

$$dI \rightarrow \frac{dY}{dI} = \frac{1}{s} - \frac{Y}{s} \frac{ds}{dI} \underset{>}{<} 0 \tag{4}$$

This is a tautological non-prediction. Economists who advance theories of this nature always tell the truth, but they cannot predict. They may impress because their models are less simple than our trivial example, but if you put a question to them and provide them with an initial condition, they answer, 'It will rain or not rain', or more sophisticatedly but nevertheless the same, *'Ceteris paribus,* it will rain', without specifying the restriction. Decisions on the acceptance or rejection of their 'pure' theories cannot be taken on the basis of tests.

Theories which merely yield tautological non-predictions abound in the history of economics. They may be useful as consistent systems of definitions, boxes of tools and elastic supports to world pictures; they are irrefutable. They comply perfectly with the idea of economics as some kind of formal system, a branch of logic which enables us to talk about the world in a specific and consistent way. Their proclaimers always have a perfect alibi (Papandreou, 1958, 142; Archibald, 1959, 61) for no test can disprove their claims.

But most economists of the present day do not behave in that non-committal way. They assume that the structural parameters are 'stable', that is, more or less constant over time, at least during a certain period within a specific area. We can then try to estimate them according to place and can construct an econometric model containing operationally-defined variables and numerical constants. Such a specific model yields predictions of events in a limited social space, such as the economy of the United States since 1867 or the port of Rotterdam since 1950, which have the form of contingent statements. Specific models are, therefore, falsifiable.

The trouble with specific models in economics is, however, that they are generally not proper instances (subrelations) of basic theories which describe sets of structures. A basic theory allows empirical investigations too much choice. They can choose how to translate theoretical concepts into operationally-defined concepts, how to apply dis-aggregation, how to plug in auxiliary hypotheses justifying the use of proxies, how to produce a dynamic version of the theory by introducing time as a variable and dating the variables (which implies a choice of lags). The mathematical forms of the relations also rest upon choices and the model is often augmented by hypotheses which are not included in the basic theory.

A specific model, in other words, is an *interpretation* of a basic theory (possibly composed of elements from more than one basic theory). If it is refuted empirically, the basic theory is not falsified. The outcome of the tests are not decisive; either the interpretation or the theory is false. Decisions on the acceptance or rejection of economic theories are taken in discussions on the *plausibility* of hypotheses. If a Keynesian model yields worse predictions than a monetarist one, Friedman need not be preferred to Keynes. The investigator who considers Keynes' theory more plausible, and more in conformity with his 'natural order' producing 'agreeable effects', will reject his interpretation, but not the theory. The assumption of stable structural parameters is: 'There exists for every area at least one specific model, which satisifies the theory and yields good predictions'. This is an existential statement. Existential propositions are not falsifiable.

Basic theories in economics are heuristic systems. We decide upon their acceptance or rejection in a discussion on plausibility. The success and failure of the estimated empirical models, as Tintner indicated, support arguments in that discussion. Statistical analysis is a contribution to the discussion on plausibility. Newton's ideal cannot be realised, but basic theories, the heuristic 'engines for discovery', are more than forms of applied logic. They are inspiring visions which tempt us again and again to draw mechanistic pictures — for that is what specific models are — of parts of the world so that we can choose a good policy.

In the letter to Harrod from which I quoted above, Keynes wrote: 'Economics is a science of thinking in terms of models joined to the art of choosing models which are relevant to the contemporary world' (CW, XIV, 296). He thereby in fact characterised heuristic theories describing generic structures. Their application is an art to be performed by those who, as Marshall recommended, trust their common sense and practical instincts. Economics contains elements of philosophy, science and art.

Economics as an Art

Reason being the slave of the passions, every science is an art, in the sense of a creative activity which rests upon flashes of intuition and fantasy. It leads to startling discoveries and changes of our world picture. Economists, too, have their brainwaves, albeit never so fantastic and so *a priori* absurd as the ideas of Newton, Einstein or Planck. Investigators of nature get repeated opportunities to be amazed. Economists encounter far fewer surprises. They are more motivated by an urge to change the world known to them than by unabated curiosity. They may utter cries of amazement at discovering the circular flow, loans that create money or the (supposed) efficiency of the market mechanism. Their surprise seems, however, to be accompanied by the pleasant effect of having rediscovered the so-familiar rationality of motivated human conduct — themselves, in other words. The economists do not land in worlds unimaginable through their research. They always stay at home. In moral science we consider ourselves (Klant, 1984, 180).

But when it comes to *predicting* with the aid of theories more artistry is usually demanded from economists than from physicists. Firstly, economists (I am thinking of macroeconomists in particular) have to devise specific models, in mathematical or natural language. This choice and interpretation of basic hypotheses also requires intuition and ingenuity.

Secondly, economic predictions depend on what Theil called 'predictions of a higher order' (1965, 17). Predictions in science are derived from theories by specifying concrete boundary conditions (initial conditions). If certain events are known, the description thereof (I) and the theory (T) together imply the description of other events (P), that is, the predicted events; $T \wedge I \rightarrow P$. In economics I, however, does not describe a set of accomplished facts. It mainly comprises events which *might* occur.

In an econometric forecasting model the values of the exogenous variables have, for the greater part at least, to be estimated on the basis of incomplete information, plausibility, imagination and subjective judgements of likelihood. Predictors also often apply feedbacks; they re-estimate exogenous variables if the determined values of the endogenous variables seem implausible. They can, therefore, even express their own feelings, optimistic or pessimistic. Their forecasts are dependent upon common sense and practical instincts. The judgement of the predictor is an indispensable complement of every prediction process and dependent upon personal talent, experience and training (Zarnowitz, 1968, 427).

The mechanistic model does not allow the application of a mechanistic prediction procedure; 'an econometric model is an objective framework into which judgmental information may be placed' (Klein, 1971, 48). The basic theory is a conjecture, the interpretation is a conjecture and the application is a conjecture. Usually the forecasts on the basis of the three-layered conjectures are not accurate but are better than those of businessmen and politicians. They are at least consistent. The predictions which they yield are neither tautological nor contradictory.

In our century physicists have crushed the mechanistic world picture. It is true that mechanical models continue to be applicable in many fields, but in many others 'science cannot make any predictions about future happenings without an appeal of the laws of chance' (Dampier, 1971, 491). This and other new ways of explaining and predicting events none the less imply that physical scientists continue to think in terms of structures and to describe relations which are characterised by universal numerical constants. The latter are missing in basic economic theories. It makes them non-falsifiable. That is presumably not a symptom of immaturity but reflects the nature of the domain, where 'motives, expectations and psychological uncertainties' reign. Historical change in the economists' domain is much more rapid than in those of the natural scientists, biologists included. Human beings learn and create, they change their world all the time in an unpredictable way. Locke's natural order was not the complex real world, but the simple world as he wished it to be.

I think that when Keynes rejected econometrics as a method of testing he was basically right, but that this should not be taken as a reason for stopping econometric research or for abandoning the use of forecasting models. They provide us with rational guesses. We should handle them for what they are, with scepticism, modesty, and care, knowing that their predictions are debatable. I also think Keynes and Marshall were basically right in considering economics as 'an engine for the discovery of concrete truth'. Basic theories are heuristic systems.

Specific models which are based on them are efforts to find the concrete truth. Basic theories are accepted if they are considered plausible. Their assumptions should be consistent with other accepted hypotheses, they should contribute to the solution of problems and be supported by experience. Inevitably they also have roots in human values and our desires to change the world. I think Keynes was essentially right in considering economics a moral science which cannot be cultivated in the same way as a natural science.

Notes

1. Elements in the set designated by the predicate P have properties which are denominated in the *intension* (meaning) of a concept. They can be specified in a definition. The *extension* (content) is the set of elements for which the defining sentence is true. If a change in extension is accompanied by a change in intension, they always take place in the opposite direction. We can, therefore, also define greater *a priori* probability, as: the larger the extension of the condition Px and the smaller the extension of the conclusion Qx, the greater *a priori* probability do we attribute to the generalisation (x) $(Px \rightarrow Qx)$.

Keynes uses the term 'comprehension' for extension and defines: 'The more comprehensive the condition g and the less comprehensive the conclusion c, the greater *a priori* probability do we attribute to the generalization g' (CW, VIII, 250).

References

Archibald, G.C. (1959) 'The State of Economic Science', *The British Journal for the Philosophy of Science, 10,* May

Dampier, W.C. (1971) *A History of Science* (1929), Cambridge

Dijksterhuis, E.J. (1961) *The Mechanisation of the World Picture,* transl. C. Dikshoorn, Oxford

Hacking, I. (1976) *Logic of Statistical Inference* (1965), Cambridge University Press, Cambridge

Hume, D. (1975) *A Treatise of Human Nature* (1739-40), ed. L.A. Selby-Biggs, London

Jeffrey, R.C. (1968) 'Probable Knowledge', in I. Lakatos (ed.), *The Problem of Inductive Logic,* Amsterdam

Keynes, J.M., CW VIII, X XII, XIV

Klant, J.J. (1984) *The Rules of the Game,* transl. I. Swart, Cambridge University Press, Cambridge

Klein, L.R. (1951) 'The Life of John Maynard Keynes', *The Journal of Political Economy, LIX,* October

— — *An Essay on the Theory of Economic Prediction,* Chicago

Lakatos, I. (1974) 'Popper on Demarcation and Induction', in P.A. Schilpp (ed.), *The Philosophy of Karl Popper,* La Salle

Marshall, A. (1961) *Principles of Economics* (1890), 8th edn, Macmillan, London

— — (1966) 'The Present Position of Economics', in A.C. Pigou (ed.), *Memorials of Alfred Marshall* (1925), London

Moggridge, D.E. (1974) *Keynes: Aspects of the Man and his Work,* Macmillan, London

Noxon, J. (1975) *Hume's Philosophical Development,* Oxford

Papandreou, A.G. (1958) *Economics as a Science,* Chicago

Popper, K.R. (1959) *The Logic of Scientific Discovery,* Hutchinson and Co., London

— — (1965) *Conjectures and Refutations* (1963), Routledge and Kegan Paul, London

— — (1983) *Realism and the Aim of Science,* ed. W.W. Bartley III, London

Robinson, J. (1948) *The Economics of Imperfect Competition,* Macmillan, London

Roll, E. (1973) *A History of Economic Thought,* Faber & Faber, London

Samuelson, P.A. (1948) *Foundations of Economic Analysis,* Harvard University Press, Cambridge, Mass

Smith, A. (1976) *The Theory of Moral Sentiments* (1759), ed. D.D. Raphael and A.L. Macfie, Clarendon Press, Oxford

Stone, R. (1978) *Keynes, Political Arithmetic and Econometrics,* The British Academy, London

Theil, H. (1965) *Economic Forecasts and Policy* (1958), North-Holland, Amsterdam

— — (1940) 'On a method of statistical business-cycle research: a reply', *The Economic Journal, L,* March

Tinbergen, J. (1968) *Statistical Testing of Business-Cycle Theories* (1939), New York

Tintner, G. (1968) *Methodology of Mathematical Economics and Econometrics,* Chicago

Zarnowitz, V. (1968) 'Prediction and Forecasting', *International Encyclopedia of the Social Sciences,* Macmillan and The Free Press

6 ARE POPPERIAN CRITICISMS OF KEYNES JUSTIFIED?

John Pheby

The main objective of this chapter is to arrive at a clearer understanding of aspects of Keynes' methodology. In order to achieve this I think it is both interesting and instructive to consider some Popperian criticisms that have been directed at Keynes' contribution. Such criticisms suggest that the methodological perspectives of Keynes and Popper are different, if not incompatible. Surprisingly, however, it seems on close examination of Keynes' and Popper's work that the two are far closer than is usually believed. One question that this conclusion raises is whether such similarities extend to shared criticisms of Friedman's instrumentalism. We know that Popper rejects this methodology, but what might Keynes' attitude have been? In what follows, I shall first outline the basic methodologies of Keynes and Popper. Then I shall consider the Popperian criticisms of Keynes and assess their validity. Finally, by extending the now established similarities between Keynes and Popper, the former's likely views on Friedman's instrumentalism will be discussed.

Keynes' Methodology

In considering Keynes' methodology it is helpful briefly to consider some of the attitudes of two of his main mentors, his father Neville Keynes, and Alfred Marshall. It seems that they both influenced some of Keynes' basic views on economic methodology.

Neville Keynes' *Scope and Method of Political Economy* was an attempt to deal with some of the methodological controversies arising from the *Methodenstreit* (conflict of methods) of the 1880s. One of his central concerns was the demand for an appropriate balance between the inductive and deductive methods in economics. He argued that different methods were appropriate 'according to the materials available, the state of investigation reached and the object in view' (Neville Keynes, 1897, 6). Consequently, a primarily theoretical discussion could rely more heavily upon a deductive approach, whereas 'concrete problems' would often involve more inductive studies. His basic tenet for economic method was that we 'must begin with observation and end with observation' (220). However it is clear that the initial observation does not necessarily require a very systematic study of facts, more a comprehension 'of elementary economic forces and the conditions under which they operate' (170). Concerning the relative roles to be attributed to induction and deduction, he suggested the following:

> It is necessary, first, to determine what are the principal forces in operation, and the laws in accordance with which they operate. Next comes the purely deductive stage, in which are inferred the consequences that will ensue from the operation of these forces under given conditions. Lastly, by a comparison of what has been inferred with what can be directly observed to occur, an opportunity is afforded for testing the correctness and practical adequacy of the two preceding steps, and for the suggestion of necessary qualifications. (212-13)

Indeed we see how the deductive method is 'aided and controlled by induction'.

Marshall often disagreed with Neville Keynes on matters of method (see Coase, 1975), despite his unwillingness to become involved in disputes over methodology. However, on the question of induction and deduction their views were similar. He too felt that there was a place for all methods within economics and that induction and deduction usually entailed each other. He also saw situations where induction would be more appropriate than deduction, and vice versa. Ultimately he regarded himself as representing a 'dull mean' between the two methods. This view is not shared by Coase, who argues that Marshall was more inclined towards induction. Maynard Keynes (CW, XIV, 296) made a similar observation.

It seems that his father and Marshall influenced Keynes on this particular question of methodology. To begin with Keynes clearly rejected both extremes of inductivism and deductivism. Here I define extreme inductivism as an approach that seeks to secure objectivity in scientific investigation by forbidding researchers to entertain any preconceived ideas or hypotheses concerning the phenomena under investigation. Instead one must proceed by carefully collecting facts. Eventually it is hoped that repeated observations will result in some regularities or causal connections being established. Keynes found little attraction in such an approach (CW, VIII, 338).

At the other methodological extreme Keynes felt unhappy about a highly abstract, deductive approach within economics, especially when it led us too far away from real-world considerations. This was something for which he castigated Ricardo (CW, X, 87-8, 98).

Not surprisingly a rejection of the extremes of induction and deduction, at least in isolation from each other, manifested itself in a belief that some combination of both approaches was desirable. For example, in a letter to Harrod, he wrote:

> It seems to me that economics is a branch of logic, a way of thinking; and that you do not repel sufficiently firmly attempts à la Schultz to turn it into a pseudo-natural-science. One can make some quite worth while progress merely by using your axioms and maxims. But one cannot get very far except by devising, new and improved models. This requires, as you say, 'a vigilant observation of the actual working of our system'. *Progress* in economics consists almost entirely in a progressive improvement in the choice of models. The grave fault of the later classical school, exemplified by Pigou, has been to overwork a too simple and out-of-date model, and in not seeing that progress lay in improving the model; whilst Marshall often confused his models, for devising which he had great genius, by wanting to be realistic and by being unnecessarily ashamed of lean and abstract outlines'. (CW, XIV, 296)

Elsewhere he referred to his approach involving 'interspersing our logic with practical judgements based on experience' (CW, XIII, 483).

Furthermore, Keynes also recognised that different approaches were appropriate depending upon the task in hand. For example, his strong criticisms of Tinbergen's econometrics were largely founded upon the inductive weaknesses that Keynes identified with this method (see Lawson in this volume for similar considerations). He argued that 'If we were dealing with the action of numerically measurable, independent forces, adequately analysed so that we knew we were dealing with independent atomic factors and between them completely comprehensive, acting with fluctuating relative strength on material constant and homogeneous through time' (CW, XIV, 286) then Tinbergen's approach might be acceptable. For Keynes, however, this was not the case. But it is interesting that these very same considerations were made by him when considering the possibility of inductive reasoning in his *Treatise on Probability* (CW, VIII, 276-8). There he argued that if these conditions were not satisfied then induction would be 'useless'.

However, he did indicate other situations where Tinbergen's methods might be more appropriate (CW, XIV, 295). Elsewhere he acknowledges that certain inductive assumptions were sometimes necessary:

> Peace and comfort of mind require that we should hide from ourselves how little we foresee. Yet we must be guided by some hypothesis. We tend, therefore, to substitute for the knowledge which is unattainable certain conventions, the chief of which is to assume, contrary to all likelihood, that the future will resemble the past. That is how we act in practice. (CW, XIV, 124)

Conversely, when considering *The General Theory* he regarded it as a work of pure theory that did not require a great deal of statistical investigation on his part (CW, XIV, 274). Indeed he emphasised the more logical, deductive nature of that work on a number of occasions (e.g. CW, XXIX, 41, 73).

That Keynes believed that both induction and deduction have a role to play in economics may strike one as unremarkable. Many other economists have argued similarly, especially since the days of the *Methodenstreit.* However Keynes' views differ from such familiar, and often glib, appeals. He was very familiar with some of the difficulties associated with induction and deduction. The more significant, for our purposes, is his interest in induction. Here Keynes not only thoroughly studied induction, but also made an original contribution within the field with his *Treatise on Probability.* Induction has always proved to be a difficult matter for philosophers of science. This arises from the very nature of inductive reasoning, whereby assertions are usually made about events, or propositions, that go beyond the evidence available. Even though inductive reasoning may support certain laws or regularities we have no means of knowing whether they will persist. In order to render existing laws, or regularities, feasible for future needs, an appeal is often made to the Principle of the Uniformity of Nature. This states that laws or regularities that have held in the past will continue to hold in the future. The difficulty with this argument is that it is circular. One is employing an inductive argument to justify induction. This is known as 'the problem of induction' and is posed by our inability to provide rational or logical grounds for justifying induction.

Keynes sought to provide rational grounds for employing inductive reasoning in his *Treatise on Probability.* He appreciated that it was necessary to start from an *a priori* finite probability concerning the truth of any generalisation, otherwise the accumulation of inductive evidence would not raise its probability above zero (CW, VIII, ch. 22). Keynes realised that one of the difficulties in obtaining such a finite *a priori* probability is that there are innumerable characteristics associated with all of the phenomena of the world. Consequently he needed to 'bind up' all of these characteristics into a finite or limited number of groups. Therefore every characteristic would need to belong to at least one group. This was achieved by Keynes' 'principle of limited independent variability'.

It is not surprising that Keynes found elegantly combining induction and deduction 'a singularly difficult art'. His advocacy was based upon an intimate understanding of both approaches. His concerns are no longer shared by the majority of economic methodologists. Interest in the induction-deduction issue has been largely replaced by consideration of other methodologies, such as those of instrumentalism, or those associated with Kuhn and Lakatos. These perspectives largely avoid detailed consideration of the appropriate balance between induction and deduction, which partly explains their popularity. However, as Keynes seems to have realised, consideration of such issues does involve difficulties which need to be met. Indeed, there are signs that some economists are endeavouring to do this. For example, Wiles (1979-80) and Eichner (1983) basically argue that economics is far too deductively oriented, and needs to be more empirical. Similar considerations can be found in Gordon (1976). He feels that a reasonable balance between theoretical and empirical work has rarely been achieved, with serious consequences for economics.

Another important methodological perspective that we can associate with Keynes is that of critical rationalism. It seems that he was prepared to invite criticism of his views in order to avoid becoming dogmatic. For example he wrote, 'I hope that in these lectures I shall show that I am not obstinate and can take advantage of criticism on substantial points of argument and exposition' (CW, XXIX, 38). This appears to be no casual comment. He had thought about the role of criticism in the development of economic theories when writing about Marshall. He was unhappy with Marshall's long delays in publication owing, in part, to fears of criticism. Keynes favoured Jevons' tendency to discuss his ideas openly and invite criticism. This approach, for Keynes, was more likely to stimulate discussion and aid progress.

Although he grew to dislike controversy, at least for its own sake, we still find him writing, 'On the other hand, controversy may assist progress and be healthy in spite of being disagreeable; whilst the avoidance of it may allow the charlatan to flourish unrebutted' (CW, XIII, 469). He continues:

> Moreover, a candid author surely enjoys criticism which comes from a thorough understanding of his thesis. There is no greater satisfaction than in the exchanging of ideas between minds which have truly met, leading to further discoveries and a shift of view in response to difficulties and objections. (CW, XIII, 470-1)

An attachment to such a critical rationalism helps to explain his dislike of dogmatism. One of his criticisms of the pervasive influence of the classical school was that he felt it to be unhealthy because it tended to 'ward off experiments, to damp enthusiasm, and keep us all in order'. To counter this he appeals for the adoption of the 'guarded and undogmatic attitude'. It seems that he genuinely adhered to such a belief in practice. On being asked why he changed his views so often he replied, 'when my information changes, I alter my conclusions'. His tendency to change his views frequently has been well catalogued and considered in Johnson (1974). She refers to an incident when Keynes was discussing differences between political parties:

> To proclaim any dogma as infallible and applicable in all cases, he [Keynes] said, debating the merits of the two parties, was 'voluntarily to shut oneself out from any scientific approach to economic problems by means of experiment and investigation' (105).

Another aspect of Keynes' method that we can identify was its problem-dependent nature. Most of Keynes' works were designed to deal with a particular problem. That economic theory should, for Keynes, be used to deal with problems is well illustrated in his biographical essay on Malthus (CW, X, 107). Here we read that Malthus' method was 'the best of all routes' by which to approach economics. This route, a combination of induction and deduction, ultimately ends in our being able 'to interpret the problem and propose the remedy'.

This section has attempted to illustrate how Keynes adopted a problem-dependent methodology that involved some combination of induction and deduction supported by a critical rationalist outlook.

We can now briefly consider Popper's methodology.

Popper's Methodology

Given the vast scope of Popper's writings we can only hope to give a brief outline of his methodology here. We shall concentrate on those features of Popper's method that have a more direct bearing on our central concern, i.e. Keynes' methodology.

One of the main concerns of Popper is to reject all attempts to justify induction. 'I hold that inductive procedures simply do not exist (not even low-level ones) and that the story of their existence is a myth' (Popper, 1983, 118). He believes firmly that we have no rational grounds for drawing wider inferences than the available evidence warrants. Also he does not regard extreme inductivism as a feasible, or desirable, methodology. He questions whether such an approach can ever lead to progress in science. This question of the growth of knowledge has always been a central concern of his. Contrary to inductivism, Popper feels that we always need some frame of reference, some point of departure (Popper, 1976a, 46-7) otherwise we are likely to continue gathering facts for the rest of our lives. Indeed if we wish to gather 'all' the evidence then our endeavours are destined to end in frustration.

Popper's misgivings regarding induction stem from his belief that searches for regularities and verifications of theories can easily result in our being reluctant to take much account of disconfirming evidence. Consequently he felt that induction could lead to dogmatism. Dogmatism is something that he had identified with Adlerian and Freudian psychology and Marxism. He found that these theories seemed always to explain away phenomena that contradicted them. Popper regarded such feats as a vice rather than a virtue.

It was with such considerations in mind that he first proposed his falsification methodology. Instead of seeking to verify theories we should actively attempt to falsify them. The hope is that bad hypotheses will be quickly dismissed and be replaced by better ones that can withstand rigorous attempts at falsification. His evolutionary view of scientific development is clearly Darwinian in the sense that a process of rational selection ensures the survival of the fittest theories. Popper recognises that we can never completely unmask the truth about the world because our knowledge is always, to some extent, tentative and fallible. However, the progressive discovery of theories containing greater verisimilitude is a step in the right direction. Theories, for Popper, are essentially devices for enabling us to draw deductive consequences.

He has schematised his methodological approach in the following manner (Popper, 1976c, 32).

$$P_1 \rightarrow TT \rightarrow EE \rightarrow P_2$$

Initially we begin with a problem that we wish to solve with the aid of a tentative theory. This theory is subjected to rigorous criticism in order to eliminate error. However the process is continuous because as the theory develops it throws up fresh problems. This schema needs to be supported by other features for it to have much chance of being successful. Firstly, we need to adhere, as with Keynes, to critical rationalism. This is a particularly crucial aspect of Popper's methodology as it lies at the heart of his distaste for dogmatism. The critical rationalist is someone who does not cling onto beliefs, but is ready to modify his/her position in the light of comments and criticisms from others. Therefore the critical attitude is marked by a willingness not only to change beliefs but to put them to rigorous tests. Secondly, Popper seeks to prevent theorists from making *ad hoc* adjustments to their theories with the sole intention of saving the theory from refutation. Such modifications he terms 'immunizing stratagems' and 'conventionalist twists'. Modifications can be permitted where they broaden the empirical scope of a theory. This is due to that theory being rendered more susceptible to falsifying evidence.

This outline of Popper's method immediately suggests likely areas of agreement and disagreement with the description of Keynes' methodology given earlier. With respect to critical rationalism there would appear to be much similarity between them. They also both favour a problem-dependent methodology. However, the similarities appear to end here. When considering the fundamental issue of induction they seem to be very far apart. When we also bear in mind Popperian-type criticisms of Keynes' views of Tinbergen's econometrics the gulf seemingly grows wider. Is this the case? Or are there really further similarities that we have not yet discovered?

Popperian Criticisms of Keynes

In order to answer these questions we need to consider whether Popperian criticisms of Keynes are justified. An obvious criticism that Popper raised against many writers, including Keynes, concerned their attempts to justify induction. This applies even to endeavours to employ induction in the context of probability relations. Popper objected to such approaches because the probability of any generalisation being true must always be zero (see Newton-Smith, 1981, 49-50). The reason for this is that any generalisation which we expect to hold into the future necessarily implies an infinite number of instances. The probability of any generalisation being true when the number of instances approaches infinity is, at the limit, zero. Any attempt to impose a probability of one on such a generalisation, which would get round this difficulty, would be unacceptable to Popper. For we can rarely possess such certain knowledge within his fallibilist framework.

We have seen that Keynes possessed some awareness of such difficulties. How successful was he in dealing with this problem? His approach does suffer from a number of limitations. One of the major difficulties concerns his need to use the Principle of the Uniformity of Nature (CW, VIII, 284). This immediately weakens his attempts to justify induction rationally. The circularity involved leads us back to the 'problem of induction'. However there are other weaknesses associated with Keynes' approach. For example, the employment of the 'principle of limited independent variability' is such a strong, and untestable, assumption that one cannot feel easy about it. Furthermore, as Barker (1957, 58-61) notes, there are other limitations. How do we arrive at the finite *a priori* probabilities that are so important? Unless Keynes could provide some meaningful way of assigning *a priori* probabilities to any connection or regularity that we are interested in, his approach lacks credibility. Even if we were happy about the use of the 'principle of limited independent variability' we are given little indication as to how we define the number of distinct groups or identify the characteristics within them. Consequently Keynes provides us with an approach that is impossible to put into operation. Indeed it is clear that he harboured doubts about the approach himself. 'I do not pretend that I have given any perfectly adequate reason for accepting the theory I have expounded, or any such theory' (CW, VIII, 293).

This suggests that Popper's criticism of Keynes' attempts to justify induction is justified, up to a point. The reason for this qualification is simple. For despite his dismissal of all forms of induction we find that Popper is not as totally divorced from this approach as he would like to be. To begin with O'Hear (1980, ch. 4) notes Popper's need to employ something like the Principle of the Uniformity of Nature for scientific activity to be at all possible. O'Hear comments, 'This is not far from admitting that there is a sense in which inductive assumptions have to be made by us in our attempt to live in, and understand the world' (62-3). Furthermore, Popper's more recent developments of degrees of corroboration and verisimilitude are not without their inductive features.

As Putnam (1981, 63) notes:

> Standard 'inductivist' accounts of the confirmation of scientific theories go somewhat like this: theory implies prediction (basic sentence, or observation sentence); if prediction is false, theory is falsified; if sufficiently many predictions are true, theory is confirmed. For all his attack on inductivism, Popper's scheme is not *so* different: theory implies predictions (basic sentence); if prediction is false, theory is falsified; if sufficiently many predictions are true, and certain further conditions are fulfilled, theory is highly corroborated.

Similar considerations, where Popper's 'whiff of inductivism' is seen to be more of a 'full-blown storm', can be found in Newton-Smith (1981, 67-70). Therefore we find that the gulf between Keynes and Popper on induction is not as wide as initially appeared and it seems that Popper also relies upon some combination of induction and deduction.

The other Popperian criticism of Keynes that we shall consider comes from Bray (1977). This relates to Keynes' criticisms of Tinbergen's pioneering work in econometrics. A detailed consideration of this aspect of Keynes' work is unnecessary here as it can be found elsewhere in this volume (see especially, Lawson, Pesaran and Smith). It is sufficient for our purposes to concentrate upon certain aspects of Keynes' view of econometrics. Bray attacked Keynes' criticisms of Tinbergen from a purportedly Popperian perspective. It is clear that Bray finds Popper's methodology more congenial than that of Keynes. He claims that Popper would approve of the use of econometrics in order to test theories. Indeed he cites Popper's approving reference, from *The Poverty of Historicism,* to Tinbergen's method of 'trial and error'.

This interpretation is misleading. Firstly, it misses the point, discussed above, that Keynes' misgivings concerning Tinbergen's work were actually along very Popperian lines. That is, Keynes felt very unhappy about the unreliably inductive nature of Tinbergen's work (CW, XIV, 229, 316). When considering statistical work Keynes was very aware of the problems associated with induction:

> the most usual error in modern method consists in treating too lightly what I have termed above the *inductive* problem, i.e. the problem of passing from series S_1, S_2 etc of which we have observed samples to the series S of which we have not observed samples. (CW, VIII, 454)

He felt that these difficulties had not been adequately dealt with by Tinbergen. Consequently a significant feature of Keynes' criticism would very probably receive Popper's endorsement.

This view is seen to be more likely when we examine closely Popper's 'approval' of Tinbergen's method of 'trial and error'. There is no mention, or discussion, of Tinbergen's econometrics in Popper's book. Indeed closer inspection of *The Poverty of Historicism* proves revealing. For example, on the use of statistics in economics, we find the following:

> In physics, for example, the parameters of our equations can, in principle, be reduced to a small number of natural constants — a reduction which has been successfully carried out in many important cases. This is not the case in economics; here the parameters are themselves in the most important cases quickly changing variables. This clearly reduces the significance, interpretability and testability of our measurements. (Popper, 1976b, 143)

These are precisely the types of arguments raised by Keynes against Tinbergen. That Popper would be sceptical about statistical techniques within economics follows from the predominantly inductive nature of such methods and his adherence to methodological individualism. Popper regards this as the most suitable methodology for the social sciences. Indeed he has intimated how marginal utility could be used in other social sciences besides economics (Popper, 1976c, 118). Methodological individualists view individuals as the ultimate consitituents of the social world. Therefore any situation or institution is the result of a complex interaction of individuals' dispositions, beliefs and situations. Methodological individualists are generally unhappy with considerations of macroeconomic phenomena, e.g. unemployment or growth, unless they relate to these types of individualistic features.

Keynes was no methodological individualist but it seems clear that their views on econometrics are similar. In fact, Popper is very scathing of attempts to 'formalise' the social sciences:

> I dislike the attempt, made in fields outside the physical sciences, to ape the physical sciences by practising their alleged 'methods' — measurement and 'induction from observation'. The doctrine that there is as much science in a subject as there is mathematics in it, or as much as there is measurement or 'precision' in it, rests upon a complete misunderstanding. On the contrary, the following maxim

holds good for all sciences: never aim at more precision than is required by the problem in hand. (Popper, 1983, 7)

These sentiments concerning formalism within economics were largely shared by Keynes. This is a theme that runs throughout his correspondence and his review of Tinbergen's econometrics. It is also well known that he had doubts about the use of much of the mathematics being employed within economics (e.g. CW, VII, 297-8; CW, XXIX, 18). What emerges from this is that the other Popperian criticism of Keynes seems wholly unjustified. Indeed our considerations so far point to some substantial similarities in the methodologies adopted by Keynes and Popper. They both, in effect, combine induction and deduction, employ a predominantly problem-dependent approach, adhere to critical rationalism and an associated dislike of dogmatism, and are highly suspicious of attempts to 'formalise' the social sciences.

We are now in a position to turn to our final consideration. This concerns Friedman's instrumentalist methodology. We know that Popper has always been critical of this methodology. It seems that Keynes and Popper have a great deal in common methodologically. Does this common ground extend to Keynes also rejecting instrumentalism?

Popper and Keynes on Instrumentalism

The methodology of instrumentalism is of some interest to economists as Friedman's widely influential position is now seen as being essentially of this nature (Boland 1979, 1982; Caldwell 1980, 1982). Popper's views on instrumentalism are clear. He has, in fact, provided us with one of the definitive statements of this methodology.

By instrumentalism I mean the doctrine that a scientific theory such as Newton's, Einstein's, or Schrödinger's, should be interpreted as an instrument, and *nothing but an instrument*, for the deduction of predictions of future events (especially measurements) and for other practical applications; and more especially, that a scientific theory should not be interpreted as a genuine conjecture about the structure of the world, or as a genuine attempt to describe certain aspects of our world. The instrumentalist doctrine implies that scientific theories can be more or less useful, and more or less efficient; but it denies that they can, like descriptive statements, be true or false. (Popper, 1983, 111-12)

Another feature of instrumentalism is that it seeks to separate observation statements from theoretical ones (Newton-Smith, 1981, 30). This enables instrumentalists to emphasise observation statements, particularly predictions, and not worry too much about awkward theoretical considerations. This is further seen to be conducive towards making progress in science, as we need only to compare the predictive power of alternative theories.

Popper feels unhappy with instrumentalism for a number of reasons (Popper, 1983, 112-18). To begin with he is a realist who believes that the ultimate aim of science is the search for truth. Although he appreciates the difficulties associated with this position he feels that realism is the best way to progress. This concern for truth leads Popper to seek explanations, and he is therefore uneasy with the instrumentalist emphasis upon prediction. Also, instrumentalists are not concerned with the truth or falsity of their theories, and therefore falsifications are not actively sought. He also regards instrumentalism as a disingenuous way of dissolving the 'problem of induction'.

Friedman's famous essay 'The Methodology of Positive Economics' is now seen by many economic methodologists as owing more to instrumentalism than positivism. Indeed Friedman accepts Boland's portrayal of his instrumentalism as 'entirely correct' (cited in Caldwell, 1982, 178). The instrumentalist flavour of Friedman's essay is clear (e.g. Friedman, 1953, 14-15). Also the very objective of positive economics, for Friedman, is to provide a method that will help us in achieving greater consensus on policy matters. He clearly seeks to do so in classic instrumentalist fashion by placing more emphasis upon observational statements. This circumvents controversies over 'basic values' on which 'men can ultimately only fight'.

We know that Popper rejects instrumentalism, but what of Keynes? The difficulty we face here is that Keynes appears never to have directly considered this methodology. However it is possible to discern that Keynes' attitude would probably have been unfavourable.

To begin with Keynes, like Popper, adhered to views that render him, in important respects, a realist. As seen above, realists are diametrically opposed to instrumentalism. Newton-Smith (1981, 29) notes that realists typically believe that 'scientific propositions are true or false . . . in virtue of how the world is independently of ourselves' and are seekers after truth. It seems that Keynes satisfies both conditions. Firstly, he wrote, 'All propositions are true or false, but the knowledge we have of them depends upon our circumstances' (CW, VIII, 3), thereby upholding the basic tenet of realism. That Keynes regarded the search for truth of paramount importance is well known (Skidelsky, 1983, 116, 133). Furthermore Keynes was genuinely interested in *explaining* the 'world in which we live' and the 'world of experience'. Therefore it would appear that he possessed marked realist inclinations.

A feature of Friedman's instrumentalism is the positive virtue of employing assumptions that are 'wildly inaccurate descriptive representations of reality'. Indeed in a perceptive article Musgrave (1981) has argued that Friedman's failure to distinguish between the different roles of assumptions is the very aspect of his methodology that renders it instrumentalist. This is interesting because Keynes gave some thought to the question of assumptions within economics. His considerations seem to suggest that he held views that would have differed from those of Friedman. It is true that Keynes recognised that in order to make the complexities of the economy more intelligible we frequently needed to make simplifying assumptions (CW, XIII, 265, 482-3). However he was unhappy with this practice when it involved assumptions that were totally unrealistic. For example, he identified the assumptions of orthodox theory as being 'a state of definite and constant expectation' and 'that there should be a state of full employment'. He was critical of the use of such assumptions as they assumed away the very problems, unemployment and the trade cycle, that we were interested in (CW, XIV, 106). Indeed he wrote that 'it is for those who make a highly special assumption to justify it' (CW, XIV, 109). Such views strongly suggest that Keynes would have felt unhappy with Friedman's view that it does not matter if assumptions are a 'wildly inaccurate descriptive representation of reality'.

Another aspect of instrumentalism that would not have found favour with Keynes is the primacy given to prediction. He felt that the 'peculiar virtue of prediction or predesignation is altogether imaginary' and that it does not matter if our hypotheses are formed to account for already existing phenomena (CW, VIII, 337).

The tendency to relegate the significance of theoretical considerations that we so often associate with instrumentalism was something else that Keynes disliked. As previously noted this aspect of instrumentalism is designed to make our empirical work more straightforward. Keynes noted this in connection with Tinbergen's econometrics. 'One feels a suspicion that the choice of factors is influenced (as is only natural) by what statistics are available, and that many vital factors are ignored because they are statistically intractable or unprocurable' (CW, XIV, 287). Elsewhere he complained, on a visit to the United

States, that some of the younger economists there (i.e. Gilbert, Humphrey and Salant) were neglecting 'certain theoretical considerations which are important in the interests of simplifying their statistical task' (CW, XXIII, 192). All these considerations indicate that Keynes probably would have rejected instrumentalism.

Conclusion

We have seen how certain aspects of Keynes' and Popper's methodologies are very similar, thereby rendering the Popperian criticisms, discussed above, largely unjustified. The clarification of important features of Keynes' methodology that our comparison has facilitated is of more than intrinsic interest. This is because some of Keynes' methodological concerns are still relevant. It would be claiming too much to suggest that complete answers to contemporary methodological problems are to be found in Keynes' writings. However, we could profit from paying them more attention. For example, the epistemological status of econometrics receives scant treatment in most text-books. Keynes appreciated that the predominantly inductive nature of much econometric work is problematic. Consequently he recommended that great care be exercised in the way we use, and interpret, data. Such sensible advice does not appear to have been heeded by many researchers (see Mayer, 1980).

Also Keynes' critical rationalism is an example to us all. He wanted economics to be a progressive science. In order to achieve this he realised that we cannot afford to cling on to outmoded theories. His partial success in avoiding this enabled him to make such a fundamental, and constructive, contribution to economic theory. However, when one surveys the current collection of economic paradigms they do not seem to be imbued with a strong spirit of critical rationalism. The result is often a dogmatic adherence to a particular world view. It is all very well economists paying lip-service to Popper, but generally there seems to be a reluctance to practice what is preached.

Finally, it is worth noting that, to his credit, Keynes never resorted to soft methodological options such as scepticism and instrumentalism, despite his awareness of the shortcomings of much empirical work. Scepticism was an unattractive perspective for such a constructive thinker. His own doubts concerning classical orthodoxy were channelled into developing a richer alternative. Many of those who, understandably, feel disenchanted with much of neoclassical orthodoxy should consider this. There is far too much negative criticism of conventional wisdom and not enough effort being made to develop opposing paradigms.

Instrumentalism is another means of escaping some of the methodological problems considered above. However such an approach can easily lead us into a cul-de-sac of shallow empiricism. We have good reason to believe that Keynes would have viewed instrumentalism in such terms. Unfortunately, it seems that too many within the economics profession do not see things, methodologically, similarly to Keynes. This is a pity, because he has provided us with several leads that are worth following.

Acknowledgements

I wish to pay particular thanks to an anonymous referee who made many helpful criticisms of an earlier version of this chapter. William Guthrie also provided me with some helpful comments. Any remaining errors and omissions are my responsibility.

References

Barker, S. F. (1957) *Induction and Hypothesis*, Cornell Univesity Press, Ithaca
Boland, L. A. (1979) 'A Critique of Friedman's Critics', *Journal of Economic Literature, 17*, 503-22
— — (1982) *The Foundations of Economic Method*, George Allen and Unwin, London
Bray, J. (1977) 'The Logic of Scientific Method in Economics', *Journal of Economic Studies, 4*, 1-28
Caldwell, B. (1980) 'A Critique of Friedman's Methodological Instrumentalism', *Southern Economic Journal, 47*, 366-74
— — (1982) *Beyond Positivism: Economic Methodology in the Twentieth Century,* George Allen and Unwin, London
Coase, R. H. (1975) 'Marshall on Method', *Journal of Law and Economics, 18*, 25-31
Eichner, A. S. (1983) 'Why Economics is Not Yet a Science', *Journal of Economic Issues, 17*, 507-20
Friedman, M. (1953) *Essays in Positive Economics*, University of Chicago Press, Chicago
Gordon, R. A. (1976) 'Rigor and Relevance in a Changing Institutional Setting', *American Economic Review, 66*, 1-14
Johnson, E. (1974) 'John Maynard Keynes: Scientist or Politician?', *Journal of Political Economy, 82*, 99-111
Keynes, J. M. CW, VII, VIII, IX, X, XII, XIV, XXIII, XXIX
Keynes, J. N. (1897) *The Scope and Method of Political Economy*, 2nd edn, Macmillan, London
Mayer, T. (1980) 'Economics as a Hard Science: Realistic Goal or Wishful Thinking', *Economic Inquiry, 18*, 165-78

Musgrave, A. (1981) '"Unreal Assumptions" in Economic Theory: The F-Twist Untwisted', *Kyklos, 34*, 377-87

Newton-Smith, W. H. (1981) *The Rationality of Science,* Routledge and Kegan Paul, London

O'Hear, A. (1980) *Karl Popper,* Routledge and Kegan Paul, London

Popper, K. R. (1976a) *Conjectures and Refutations,* 4th edn, Routledge and Kegan Paul, London

— — (1976b) *The Poverty of Historicism,* Routledge and Kegan Paul. London

— — (1976c) *Unended Quest,* Fontana, London

— — (1983) *Realism and the Aim of Science*, Hutchinson, London

Putnam, H. (1981) 'The Corroboration of Theories', in Ian Hacking (ed.), *Scientific Revolutions*, Oxford University Press, Oxford

Skidelsky, R. (1983) *John Maynard Keynes: Hopes Betrayed 1883-1920*, Macmillan, London

Wiles, P. (1979-80) 'Ideology, methodology and neoclassical economics', *Journal of Post Keynesian Economics, 2*, 155-80

7 KEYNES, PREDICTION AND ECONOMETRICS

Tony Lawson

Introduction

The object of this chapter is to suggest that, although prominent contributions on the nature and usefulness of econometrics have made significant reference to Keynes' views on this topic (see e.g. Patinkin, 1976; Hendry, 1980), it remains the case that Keynes' more 'fundamental' criticisms of econometrics are in the main neglected. Thus, whilst such contributions have tended to concentrate on Keynes' comments on econometrics that deal with 'technical issues' (such as, in modern terminology, problems of omitted variable bias, simultaneous equation bias and so on), I wish to argue that the main thrust of Keynes' criticisms are of a more philosophical or methodological nature deriving from the theories and arguments which he developed in his *Treatise on Probability*.

It is also worth noting that studies which do, in fact, examine Keynes' ideas as presented in the *Treatise on Probability* tend not to relate them to his later views on econometrics. Indeed, a recent relatively extensive contribution by O'Donnell, which does trace the relationship between Keynes' philosophical and other writings, admits that a 'detailed discussion of Keynes theory of induction [which I shall argue is necessary in order to understand his comments on econometrics] has been omitted' (1982, 38), and O'Donnell suggests that a 'further study, "Keynes: Philosophy and Econometrics" would be a further worthwhile enterprise' (1982, 41).

This chapter, therefore, can be interpreted either as an attempt to fill part of a gap, or, given recent accounts of Keynes' views on econometrics, an attempt to redress an imbalance of emphasis. To this end Keynes' account of probability and induction is summarised below and some implications of this account are illustrated in the important context of 'prediction' and 'predictive accuracy'. Following on from this an assessment is made of the assumptions that, according to Keynes, are fundamental if inductive methods are to be employed legitimately. The relevance of these issues to Keynes' criticisms of econometrics is analysed next and finally some conclusions are drawn.

116

Keynes and the 'Treatise on Probability'

Keynes' theory of probability represents a major development within the logical tradition of probability. In this account, even if it is not possible to argue demonstrably from any one proposition to another one, there still exists a logical relation between the two propositions. This is the probability relation. If a conclusion a is related to a premise h with probability p then the probability relation — sometimes called the argument — is written $a/h = p$. The probability of the conclusion a is *always* relative to some evidence h. The discovery of new evidence h_1 does not entail that the previous 'argument' was wrong, it just gives rise to a new argument $a/h\ k$.

The logical view of probability is to be contrasted with the more common notion held within the 'scientific tradition'. In this account probability is usually treated as the relative frequency of a property within a population or as the limit of a relative frequency in an infinite series. Thus the main difference between the two accounts is that in the scientific or relative frequency view probability is, in effect, a property of the actual physical world, whilst in the logical account it is a property of the way people think about the world.

The logical account of Keynes is also to be contrasted with subjectivist accounts, in which people are logically free to set their own values for degrees of belief on the basis of human caprice. Keynes explicitly denies that probability is subjective in this sense. Rather it is objective in that it is concerned with the degree of belief it is *rational* to hold in certain conditions. To the extent that different individuals will be aware of different amounts and types of evidence the probability relation concerning a given hypothesis will be different for these individuals, but in each case, however, the various probability relations or rational degrees of belief will be determined objectively.

Unlike many contributors whose logical accounts of probability followed Keynes' contribution — notably Carnap (1950) and Jeffreys (1939) — Keynes does not think that numerical values can be assigned to probability relations in most situations. In fact he argues that between some pairs of probabilities no comparison of magnitude is possible, whilst between other pairs it may be possible to say which is the greater probability but without being able to measure the difference. A numerical measure of probability can only be obtained when the conclusion relative to the evidence is one of a number of equi-probable, exclusive and exhaustive alternatives.

Induction and Analogy

Having 'described probability as comprising that part of logic which deals with arguments which are rational but not conclusive', Keynes suggests that by 'far the most important types of such arguments are those which are based on the methods of induction and analogy' (CW, VIII, 241). According to Keynes the inductive argument is a combination of analogy — which refers to the likeness of the objects being compared — and pure induction — which depends upon the number of 'instances' or observations made.

The objective of Keynes' inductive method (here drastically simplified) is to develop generalisations and to analyse ways of increasing their probability both by limiting their universality and by examining the greatest possible diversity of instances. In situations where it is not possible to increase the knowledge of the instances already 'observed', then the inductive argument can be strengthened by increasing the mere number of instances — or by pure induction. The advantage of increasing the number of instances is that the conditions under which they are observed may be different, adding to existing knowledge. As Keynes writes

> The object of increasing the number of instances arises out of the fact that we are nearly always aware of *some* difference between the instances, and that even where the known difference is insignificant we may suspect, especially when our knowledge of the instances is very incomplete that there may be more. (CW, VIII, 259)

The final element in Keynes' account is that of a 'prior probability which must always be found, before the method of pure induction can be usefully employed to support a substantial argument' (CW, VIII, 259). Keynes demonstrates formally that, with pure induction, the probability of a generalisation will approach certainty as a limit, only if 'we have, from some other source a finite probability in favour of the generalisation' (CW, VIII, 264). Keynes believes the prior probability will usually be obtained from considerations of analogy. However, he also considers that certain things are self-evident, and that the prior probability can be obtained, on occasion, by introspection.

Thus Keynes sets forth a logic of rational argument based mainly on induction and analogy. It is concerned not so much with truth as with what it is rational to believe given the evidence. It is a theory of opinion and belief based on probability.

In order to bring out significant features of Keynes' account and to pave the way for examining his views on econometrics it is useful to consider Keynes' attitude to the role of prediction and predictive accuracy in the acquisition of knowledge. This focus, through facilitating a comparison between Keynes' account, as set out in his *Treatise on Probability*, and alternative accounts which *emphasise* attempts at 'testing' or falsifying hypotheses, helps illustrate the significance both of the view that the probability relation is a logical one and of Keynes' belief that empirical sciences rest on inductive methods.

Prediction

To understand the significance of different attitudes to 'predictability' it is instructive to examine how econometricians use 'predictive accuracy' as a criterion in deciding whether a proposed hypothesis or model can be provisionally 'accepted'; and why, adopting Keynes' account, even if econometric methods could be justifiably used (and I shall argue below that Keynes believed that this was not the case), the use of 'predictive accuracy' in this way is still not acceptable.

A glance at prominent econometric articles in recent economics journals is sufficient to reveal the widespread practice of splitting a data sample into two (or more) parts so that a model 'constructed' using one part of the sample can then be 'tested' using the other. The intuition involved is that a model that predicts part of the data is, in some sense, better than one that merely accommodates the data. Predictive accuracy in this sense has become a generalised criterion of model evaluation and the practice of partitioning the sample in this way is recommended in most econometric text books. Thus for example Theil, (1971, 603) writes:

> a plea can be made to divide the available observations into *three* parts, the first of which is used for the choice of specification, the second for the estimation, and the third for conditional prediction based on the estimated equation in order to verify whether the method actually works.

In contrast, Keynes' clearly contradictory view is that the

> peculiar virtue of prediction . . . is altogether imaginary. The number of instances examined and the analogy between them are the

essential points, and the question as to whether a particular hypothesis happens to be propounded before or after their examination is quite irrelevant. (CW, VIII, 337)

To account for this difference it is useful to examine why it is that a model which predicts part of the data sample is usually presumed to be better than one which merely accommodates the data. Part of the answer is that a model which merely accommodates the data sample is often considered to be *ad hoc* in the literal sense that it is specifically designed only for that purpose and has no further usefulness. Thus accommodation of data bestows no particular value on the model. On the other hand a prediction represents a *bold* claim, one that is likely to be refuted. Thus a test of predictive accuracy may be construed to be an example of a *severe* test, and non-rejection of a model on such a test might be interpreted as a remarkable, indeed surprising, event. All of these attributes — bold claims, severe tests, remarkable outcomes — are interpreted as bestowing particular value on any model or hypothesis that is not rejected in the process. To this list we might add the prediction of novel 'facts' in which the context of the predicted outcomes might also be unusual. It is difficult to imagine how an example of this could be construed to have arisen in the context of econometrics, but one can be drawn from elsewhere. Thus Chalmers argues:

it would surely seem reasonable to suggest that a theory that anticipates and leads to the discovery of new phenomena, in the way Clerk Maxwell's [electromagnetic] theory led to the discovery of radio waves, is more worthy of merit and more justifiable than a law or theory devised to account for the phenomena already known and not leading to the discovery of new ones. (1978, 35)

We can also note that Thales predicted an eclipse, and in doing so became one of the Seven Sages.

Consider then how these claims are to be interpreted in accordance with Keynes' account, turning first to the issue of whether a model which accommodates the data sample is *ad hoc*. If the presumption that such a model 'has no further usefulness' means — as is sometimes implied — that it *cannot* lead to further 'testable' hypotheses, then the claim is just incorrect, as a moment's reflection should confirm. Ultimately the question as to whether a theory is *ad hoc* revolves around the issue of whether or not there is any *motivation* for the theory's postulation other than a desire to accommodate the data. An *ad hoc* theory or model is one whose *sole* purpose is to accommodate the data. A theory which receives prior support on the basis of existing knowledge cannot, therefore, be *ad hoc* for this constitutes further grounds for its postulation.

In Keynes' account, however, the inductive argument is only possible when a theory or model receives prior support derived from existing knowledge — usually by analogy. Thus, in the example of assessing an econometric model, if the latter can be 'obtained' using only part of the data sample this may well reflect the fact that there exists a strong *a priori* probability in its favour. If, however, the model is a mere guess that happens to be consistent with the data then, by Keynes' account, the conditions for inductive argument are not present. The issue of whether data or hypothesis appeared first, however, remains irrelevant. As Keynes puts it:

> If an hypothesis is proposed *a priori*, this commonly means that there is some grounds for it, arising out of our previous knowledge, *apart from* the purely inductive ground, and if such is the case the hypothesis is clearly stronger than one which reposes on inductive grounds only. But if it is a mere guess, the lucky fact of its preceding some or all of the cases which verify it adds nothing to its value. (CW, VIII, 337)

Turning to the next issue, the notions of bold claims, remarkable events and severe tests are connected. Bold claims concern events which seem improbable on the available evidence; remarkable events are those which, before their occurrence, did seem improbable on the available evidence; and severe tests are those which make events more improbable on the available evidence. These attributes, therefore, appear to turn on the issue of whether an event in question is improbable given the initial evidence. This certainly seems to be a necessary feature but it is sometimes thought to be insufficient. Suppose, for example, that an apparently 'fair' coin is tossed 100 times and a sequence of 100 heads is observed. To many this outcome would probably seem more surprising than a particular irregular sequence containing, say, 50 heads and 50 tails. Yet on the evidence of a fair coin that particular irregular sequence is just as improbable, or so it is usually argued, as the one producing 100 heads, and yet apparently less surprising. From examples such as this Horwich (1982) has argued that for an event to be surprising the condition of prior improbability is not sufficient. Horwich in fact proposes an additional condition: that there must exist an initially implausible alternative hypothesis relative to which the evidence would be highly probable — in this case, perhaps, a highly biased (if not two-headed) coin. I believe that this additional condition is unwarranted, and that the only remarkable aspect of the sequence of 100 heads, compared with any other *particular* sequence, is the (possibly psychological) fact that it represents a recognisable pattern that could have been comprehended before the experiment. If, for example, someone unconnected with this experiment predicts a *particular* irregular pattern of 50 heads and 50 tails, prior to the experiment, and this sequence is eventually observed, then I suspect that this will be viewed as equally surprising or remarkable an event as the sequence of 100 heads. Being remarkable, therefore, seems for our purposes, to mean merely being improbable on the available evidence.

I am, therefore, once again, in agreement with Keynes:

> Uninstructed common sense seems to be specially unreliable in dealing with what are termed 'remarkable occurrences'. Unless a 'remarkable occurrence' is simply one which produces on us a particular psychological effect, that of surprise, we can only define it as an event which *before* its occurrence is very improbable on the available evidence. (CW, VIII, 334)

The question does arise, however, as to whether, in Keynes' account, the occurrence of an improbable event increases the probability of the hypothesis or model which is being considered, and which is consistent with this event. The answer in general is that it does; but that this does not imply that such an occurrence leads to an appreciable probability. The probability relation concerning the model cannot be measured after the occurrence of the 'surprising event', unless it can be measured before that event, that is unless there is initially an *a priori* probability in its favour. The argument thus tells us that the estimated model is indeed more likely after the event than before it, but unless there is an appreciable probability first there cannot be one afterwards.

In this discussion of improbable events, however, there is nothing which from the point of view of Keynes' account suggests that a model that predicts the evidence should receive greater support than a model that is constructed after the evidence is obtained. For Keynes, the relation between hypothesis and evidence is purely logical and that is the end of the matter; the issue of which appeared first, the hypothesis or the evidence, is unimportant.

Inductivism *vs* Falsification

The differences noted above arise in part because, implicitly, I have been contrasting inductivist with falsificationist accounts. I use the word falsificationist loosely. It is not entirely suitable, but other labels commonly used, such as positivist, empiricist or scientific all contain their inadequacies. However, I do not wish to consider only naive falsification accounts and I am including accounts in which theories are considered as organised structures of some kind, but in which falsification plays a prominent role. In all these accounts rash speculations or bold conjectures or novel predictions are to be encouraged provided they are falsifiable and provided that they are, at least in part, rejected when falsified. Indeed, significant scientific advances, in these accounts, are marked by the non-falsification of bold conjectures. For Keynes, as was mentioned above, the requirement for obtaining a high probability of a generalisation is its least possible universality and the greatest possible diversity of instances. The bolder the claim the smaller the probability it is entitled to, given the evidence. The tendency, in this account, is to develop more 'reasonable' arguments.

The importance of the successful prediction of novel 'facts' makes the historical context of prediction important in the falsificationist account. In the inductivist account, as we have seen, the significance of 'confirming instances' of a theory is determined solely by the logical relationship between the observation statements that are confirmed and the theory which they support. The historical context in which the evidence is acquired is irrelevant.

Econometricians seem universally to report their results as if they interpret themselves as working within the falsificationist bold predictions framework. Hendry for example, writes that 'restrictiveness increases the hazards of possible rejection and hence augments "plausibility" if disconfirmation does not occur' (1980, 388). Attempts to falsify hypotheses are usually referred to as 'tests' and Hendry goes on to state that the 'three golden rules of econometrics are test, test, and test' (403). For Keynes, as we have seen, the object is to be much more cautious: to attempt to obtain a generalisation that has strong *a priori* support and to reduce the 'hazards of possible rejection'. In fact for Keynes the 'testing' of a hypothesis has more to do with putting into effect an economic policy that is based upon it (see e.g. Lawson, 1985a).

The important point which underlies these contrasts — but which seems frequently to be missed — is that the falsificationist account is really attempting to say something about the usefulness or validity of the *hypothesis* itself whilst Keynes' inductive account is concerned with the opinion or degree of belief in a hypothesis that a person is entitled to hold, given the available evidence. If, for example, two 'falsificationists' arrive simultaneously at the same hypothesis and proceed to test it by trying to falsify it, then the person who, initially, is relatively ignorant of the available supportive evidence will, once he or she has obtained his evidence, be able to 'corroborate' the hypothesis much more 'strongly' than the person who was aware of this evidence before the hypothesis was constructed. In the falsificationist account, therefore, the value of any particular theory seems to depend upon the situation of the person creating it, and thus, in part, is a matter for historians to determine. (For other 'interesting' properties of this historical approach to confirmation see Lawson, 1985b.) For Keynes there is no such problem for, as noted above, what is being considered is the degree of belief that can be bestowed in a hypothesis. A person relatively ignorant of supportive evidence for a hypothesis will attach a lower degree of belief to it than a person who is knowledgeable about such evidence. It is this degree of belief that is related to the available evidence, not the theory's objective validity, and there is no role in its determination for the historian to play.

To sum up, in Keynes' inductive account the validity of the methods does not depend on the boldness, historical context or success of predictions. An inductive argument affirms 'not that a matter of fact *is* so, but that *relative to certain evidence* there is a probability in its favour' (CW, VIII, 245). It is a theory of knowledge concerning what, in a given situation, it is rational to believe. In this account all empirical arguments require an intitial probability which is usually acquired by analogy, but which may be raised towards certainty by methods of pure induction.

On Attempting to 'Justify' the Method of Induction

Having examined the role that Keynes attributes to inductive methods in the process of reasoning, it is important to enquire whether Keynes believed that people could ever be justified in using such methods.

In his discussion on this topic Keynes first attempts to identify an assumption made by scientists concerning the character of material laws which, if true, would support the use of inductive methods. This fundamental assumption, according to Keynes, is that the 'system of the material universe must consist . . . of bodies . . . [or] *legal atoms,* such that each of them exercises its own separate, independent, and invariable effect . . . [If this were not the case] . . . predictions would be impossible and the inductive method useless' (CW, VIII, 277). Referring to this assumption as the hypothesis of atomic uniformity Keynes writes:

> We do not have an invariable relation between particular bodies, but nevertheless each has on the others its own separate and invariable effect, which does not change with changing circumstances, although, of course, the total effect may be changed to almost any extent if all the other accompanying causes are different. Each atom can, according to this theory, be treated as a separate cause and does not enter into different organic combinations in each of which it is regulated by different laws. (CW, VIII, 276)

The identification of this 'fundamental' assumption (facilitating the use of inductive methods if true), which Keynes attributes to scientists concerning material laws, leads Keynes to put forward a similar fundamental assumption concerning any system of 'facts or propositions'. Keynes first observes that for any such system the *ultimate constituents* or indefinables of the system, which all the members of it are about, are fewer in number than the members of the system themselves. Further, Keynes argues that there are *laws of necessary connection* between the members of such a system whereby the truth or falsity of each member can be determined from a knowledge of the laws of necessary connection together with a knowledge of the truth or falsity of some, but not all, of the members.

For Keynes, the ultimate constituents together with the laws of necessary connection make up what he terms the *independent variety* of the system. It is this which Keynes focuses upon when arguing that 'if the premises of our argument permit us to assume that the facts or propositions, with which the argument is concerned, belong to a *finite* system, [by which Keynes is explicit that he means that the independent variety should be finite] then probable knowledge can be validly obtained by means of an inductive argument' (CW, VIII, 280). The assumption that a system be finite in this sense Keynes terms a hypothesis of the limitation of independent variety.

The assumption that the system of nature is finite is clearly similar to the assumption of atomic uniformity that Keynes attributes to scientists concerning the character of material laws. As Keynes writes:

> The hypothesis of atomic uniformity, as I have called it, while not

formally equivalent to the hypothesis of the limitation of independent variety, amounts to very much the same thing. If the fundamental laws of connection changed altogether with variations, for instance, in the shape or size of bodies, or if the laws governing the behaviour of a complex had no relation whatever to the laws governing the behaviour of its parts when belonging to other complexes, there could hardly be a limitation of independent variety in the sense in which this has been defined. And, on the other hand, a limitation of independent variety seems necessarily to carry with it some degree of atomic uniformity. The underlying conception as to the character of the system of nature is in each case the same. (CW, VIII, 290)

Whilst Keynes recognises the difficulty of 'justifying' such fundamental assumptions he in any case acknowledges that the finite character of all such systems cannot be assumed:

Now an assumption, that *all* systems of fact are finite . . . cannot, it seems perfectly plain, be regarded as having absolute, universal validity in the sense that such an assumption is self-evidently applicable to every kind of object and to all possible experience. . . The most that can be maintained is that this assumption is true of *some* systems of fact, and further, that there are some objects about which, as soon as we understand their nature, the mind is able to apprehend directly that the assumption in question *is* true. (CW, VIII, 291)

Keynes is equally clear that he believes that there are some kinds of objects of our experience about which we have no direct assurance that such an assumption is legitimate, and thus that there are situations for which 'inductive methods are not reasonably applicable' (CW, VIII, 293).

In sum, therefore, Keynes suggests that the 'fundamental assumptions' being made by those employing inductive methods can, on occasion, be recognised as legitimate, whilst on other occasions they are patently not so. It is this belief, I shall argue, that is central to, and underlies, Keynes' analysis when, thirty years after writing the *Treatise on Probability,* he engages in debate with Tinbergen over the potential usefulness or otherwise of the developing methods of econometrics.

Keynes' Comments on Tinbergen's Method

A perusal of the 'debate' between Keynes and Tinbergen reveals that Keynes was particularly interested in the logic of justification of Tinbergen's methods. In the light of the discussion outlined above it seems appropriate that Keynes should focus upon the inductive aspects of Tinbergen's analysis and examine whether the implicit 'fundamental assumptions' being made (which, if true, would justify inductive methods) could be considered legitimate. This, in fact, is what Keynes does, and the related arguments provide, I believe, the more fundamental part of his contribution to the debate.

Keynes' initial comments are made in response to R. Tyler of the League of Nations who requested that Keynes give his views on (the proofs of) Tinbergen's book on 'Business Cycles in the United States of America'. In this response Keynes writes:

> There is first af all the central question of methodology, — the logic of applying the method of multiple correlation to unanalysed economic material, which we know to be non-homogeneous through time. If we were dealing with the action of numerically measurable, independent forces, adequately analysed so that we were dealing with independent atomic factors and between them completely comprehensive, acting with fluctuating relative strength on material constant and homogeneous through time, we might be able to use the method of multiple correlation with some confidence for disentangling the laws of their action . . .
>
> In fact we know that every one of these conditions is far from being satisfied by the economic material under investigation . . .
>
> To proceed to some more detailed comments. The coefficients arrived at are apparently assumed to be constant for 10 years or for a larger period. Yet, surely we know that they are not constant. There is no reason at all why they should not be different every year. (CW, XIV, 285)

These sorts of comments are variously repeated in his correspondence, throughout the period of the late 1930s, both with Tinbergen and with Harrod. However, the view that it is an inductive argument that is required is most explicitly stated in the 1939 *Economic Journal* review of Tinbergen's book. After passing through various 'technical criticisms', Keynes moves 'in conclusion to a different department of the argument'. Here he writes:

Put broadly, the most important condition is that the environment in all relevant respects, other than the fluctuations in those factors of which we take particular account, should be uniform and homogeneous over a period of time. We cannot be sure that such conditions will persist in the future, even if we find them in the past. But if we find them in the past, we have at any rate some basis for an inductive argument.

and he adds

[The] main *prima facie* objection to the application of the method of multiple correlation to complex economic problems lies in the apparent lack of any adequate degree of uniformity in the environment. (CW, XIV, 316)

A Clear Statement of Tinbergen's Own Logic

Failing to find a justification for the methods used by Tinbergen within Keynes' own inductive account, Keynes' second underlying criticism is that Tinbergen fails to provide a comprehensive or coherent alternative logic of justification (a matter which Koopmans (1941) attempted to redress two years later). The point is made initially in a letter to Kahn where Keynes describes Tinbergen's work as 'hocus' complaining that there 'is not the slightest explanation or justification of the underlying logic' (CW, XIV, 289); it is repeated in correspondence with Harrod, and finds its fullest expression in the published review of Tinbergen's book:

The second chapter, which gives in brief compass a most lucid account of the statistical method to be employed, is very good indeed. But the first chapter, which should deal with the difficult logical problems involved in applying to economic data methods which have been worked out in connection with material of a very different character, is grievously disappointing. So far as it goes, it is helpful; but it occupies only four pages, and it leaves unanswered many questions which the economist is bound to ask before he can feel comfortable as to the conditions which the economic material has to satisfy, if the proposed method is to be properly applicable . . . I would urge that the next instalment should be primarily devoted to the logical problem, explaining fully and carefully the conditions which the economic material must satisfy if the application of the method is to be fruitful. (CW, XIV, 306)

Economics, Induction and Science

If the methods of Tinbergen are believed by Keynes to be *prima facie* inappropriate for dealing with economic material within Keynes' own inductive account, and if Keynes can find no alternative logic of justification in Tinbergen's work, then it would seem that Keynes ought to conclude that the work has little value. This Keynes comes close to asserting, for he writes:

> Professor Tinbergen is obviously anxious not to claim too much. If only he is allowed to carry on, he is quite ready and happy at the end of it to go a long way towards admitting, with an engaging modesty, that the results probably have no value. (CW, XIV, 307).

Keynes, of course, is not making the general claim that empirical evidence has no relevance to economic analysis (on this see e.g. Meeks, 1978; Lawson, 1985a). Nor, of course, does he reject the usefulness of inductive methods in general; he merely doubts their legitimacy in the form of correlation analysis using economic material comprising observations on given 'variables' over time. Indeed it would seem that Keynes is of the opinion that such methods are generally useful in the natural sciences, but that the relevant situation in this field of study differs markedly from that found in economics:

> unlike the typical natural science, the material to which [economics] is applied is, in too many respects, not homogeneous through time. (CW, XIV, 296)
>
> In chemistry and physics and other natural sciences the object of experiment is to fill in the actual values of the various quantities and factors appearing in an equation or a formula; and the work when done is once and for all. In economics that is not the case, and to convert a model into a quantitative formula is to destroy its usefulness as an instrument of thought. Tinbergen endeavours to work out the variable quantities in a particular case, or perhaps in the average of several particular cases, and he then suggests that the quantitative formula so obtained has general validity. Yet in fact, by filling in figures, which one can be quite sure will not apply next time, so far from increasing the value of his instrument, he has destroyed it. (CW, XIV, 299)
>
> The pseudo-analogy with the physical sciences leads directly counter to the habit of much which is most important for an economist proper to acquire. (CW, XIV, 300)

A question often posed in this connection is whether or not economics can ever be considered a science. Now Hendry has written:

Taken literally, Keynes comes close to asserting that no economic theory is ever testable, in which case, of course, economics itself ceases to be scientific — I doubt if Keynes intended this implication. (1980, 396)

If by 'scientific' the usual implicit comparison with the methods and material of the 'natural sciences' is being made then clearly Keynes intends precisely the implication Hendry has noted. In any case, as I have discussed above, Keynes' inductive account does not place significant emphasis on 'testing', interpreted as attempts at falsification (and Keynes views all empirical sciences as resting on methods of induction) (CW, VIII, 241). In fact, however, Keynes actually believes that economics *is* a science, but opposes the reduction of all sciences to one type (see Carabelli, 1982). In fact, for Keynes 'economics is essentially a moral science and not a natural science. That is to say, it employs introspection and judgements of value' (CW, XIV, 297).

The issues focused upon above, I suggest, represent the fundamental bases of Keynes' criticism of econometrics, and stem from a philosophical perspective developed in his *Treatise on Probability*. The 'technical' criticisms that Keynes also made (for a useful summary see Hendry, 1980, 396) are also important of course, but from Keynes' point of view they represent overkill. If econometric study *could* be given *a priori* support then 'technical' criticisms of methods are, within Keynes account, in order; but Keynes does not seem to believe that this is the case.

Final Comments and Conclusion

The object of this paper has been to emphasise the fundamental connection between Keynes' views on econometrics as revealed in the 'debate' with Tinbergen and the theories he developed in the *Treatise on Probability*. Given this perspective it seems worthwhile inquiring into the status of Keynes' *Treatise on Probability* account today.

It is perhaps an implication of this chapter that the *Treatise on Probability* has been overly neglected by economists. As Levy has recently noted 'the work on probability of Maynard Keynes . . . is, for the most part, seriously underestimated outside philosophical circles' (1981, 15). Certainly his work does seem to be taken seriously within philosophical circles, although it may well be too intuitive an account for most philosophers of the present Anglo-American generation — especially as probability judgements are based on some form of direct perception or intuition. Recent accounts that compare the different traditions in the philosophy of probability do, however, tend to emphasise Keynes' work. Weatherford (1982), for example, in comparing logical, relative frequency, subjectivist and classical theories, focuses in the former case mainly on the contributions of Keynes and Carnap. In concluding his comparative analysis in favour of the logical interpretation Weatherford feels that 'Keynes has not so much waned as been eclipsed' (133) by the theories of Carnap although, as Weatherford points out, the latter are flawed. Popper, of course, devoted energy to criticising 'the logico-subjective theory, of which Keynes is the principle exponent' (1975, 149), and it remains noticeable that, as new accounts of probability appear, Keynes' theory is often set out as a standard of comparison (see for example Gillies, 1973). In sum, therefore, Keynes' account would seem to be thought to retain some relevance (see also Meeks, 1983), as indeed might the following remark concerning the *Treatise on Probability* made by Harrod:

> Keynes' work, which is likely in any case to be for long unmatched in its scope and erudition, will remain of living importance as a starting-point for discussion, until a more satisfying logical solution of the central problem of human knowledge is found. (1972, 778-9)

If prominent articles about econometrics are to continue to refer to Keynes' criticisms so that Keynes' views are to be interpreted as maintaining relevance, what is the form of constructive response that econometricians can make? The answer to this question follows, I think, from the discussion above: if econometrics is not to be rejected as being of little value, then econometric practice must be justified within Keynes' own account. If Keynes' account, or indeed any analytic/*a priori* account, is adopted then there must, it seems, be some intuition provided as to why, in the given context, the 'material can be treated as constant and homogeneous' through time. This may require a particularly ahistorical, perhaps 'mechanical', view of social development with no clear place for any notion of a human subject (although for a possible reconciliation see Lawson, 1985a). Amongst other things it is difficult to see how by this account a research programme can avoid being committed to investigating the real possibility of frequent 'structural breaks' given any preconceived theoretical framework.

The remaining possibility is to ignore Keynes' criticisms altogether.

As is well known, the 'technical' criticisms made by Keynes in effect form chapter headings in many econometric text-books and they gain no particular value from being associated with Keynes' terminologically dated account. To ignore Keynes' account, and indeed any account involving 'belief' is, of course, quite legitimate. Van Frassan (1980), amongst others, frequently contends that the business of science is to produce models that are *empirically adequate* — it is concerned with the possible — and that it has absolutely nothing to do with belief. Of course, if people are concerned with action, and the path to action is perceived as being, at least in part, through belief or opinion, then something more than empirical adequacy is required. It was this something more, of course, that Keynes was concerned with.

A main reservation I have with the emphasis of the above account of Keynes' views on econometrics derives from the lecture by Stone (1978) presented to the British Academy. Stone is someone who clearly knew Keynes well and was sensitive to Keynes' intellectual and social development. Yet he remains surprised at how negative were Keynes' remarks on econometrics. Indeed he puts forward as possible explanations Keynes' 'irresistible urge to overstate', the fact that 'by the thirties Keynes' mathematics had become pretty rusty' and that Keynes' personality was such that his 'reaction to anything new was to look for weak spots and shoot them full of holes' (1978, 62, 63). Such features may indeed partly explain at least the *virulence* of Keynes' remarks. Nevertheless the content of Keynes' criticisms, as I think I have demonstrated, were at least consistent with his views developed thirty years earlier in his *Treatise on Probability*. Thus I maintain that for any full account of Keynes' opposition to econometrics his views developed in the *Treatise on Probability* must at least be taken into account.

References

Carabelli, A. (1982) 'On Keynes's Method: Practical   Rationality', Cambridge, mimeo

Carnap, R. (1950) *Logical Foundations of Probability,* University of Chicago Press, Chicago

Chalmers, A.F. (1978) *What is This Thing Called Science?,* University of Queensland Press, Queensland

Gillies, D.A. (1973) *An Objective Theory of Probability,*   Methuen & Co. Ltd, London

Harrod, R.F. (1972) *The Life of John Maynard Keynes,* Penguin Books, Harmondsworth

Hendry, D.F. (1980) 'Econometrics — Alchemy or Science?', *Economica,* vol. 47, 387-406

Horwich, P. (1982) *Probability and Evidence,* Cambridge University Press, Cambridge

Jeffreys, H. (1939) *Theory of Probability,* Oxford Press

Keynes, J.M. CW, VII, VIII, XIV

Koopmans, T. (1941) 'The logic of econometric business-cycle research', *The Journal of Political Economy,* xlix, no. 2, 157-81

Lawson, T. (1985a) 'Uncertainty and Economic Analysis', *Economic Journal*

— — (1985b) 'The Context of Prediction (and the Paradox of Confirmation)', *British Journal for the Philosophy of Science,* forthcoming

Levy, P. (1981) *Moore (G.E. Moore and the Cambridge Apostles),* Oxford University Press, Oxford

Meeks, J.G.T. (1978) 'Bray on Keynes on Scientific Method: A Comment', *Journal of Economic Studies*

— — (1983) 'Keynes on the rationality of the investment decision under uncertainty', *Scottish Journal of Political Economy,* forthcoming

O'Donnell, R.M. (1982) 'Keynes: Philosophy and Economics (An approach to rationality and uncertainty)', Ph.D. Dissertation, Cambridge University

Patinkin, D. (1976) 'Keynes and econometrics: on the interaction between the macroeconomic revolutions of the interwar period', *Econometrica*, 44, 1091-1123

Popper, K.R. (1975) *The Logic of Scientific Discovery,* Hutchinson and Co. Ltd., London and John Wiley, New York and London

Stone, R. (1978) *Keynes, Political Arithmetic and Econometrics,* The British Academy, London

Theil, H. (1971) *Principles of Econometrics*, John Wiley and Sons, Inc., New York

van Frassan, B.C. (1980) *The Scientific Image,* Clarendon Press, Oxford

Weatherford, R. (1982) *Philosophical Foundations of Probability Theory,* Routledge and Kegan Paul, London

8 KEYNES ON ECONOMETRICS

Hashem Pesaran and Ron Smith

Introduction

The review by Keynes (CW, XIV, 306) of the first volume of Tinbergen's study of business cycles for the League of Nations (Tinbergen, 1939) has been widely discussed — e.g. Patinkin (1976), Stone (1978), Hendry (1980). Rather like military historians re-fighting Waterloo, econometricians dissect this debate for its lessons. Despite the merits of his campaign, Napoleon loses every time the battle is re-fought, and so does Keynes. His conclusion that econometrics was 'black magic' or 'statistical alchemy' (CW, XIV, 320) did little to hinder the growth of the enterprise. Rather, Keynes' stimulus to macroeconomics, national income accounting, and interventionist policy provided a major impetus to the very same activity he attacked. As a result, Keynes' judgement — 'I have a feeling that Professor Tinbergen may agree with much of my comment, but that his reaction will be to engage another ten computers and drown his sorrows in arithmetic' (CW, XIV, 318) — was to prove true for econometricians in general, albeit with electronic rather than human computers.

Like military historians, our purpose in re-fighting this battle is not to change the result, but to learn its lessons. This involves examining the positions and strategies of the two combatants. This is not a straightforward activity. Tinbergen was a pioneer, and his work needs to be assessed in terms of both current practice and the knowledge available in the late 1930s. Keynes uses a different terminology from that now common. On a number of details both of them seem confused, which is not surprising given the state of the art at the time. These difficulties mean that Keynes' review can be read in very different ways. On an uncharitable interpretation, he was merely ignorant of a range of possible statistical solutions to his problems. On a charitable one he pinpointed the methodological weaknesses of econometrics with characteristic clarity, provided a perceptive research agenda, and accurately predicted the chapter headings of econometrics text books to come.

The debate can be examined at three levels. At a technical level,

Keynes raised a set of 'logical problems' covering Tinbergen's method. These occupy the bulk of the review. After briefly describing Tinbergen's method, we shall discuss these technical issues. In particular, we shall examine how sensitive Tinbergen's results were to these problems. In addition, at a philosophical level, Keynes' critique reflected strong views about the appropriate manner of economic analysis. This comes out most clearly in his letters to Harrod about Tinbergen's work. In these he criticises Harrod for not repelling sufficiently firmly attempts to turn economics into a 'pseudo-natural-science' (CW, XIV, 296). We also discuss these methodological issues.

At an instrumental level, Keynes raised the fundamental question of the purpose of the activity. 'If the method cannot prove or disprove a qualitative theory, and if it cannot give a quantitative guide to the future, is it worth while? For assuredly, it is not a very lucid way of describing the past' (CW, XIV, 315). We argue that this question of purpose is central both to an understanding of the debate, and to drawing the lessons of the review for current practice.

Tinbergen's Method

Before embarking upon a discussion of Keynes' views on econometrics it is important to have a fresh look at Tinbergen's business cycle research which led Keynes to his criticisms. In this way we are in a better position to identify those aspects of Keynes' criticisms of econometrics that are specific to the pioneering nature of Tinbergen's attempt and those aspects that are of general validity and are directly relevant to current econometric practice.

The first macroeconometric model built by Tinbergen (or, as far as we are aware, by anyone) was a model for the Dutch economy originally published in Dutch as a memorandum submitted to the Dutch Statistical and Economic Society in 1936.[1] A simplified presentation of this model was subsequently published in English in a volume entitled *An Econometric Approach to Business Cycle Problems*.[2] In this slim volume Tinbergen not only shows how a macroeconometric model may be constructed in practice, but also goes on to discuss the possible ways that econometric models can be used for simulation and policy analysis, thus paving the way for most of the subsequent developments. In this and in his later works Tinbergen is clearly motivated by the need to give concrete answers to policy problems, and rejects the 'purely verbal treatment' of the policy questions on the grounds that it inevitably leads to a 'dead end'. He readily admits, however, that a mathematical and quantitative approach may not always be appropriate as it invariably involves a more or less arbitrary degree of simplification and schematisation. Tinbergen defends macro-econometric modelling not because he believes that it provides a *logical* solution to the problem of policy analysis, but because it pro- vides a reasonable framework within which policy issues can be studied and debated. In his own words.

> The establishment of a system of equations compels us to state clear- cut hypotheses about every sphere of economic life and, in addition, to test them statistically. Once stated, the system enables us to distinguish sharply between all kinds of different variation problems. And it yields clear-cut conclusions. Differences of opinion can, in principle, be localised, i.e. the elementary equation in which the dif- ference occurs can be found. Deviations between theory and reality can be measured and a number of their consequences estimated . . . (Tinbergen, 1937, 73)

Tinbergen's emphasis on the practical aspects of modelling, as opposed to its logical foundations, should be borne in mind when we come to consider Keynes' criticisms.

Despite the apparent importance and novelty of Tinbergen's approach for practical policy analysis, Keynes chose to focus almost exclusively on the first volume of Tinbergen's League of Nations studies, which dealt with the application of the multiple correlation technique to the explanation of fluctuations in total investment, invest- ment in residential building, and new investment in railway rolling- stock. Keynes' central concern in his review, and in his correspondence with Harrod that led to it, was with the question of methodology, i.e. 'the logic of applying the method of multiple correlation to unanalysed economic material, which we know to be non-homogeneous through time' (CW, XIV, 286). To understand more fully the nature of Keynes' *logical* objections to Tinbergen's methodology we need to look at the latter in some detail.

The object of Tinbergen's volume on methodology was 'to submit to statistical test some of the theories which have been put forward regard- ing the character and causes of cyclical fluctuation in business activity' (Tinbergen, 1939, 11). This is what he had been asked to do by the League of Nations, and represents a rather different objective from the more practical ones advanced in Tinbergen (1937). In fact, after stating this objective of testing theories, he rapidly qualifies it, pointing out all the difficulties involved. In the process of testing a theory, Tinbergen envisages a rather limited role for the statistician and argues that it is with the economist that the responsibility for the specification of theories must remain. For him it is essential that the explanatory variables of each equation be known on *a priori* grounds. The function of the statistician (or econometrician) is then confined to computing the regression coefficients that determine the relative quantitative importance of all the *a priori* postulated variables in the explanation of the phenomenon under consideration.

Tinbergen subjected his equations to more statistical testing than was common at the time, though his view of these tests is rather difficult to discern from his writings. At a formal level he adopts two different statistical frameworks, namely the classical regression model and the errors-in-variables model as analysed by Frisch. In his work Tinbergen uses both these approaches in a more or less complementary fashion. But for the decision concerning the choice of regressors Tinbergen relies on a less formal procedure and adopts the following judgemental procedure:

(1) whether or not the variate in question increases the correlation coefficient to any considerable extent;
(2) whether or not the sign of a fairly stable regression coefficient is right; and
(3) whether or not the influence of that variate is perceptible
                                        (Tinbergen, 1939, 50)

Thus in Tinbergen's methodology judgement is allowed to play an important role in the process of deciding whether an explanatory variable should be retained or discarded. Tinbergen does not, however, propose any explicit method of combining formal statistical results with judgemental and other non-quantifiable data. The problem of how to do this still bedevils applied econometrics. Tinbergen also discusses the determination of lags, the use of time trends, problems of structural instability and the choice of functional form. Again he does not offer any systematic methodology for dealing with these problems. Keynes recognised the lacunae and attacked them with spirit.

Keynes was not alone in his criticisms of Tinbergen's work. In many respects he echoed the views of others, not only on the problems involved in the application of statistical methods to economic time series, but also on the use of probability calculations for the purpose of induction. Haavelmo clearly summarises these two strands of criticism.

Since the days when Yule discovered that correlation between time series might be nonsense, very few economists have dared break the ban on time series as an object of statistical inference. So far, Tinbergen's pioneer work stands almost alone. As one might expect, his methods and results have raised a storm of criticism. But this criticism did not attack Tinbergen only for his short cuts in statistical methods, for his omission of rigorous formulation of the probability models involved and the statistical hypotheses to be tested. The criticisms came largely from another angle, arguing that Tinbergen had tried to go too far in using statistical methods; that inference of this sort was inferior, if not worthless, compared with the noble art of theoretical deductions based on general economic considerations. (Haavelmo, 1943, 13)

The prominence given to Keynes' attack on Tinbergen's work stemmed from the comprehensive nature of his critique and the effectiveness of his rhetoric, not to mention the eminent position which seems to have led Tyler of the League of Nations to solicit comments on Tinbergen's work from a rather reluctant Keynes (CW, XIV, 289).

Had Tyler not made this request, Keynes would perhaps not have been provoked to write the *Economic Journal* review, and the criticisms of those less eminent economists with similar opinions would now be forgotten. A useful discussion of the views on econometrics prevalent at the time can be found in Morgan (1984).

Keynes' Critique: the Technical Issues

The bulk of Keynes' review of Tinbergen's book is occupied with raising six questions about a range of technical difficulties.

His first five questions concern the specification of econometric equations, his sixth, which he believed to be in a 'different department of the argument' (CW, XIV, 315), concerns the inductive and predictive value of the estimates. The first question asked about the inclusion of all relevant factors in the equation. Unless all are included, and this can never be known, the estimated coefficients suffer from omitted variable bias. The second question is about the measurability of the factors. Many theoretical concepts such as supply and demand variables are unobservable and this creates severe difficulties. Elsewhere, he also comments on 'the frightful inadequacy of most of the statistics employed' (CW, XIV, 317). The third question is about the independence of the factors. Here he raises the problems of spurious correlation, simultaneity and multicollinearity. The fourth question is about functional form, and in particular the implausibility of the widespread assumption of linearity. The fifth question is about time-lags and trends and the general problem of dynamic specification. The sixth question is about the likely structural instability of the relationships.

Whatever judgement one makes on the implications Keynes drew, it must be recognised that the problems Keynes raised were real enough, and that these problems impose important limitations on the inferences that can be drawn from econometric results. It must also be recognised that in many respects econometric practice remains poor, the problems and limitations are ignored, and therefore Keynes' warnings retain their relevance. However, considerable efforts have been made to overcome the difficulties, with some success. These efforts have followed two main paths.

The first path involves recognising the problem and constructing a formal statistical model to deal with it. Examples include errors-in-variables models to deal with unobservables; simultaneous equations models to deal with interdependence; Box-Cox type transformations to deal with uncertain functional forms; distributed-lag and time-series methods to deal with dynamics; and random coefficient models to deal with parameter change. Although such techniques increase the flexibility with which the problems can be approached, they do not solve them. In each case the results remain conditional on specific prior assumptions which can be questioned. These assumptions include those about exogeneity, the distribution of the measurement errors, the class of transformations considered, the structure of the lags, the assumed patterns of parameter change, etc.

The second path involves specification testing and sensitivity analysis. One might have more faith in the econometric results if the model were to fit the data well, in some sense, and if the estimates should prove to be robust to changes in the auxilliary assumptions. These procedures can be interpreted as data-based guides to our degree of belief in the results. Econometricians have devoted considerable ingenuity to devising diagnostic statistics and specification tests which will signal if the data are not consistent with the estimated model. Likewise if very similar estimates are obtained with different sets of data, different *ceteris paribus* assumptions, or different stochastic specifications, then the confidence with which they are used will be increased.[3] An important aspect of data-based evaluation is replicability. Keynes put considerable weight on replication.

It will be remembered that the seventy translators of the Septuagint were shut up in seventy separate rooms with the Hebrew text and brought out with them, when they emerged, seventy identical translations. Would the same miracle be vouchsafed if seventy multiple correlators were shut up with the same statistical material? And anyhow, I suppose, if each had a different economist perched on his *a priori*, that would make a difference to the outcome. (CW, XIV, 319-20)

The experience of the past 40 years suggests that few econometric results are robust, and that replication is achieved only when the various econometricians are looking for the same result.

Since most econometrics text books discuss these problems we need not pursue the technical issues; it is now generally recognised that these problems present severe difficulties for econometric inference in general. There is however the question of whether these problems were serious in the particular case that concerned Keynes. Were Tinbergen's results robust to these problems? We shall consider one example, the issue of trends.

Tinbergen's treatment of time trends is particularly unsatisfactory and is based on the implicit assumption that all economic variables are subject to a nine-year cycle,[4] and he therefore bases his regressions on deviations from nine-year moving average trends. This method causes the dependent and the explanatory variables to pass through a complicated filter which can have a distorting impact upon the estimates of the regression coefficients and the dynamic specification of the relations concerned.

In order to show the effect of 'detrending' on Tinbergen's results we chose as an example the explanation of the UK net investment in railway rolling-stock, the case discussed in some detail by Keynes in his letter to Tyler.[5] Tinbergen considers three basic hypotheses for the explanation of investment in rolling-stock; namely the 'acceleration principle', the 'profit principle', and their linear combination which he refers to as the 'mixed principle'. All the variables in his pre-war regressions are measured either as absolute deviations or as relative deviations from a nine-year moving average trend. The original data underlying these deviations are denoted by $\bar{\bar{v}}_R$ (percentage increase in number of locomotives and of carriages, wagons and tracks, weighted by 1 and 4 respectively), $\Delta\bar{\bar{u}}_R$ (percentage increase in ordinary passenger journeys and in tonnage of goods conveyed, weighted by 4 and 5 respectively), $\bar{\bar{Z}}_R$ (ratio of net receipts to paid-up capital), $\bar{\bar{q}}_i$ (price index of pig iron, $1782 = 100$), and $\bar{\bar{m}}_{Lb}$ (yields on British consols). The corresponding variables measured as deviations from a nine-year moving average trend are represented by v_R, Δu_R, Z_R, q_i and m_{Lb} respectively.[6]

Tinbergen's results are summarised in his Tables V.1 to V.3 (Tinbergen, 1939, 124-7), and those results that allow for the effect of what Tinbergen calls 'secondary' explanatory variables are reproduced below for ease of comparison.

(a) Acceleration principle
$$v_R = + 0.27\ \Delta u_R(-3/2) + 0.02\ q_i(-3/2) - 0.04\ m_{Lb}(-3/2), \quad (1)$$
$R = 0.75$, where R stands for (multiple) correlation coefficient of the regression. The bracketed figures (next to the regressors) specify the average lag imposed on the regressors.

(b) Profit principle
$$v_R = + 3.8\ Z_R(-3/2) - 1.35\ Z_R(-5/2) + 0.02\ q_i(-3/2)$$
$$-0.03\ m_{Lb}(-3/2), \quad (2)$$
$$R = 0.70$$

The estimates reported by Tinbergen for the 'mixed principle' exclude the secondary factors (i.e. the price of pig iron and the long-term rate of interest) and will not be considered here.

Since our purpose is primarily to examine the effect of 'detrending' on Tinbergen's results, we chose in the first instance to re-estimate relations (1) and (2) above, retaining the same functional form and time lags, by the Ordinary Least Squares (OLS) method using the original un-detrended series. The results are summarised in the first columns of Tables 8.1 and 8.2 respectively. These estimates support Tinbergen's contention that both the profit and acceleration principles are important in the determination of investment. But, in contrast to his findings the un-detrended estimates favour the profit principle as the more effective explanation of the investment in rolling-stock. Tinbergen's detrended estimates are, however, much smaller in magnitude than the un-detrended estimates given in Tables 8.1 and 8.2.

But the un-detrended OLS results suffer from a significant degree of residual autocorrelation which sheds considerable doubt on the size and the statistical significance of the estimated regression coefficients. The Durbin-Watson statistics computed for both regressions are considerably lower than the values one would expect under the null hypothesis of non-autocorrelated disturbances. The method of detrending employed by Tinbergen can, and often does, deal with the problem of residual autocorrelation. But, as pointed out above, its application can also introduce erroneous dynamics into the relation and its residuals. A more satisfactory procedure would be to allow explicitly for the existence of residual autocorrelation in the estimation of the regression coefficients.[7] Such estimates, which account for a second

Table 8.1: Re-estimation of Tinbergen's Equation for the UK Net Investment in Railway Rolling-stock: the Acceleration Principle

Dependant Variable is $\bar{v}_R$	Whole period 1875-1912		Sub-period I 1875-1892		Sub-period II 1893-1912	
	(1) OLS	(2) AR2	(3) OLS	(4) AR2	(5) OLS	(6) AR2
Cons.	−0.602	7.53	30.08	27.45	16.67	16.41
	(−0.20)	(1.17)	(3.69)	(4.89)	(5.57)	(5.60)
$\Delta\bar{\bar{u}}_R(-3/2)$	0.488	−0.018	0.291	0.511	0.050	0.070
	(4.57)	(−0.22)	(2.18)	(4.80)	(0.55)	(0.81)
$\bar{\bar{q}}_i(-3/2)$	−3.75	2.58	7.45	3.73	−4.25	−5.14
	(−1.49)	(0.71)	(2.30)	(1.38)	(−1.78)	(−1.98)
$\bar{\bar{m}}_{Lb}(-3/2)$	0.960	−2.20	−10.27	−9.16	−4.94	−4.74
	(0.87)	(−0.95)	(−3.49)	(−4.40)	(−4.30)	(−4.18)
$\hat{\rho}_1$	—	1.108	—	−0.177	—	0.335
		(7.26)		(−0.94)		(1.51)
$\hat{\rho}_2$	—	−0.371		−0.599		−0.255
		(−2.43)		(−3.17)		(−1.13)
DW	1.13	1.98	1.75	1.93	1.34	2.01
$\hat{\sigma}$	1.161	0.845	0.912	0.799	0.508	0.477
$\bar{R}^2$	0.334	0.648	0.564	0.665	0.796	0.820
LL	−3.42	7.68	3.92	5.85	15.12	16.20

Source: Tinbergen (1939, 148-9).
Notations: $\bar{v}_R$ = percentage increase in number of locomotives and of carriages, wagons and trucks
   $\Delta\bar{\bar{u}}_R$ = percentage increase in railway traffic
   $\bar{\bar{q}}_i$ = price of pig iron
   $\bar{\bar{m}}_{Lb}$ = long-term interest rate
$\hat{\rho}_1$ and $\hat{\rho}_2$ = maximum likelihood estimates of the parameters of AR2 error specification
   DW = Durbin-Watson statistic
   $\hat{\sigma}$ = estimated standard error of the regressions
   $\bar{R}$ = adjusted multiple correlation coefficient
   LL = maximised value of the log-likelihood function
   () = t-ratios

Table 8.2: Re-estimation of Tinbergen's Equation for the UK Net Investment in Railway Rolling-stock: the Profit Principle

Dependant Variable is $\bar{v}_R$	Whole period 1875-1912		Sub-period I 1875-1892		Sub-period II 1893-1912	
	(1) OLS	(2) AR2	(3) OLS	(4) AR2	(5) OLS	(6) AR2
Cons.	−23.73	−20.33	22.55	34.21	1.55	3.01
	(−4.34)	(−3.06)	(1.48)	(1.55)	(0.19)	(0.41)
$\bar{\bar{Z}}_R(-3/2)$	7.49	2.49	5.89	−7.83	0.768	−0.480
	(3.52)	(1.18)	(1.57)	(−1.74)	(0.52)	(−0.35)
$\bar{Z}_R(-5/2)$	−0.341	4.12	−4.48	5.23	2.23	3.34
	(−0.17)	(2.18)	(−1.25)	(1.43)	(2.05)	(3.72)
$\bar{q}_i(-3/2)$	−4.48	−7.92	8.90	4.92	−4.49	−4.47
	(−1.83)	(−2.88)	(1.90)	(0.77)	(−2.29)	(−3.59)
$\bar{\bar{m}}_{Lb}(-3/2)$	−0.80	−0.74	−9.62	−7.42	−3.87	−4.20
	(−0.81)	(−0.62)	(−2.73)	(−1.49)	(−3.84)	(−4.99)
$\hat{\rho}_1$	—	0.908	—	1.165	—	−0.198
		(6.79)		(7.66)		(−1.01)
$\hat{\rho}_2$	—	−0.582	—	−0.764	—	−0.525
		(−4.35)		(−5.02)		(−2.69)
DW	0.91	2.24	1.38	2.18	2.09	2.57
$\hat{\sigma}$	1.06	0.786	1.00	0.778	0.438	0.378
$\bar{R}^2$	0.442	0.695	0.474	0.683	0.848	0.887
LL	0.48	10.97	2.89	6.30	18.60	21.07

Note: $\bar{Z}_R$ =Ratio of the net receipt to paid-up capital. The rest of the notations are as defined at the foot of Table 8.1.

Source: Tinbergen (1939, 148-9).

order autoregressive residual autocorrelation (AR2) are given in the second columns of Tables 8.1 and 8.2. The results for the acceleration principle are very disappointing. The coefficient of the rate of increase of the volume of rail traffic drops substantially from 0.488 to 0.066 and completely loses its statistical significance. The situation is not as disastrous for the profit principle. The profit rate still plays a significant part in the explanation of investment, albeit with a significantly altered lag pattern.

The presence of residual autocorrelation can, however, be due to omitted variables, functional form misspecification, structural change and a host of other factors all of which are highlighted in Keynes' review. One important problem especially stressed by Keynes is the issue of parameter stability. Just to show the degree of sensitivity of the results to the particular period chosen for estimation and testing, we also re-estimated the two investment equations over the sub-periods 1875-1892, and 1893-1912. As is clear from the results given in columns (3)-(6) of Tables 8.1 and 8.2, there is definite evidence of a structural break, both in the case of error variances and regression coefficients. The estimated coefficients move all over the place. The autocorrelation patterns of the residuals also undergo a significant change. It should be noted that Tinbergen also examined his equations for structural breaks (Tinbergen, 1939, 67-72).

The above is just an *example* of the type of technical issues that surround Tinbergen's pioneering work, to part of which Keynes paid particular attention. But it should not be construed as a downgrading of Tinbergen's important and significant contributions. Given the statistical and computational technology available to Tinbergen, the importance of his achievements is undeniable, and in our view is justly reflected in his being awarded (jointly with Frisch) the first Nobel prize for economics. None the less, it does make the point that the problems Keynes raised were real, despite his occasional technical confusions.

Keynes' Critique: the Methodological Issues

If it is accepted that Keynes' technical criticisms were largely correct, and in general econometricians have praised his grasp of these issues (e.g. Hendry, 1980), what are the implications? To Keynes they were clear. The weight of the difficulties was such as to preclude econometric methods of inference for most cases of real interest. The reasons for this strong conclusion are rooted in a methodology originally articulated in the *Treatise on Probability*.[8] Keynes rejected the frequency as well as the subjective interpretations of probability in favour of a rational or logical theory. While arguing that the probability of a proposition (for given premises) is not 'subject to human caprice' (CW, VIII, 4), he also doubted the possibility of making 'the transition from an observed numerical frequency to a numerical measure of probability' (CW, VIII, 400). This 'logical' theory of probability, together with his insistence that most probability relations are not measurable, inevitably led Keynes to the view that, save in special circumstances, statistical analysis for purposes of induction lacks the necessary logical foundations and should be embarked on with a great deal of care. In highlighting his views he distinguished between that part of the statistical analysis which was purely 'descriptive' and the part which was 'inductive' (CW, VIII, 359-63). While he welcomed 'numerical and diagrammatic methods' for the purpose of summarising the important features of large bodies of data, he strongly warned against mistaking 'the statistical description for an inductive generalisation'. It was against this broad philosophical background on inference that Keynes reviewed Tinbergen's work

It was not therefore surprising that the main focus of Keynes' attack was the claim that econometricians were able to estimate and *test* the relationships provided by economic theory. Tinbergen tentatively advanced this interpretation and the fiction still survives in the introductions to elementary econometric text-books. Economic theory operates with unrestricted *ceteris paribus* clauses, unobservable theoretical variables, generally under-identified interdependent equilibrium formulations, general functional forms, and unspecified adjustment processes. This means that it is immunised against refutation and cannot provide relationships suitable for estimation or testing. The econometrician then has the task of intermediate specification in order to obtain an equation which can be subjected to statistical analysis. This involves making a set of auxilliary assumptions, about other relevant factors, functional form, dynamic specification, etc., and it is these assumptions which provide the answer to Keynes' questions.

A consequence of this procedure is that one cannot know whether the results of the statistical analyses reflect inferentially on the economic theory or on the auxilliary assumptions. It may be useful to reject a specific formulation or hypothesis, but the significance of this for the more general underlying economic theory will always be ambiguous. Keynes seemed to believe very strongly in the untestable nature of economic theories, and this brings us to another methodological aspect of his critique, his belief that economics is a moral science, and not a pseudo-natural science (CW, XIV, 296).

Keynes' view of economic methodology, as it was expressed in the letters to Harrod, is so different from the philosophy currently prevailing that an immediate reaction tends to be that he cannot really have meant it. For instance Hendry (1980, 396) says 'Taken literally, Keynes comes close to asserting that no economic theory is ever testable, in which case, of course, economics itself ceases to be scientific — I doubt if Keynes intended this implication.' In fact, Keynes' letters have exactly that implication.

Economics had been originally taught in Cambridge as part of Moral Sciences along with philosophy, logic and ethics. To Keynes it was still 'a branch of logic, a way of thinking' (CW, XIV, 296), 'essentially a moral science and not a natural science. That is to say it employs introspection and judgements of value' (CW, XIV, 297), 'I might have added that it deals with motives, expectations, psychological uncertainties' (CW, XIV, 300). Despite this, economics was to be empirical: 'The specialist in the manufacture of models will not be successful unless he is constantly correcting his judgement by intimate and messy acquaintance with the facts to which his model has to be applied' (CW, XIV, 300). Yet even so he criticised Marshall who 'often confused his models, for devising which he had great genius, by wanting to be realistic and by being unnecessarily ashamed of lean and abstract outlines' (CW, XIV, 296).

The power of Popperian norms and the attractions of the natural sciences as models for economic methodology make it difficult for current econometricians to understand Keynes' position. In practice, as we shall see, Keynes and econometricians conduct their empirical and policy analysis in quite similar ways, but use orthogonal rationalisations for the activity. Perhaps an analogy might be to regard economic models as tools rather than representations of reality. The skill of the economist was in collecting a wide range of tools and knowing which one was appropriate for the job at hand. To Keynes it made no sense to say that a tool was right or wrong in isolation, the question was whether it was useful or not. However, the choice of an appropriate tool required a feel for the psychological, empirical and institutional dimensions of the problem at hand. '*Progress* in economics consists almost entirely in a progressive improvement in the choice of models' (CW, XIV, 296).

From this perspective econometrics leads to two errors. First, it regards the model as a testable representation of reality, confusing the tool with the object for which it is used. Second, its premises (stable coefficients, measurable variables, etc.) exclude from consideration the interesting and important dimensions of economic problems. Thus there was a danger that mechanical procedures would displace insight and intuition and confine the scope of economics. The most restrictive assumption of the procedure, and the one to which Keynes objected most vehemently, was the premise of structural stability.

Some degree of homogeneity over space and time in the relationships considered is a prerequisite for statistical inference, just as the presumed constancy of natural laws, whether deterministic or probabilistic, is a prerequisite for physics. If the relationships are not stable then a historical rather than a statistical approach is necessary. Kalečki (1965) discusses the relation between historical materialism and econometrics in terms of the stability of the functions involved. Keynes argued strongly that the material was 'non-homogenous through time' and that the coefficients were not constant. In fact he saw 'no reason at all why they should not be different every year' (CW, XIV, 286). He had made a very similar point in his *Quarterly Journal of Economics* article (CW, XIV, 109), which can be read as suggesting that the lesson of *The General Theory* is that there are no stable economic relations.

Given that there are not strong *a priori* reasons for believing economic relationships to be stable over time, and the fact that estimated equations are prone to structural change, one is forced to agree with Keynes that at a logical level econometric inference, like other forms of induction, is insupportable. However, having given Keynes victory on both the technical and logical arguments, it still does not follow that econometrics is worthless.

Action and Induction

To interpret the significance of Keynes' critique for econometrics it is necessary to consider what the objective of econometrics is. Tinbergen proposed two broad objectives. In Tinbergen (1937) he emphasised its practical usefulness in decision making and policy formation, its ability to organise and structure thought, clarify the issues under dispute, use the available information efficiently, and provide a framework for action. But Tinbergen (1939) began with the stated purpose of testing economic theories. In the light of Keynes' work on policy, and his attitude to Tinbergen and other econometricians later in his life (e.g. Stone, 1978), it can be argued that, had merely the practical purpose been emphasised, Keynes might have welcomed econometrics. It was the unjustifiable inductive pretensions that provoked his venom.

The work Keynes did on policy, such as 'The Economic Consequences of Mr Churchill' (CW, IX, 207), 'Can Lloyd George Do It?' (CW, IX, 86), and 'How to Pay for the War' (CW, IX, 367) all involved setting up models, calculating parameters and solving for the effects of policy action. Exactly the process described in Tinbergen (1937). Although Keynes did not express his models formally, did not estimate the parameters by regression techniques, and did not use numerical simulation routines to obtain his solutions, the underlying procedures are the same. In each case Keynes assumed some homogeneity in the underlying responses of the economy, and had no hesitation in predicting the consequences of policy actions. Nor can one contrast Keynes' judgemental procedure with Tinbergen's mechanical one, for Tinbergen also used considerable judgement in the development and use of his models. In fact Keynes' comments to Harrod on the characteristics of a good model-builder echo many of Tinbergen's remarks.

The contemporary relevance of the methodological aspects of the Keynes-Tinbergen debate arises because there is still a great deal of confusion and controversy concerning the objectives and limitations of econometric methods. It has, however, become more widely recognised recently that there is a marked disparity between what econometricians practice and what they profess. The work of Mayer (1980) and Leamer (1978, 1983) is particularly significant in this respect. McCloskey (1983) raises similar issues with respect to economics in general. The dynamic behind the rapid growth in econometrics has been its practical value to policy makers and economic commentators. The ideology which has been used to justify it has, however, been inductive, the search for 'truth' through testing economic theories.[9] Keynes' critique of the inductive claims for econometrics neither stopped the flow of useful practical work, nor disturbed the equanimity with which some economists professed their unattainable ideal of testing economic theory. Econometric practice expanded not because Keynes was wrong in his technical and methodological criticisms of Tinbergen's work, but because it happened to fill a vacuum that was created by the need to formulate and implement the type of interventionist policies that Keynes himself had advocated. As a tool of economic analysis, Tinbergen's method serves an important purpose and it is unlikely that it will be discarded. The challenge lies in recognising its limitations and in using it with care.

Acknowledgements

The authors wish to acknowledge helpful comments by Mary Morgan on a previous version of this chapter.

Notes

1. An English translation of this memorandum later appeared in Tinbergen's *Selected Essays* edited by Klaassen *et al.* (1959). On this see also Hansen's essay on Tinbergen.
2. Note, however, that in his account Hansen (1969, 329) overlooks the fact that an English version of Tinbergen's original model of the Dutch economy (albeit in a revised

and simplified presentation) was made available by Tinbergen (1937).

3. For a more detailed discussion of specification tests and related references to the literature, see Pesaran and Smith (1985).

4. In his analysis of post World War I data Tinbergen employs a simple linear trend, on the ground that the data are too short to allow extraction of a nine-year moving average trend.

5. See Keynes (CW, XIV, 288) as well as Tinbergen's response (CW, XIV, 293).

6. The relationship between the 'barred' and 'unbarred' variables is given (for example) by

$$v_R = -\frac{1}{9}(1 - L)^2 L^{-4}(L^6 + 3L^5 + 6L^4 + 10L^3 + 6L^2 + 3L + 1)\bar{\bar{v}}_R$$

where L and L stands for one-period backward and forward operators.

7. An alternative approach would be to interpret the existence of residual autocorrelation as evidence of structural change, omitted variables, non-linearities, etc. But since our aim here is not to come up with a satisfactory explanation of investment in pre-war UK rolling-stock we shall not pursue this line of investigation.

8. An extensive review of Keynes' *Treatise on Probability* can be found in O'Donnell (1982). This work does not, however, cover Keynes' views on statistical inference and econometrics.

9. These issues are discussed further in Pesaran and Smith (1985).

References

O'Donnell, R.M. (1982) 'Keynes: Philosophy and Economics (an approach to rationality and uncertainty)', Ph.D Dissertation, Cambridge University

Haavelmo, T. (1943) 'Statistical Testing of Business-Cycle Theories', *Review of Economics and Statistics, 25*, 13-18

Hansen, B. (1969) 'Jan Tinbergen: An Appraisal of His Contributions to Economics', *The Swedish Journal of Economics, 71*, 325-36

Hendry, D.F. (1980) 'Econometrics: Alchemy or Science', *Economica, 47*, 387-406

Kalecki, M. (1965) 'Econometric Model and Historical Materialism', in *On Political Economy and Econometrics: Essays in Honour of Oskar Lange,* Pergamon Press, 233-8

Keynes, J.M. CW VIII, IX, XIV

Klaassen, L.H., Koyck, L.M. and Witteveen, H.J. (1959) *Jan Tinbergen: Selected Papers,* North-Holland, Amsterdam

Leamer, E.E. (1978) *Specification Searches: Ad Hoc Inference with Non-Experimental Data,* Wiley, New York

— — (1983) 'Lets Take the Con out of Econometrics' *American Ecomomic Review, 73*, 31-43

Mayer, T. (1980) 'Economics as hard science: realistic goal or wishful thinking?', *Economic Inquiry, 18*, 165-77

McCloskey, D.N. (1983) 'The Rhetoric of Economics', *Journal of Economic Literature, 21*, 481-517

Morgan, M. (1984) 'The probabilistic revolution: Haavelmo's contribution to econometrics', London School of Economics, mimeo.

Patinkin, D. (1976) 'Keynes and Econometrics: on the interaction between the macroeconomic revolutions of the inter-war period', *Econometrica, 44*, 1091-123

Pesaran, M.H. and Smith, R.P. (1985) 'Evaluation of macroeconometric models', *Economic Modelling*, forthcoming

Stone, R. (1978) 'Keynes' Political Arithmetic and Econometrics', *British Academy Seventh Keynes Lecture in Economics*

Tinbergen, J. (1937) *An Econometric Approach to Business Cycle Problems,* Herman and Cie, Editeurs, Paris

— — (1939) *A Method and its Application to Investment Activity,* Statistical Testing of Business Cycle Theories I, League of Nations

KEYNES ON CAUSE, CHANCE AND POSSIBILITY

Anna Carabelli

Introduction

Cause and chance have long been the object of secular controversy concerning both their epistemological status and their role in the various fields of knowledge. Recently they have again been at the centre of debate in economic theory (e.g. Pasinetti, 1974; Hicks, 1979) — a debate in which attention has focused on the thought of the so-called Keynesian economists. It therefore seems useful to examine Keynes' own views on cause and chance. I shall consider mainly *A Treatise on Probability* and the position Keynes took concerning contemporary science, principally concerning the use of the calculus of probability.

As we shall see, Keynes' position had two main features. First, the focus of analysis of the problem of cause and chance is shifted from the field of explanation by material and physical connection to the study of the effective processes of knowing and believing. Second, his theory of probability led him to develop an organic analysis based on non-demonstrative logic and ordinary discourse, rather than an atomic one based on deductive logic and mathematics.

Keynes' cognitivism, I shall argue, was anti-empiricist. However, it did not constitute rationalism either: Keynes' view, though a cognitive one, was not grounded in the certainty of deductive logic. This mixture of anti-empiricism and anti-rationalism was the core of Keynes' peculiar epistemological position and makes Keynes' position difficult to describe in simple terms. Keynes too rejected positivism, refusing both its empiricist and its logicist versions.

These attitudes were also reflected in Keynes' economics, so that his contributions on economic method, theory and policy are characterised by a sense of what is possible rather than that which is necessary.

Cause

Though the concept of cause is a recurrent issue in *A Treatise on Probability*,[1] the reader looking for a reasoned definition of it has to wait until Part III. There he/she can take delight in a three-page Note, entitled 'On the Use of the Term "Cause" ' (CW, VIII, 305-8).[2]

In this Note Keynes explained that up to that point he had not found it necessary to clarify what he thought about the concept of cause, though he managed to avoid 'the metaphysical difficulties which surround the true meaning of cause'. (However, on p. 182 he had already noted: 'A partial or possible cause involves ideas which are still obscure'.)

In the Note he openly stated that he had been using the expression 'in a broader sense' than that involved in technical expressions like 'sufficient cause' or 'necessary cause'. He had been referring to causal relations between objects which did not stand strictly in a position of cause and effect, or to probable causes where there was no implication of necessity and where the antecedents would sometimes have led to particular consequences and sometimes not.

In this, Keynes argued that, although he was departing from the narrow technical standard, he had followed a not uncommon usage among students of probability, using 'cause' where the term 'hypothesis' might have seemed more appropriate. One such student was E. Czuber (1903, 139; quoted in CW, VIII, 306), who by possible cause meant the various sets of conditions *(Bedingungskomplexe)* from which cause could result. Keynes' reason for following Czuber was that the latter's use reflected the way the term was employed in current practice and ordinary language.

In defending such a position, Keynes manifested an attitude which he had consistently shown in his usage of the notion 'probability' throughout the *Treatise.* Probability was treated from a practical point of view, notably that of ordinary discourse, rather than as an artificial language of formal logic. He spoke of 'the practice of ordinary argument' and of the 'actual exercise of reason' (CW, VIII, 37, 3). In the preface to the 1908 draft he had already remarked that 'the logic of probability is of the greatest importance, because it is the logic of ordinary discourse, through which the practical conclusions of actions are often reached' (MSS, MLC, 1908 draft, iv). Throughout the *Treatise* he attended particularly to the broad and ordinary use of probability because, as we shall see later, he thought that probability was only susceptible to mathematical treatment (i.e. numerical measurement) in a restricted range of cases.

Keynes' reason for adopting the practical sense of the term 'cause' was similar. As he explained in the Note, necessary causation of particulars by particulars is rarely apparent to us. The 'antecedent circumstances', he added, 'which we are usually content to accept as causes, are only so in strictness under a favourable conjunction of innumerable other influences'. Therefore 'the strict sense' of the term cause 'has little utility' (CW, VIII, 306).

This particular approach to cause is connected to Keynes' analysis of the relation between probability and limited knowledge. He considered probability as essentially relational, consisting of a logical relation between propositions (rather than an ontological connection), and variable according to the amount of knowledge available. The knowledge we have of the relation between propositions, he explained, 'depends on our circumstances; and while it is often convenient to speak of propositions as certain or probable, this expresses strictly a relationship in which they stand to a *corpus* of knowledge, actual or hypothetical and not a characteristic of the propositions in themselves' (CW, VIII, 3-4).

Similarly, cause too was seen by Keynes as a relation, variable according to the amount of knowledge available. He wrote: 'As our knowledge is partial, there is constantly in our use of the term *cause*, some reference implied or expressed to a limited body of knowledge . . . This intimacy is relative, I think, to particular information, which is actually known to us, or which is within our reach' (CW, VIII, 306). That is to say, that the notion of cause showed the characteristics of 'distance' which in the *Treatise* were used as an analogy for the characteristics of probability. A place is not intrinsically distant, a proposition is not intrinsically probable: 'No proposition is in itself either probable or improbable, just as no place can be intrinsically distant; and the probability of the same statement varies with the evidence presented' (CW, VIII, 7).

Thus the narrow use of the term 'cause' appeared to Keynes less rewarding than the broad one. The distinction between these two mirrored the contrast which was the pivot of his approach to cause throughout *A Treatise on Probability* and was to be crucial also in his economic analysis. He countered the focus on the material causal connection between events with a new focus on the actual and relational cognitive conditions in which the connection is asserted and which give grounds for a belief on which action and practice can be based. This contrast was also expressed by Keynes in various other forms, all of them substantially interchangeable, reflecting this main concern.

One formulation, derived by Keynes from the scholastic jargon of the Middle Ages was between what is implied by the conception of cause as *'causa essendi'* and what is implied by the conception of cause as *'causa cognoscendi'*. We find it both in the Note of the *Treatise* (CW,

VIII, 308) and in two rather sketchy and convoluted passages of his manuscript notes bearing the title, 'Induction, Causation, and Hypothesis'. In the note on 'Ground and Cause' we read:

> Ground or Reason is that upon which a judgement is based as an act of thought. Every relation of causation is a ground. Still there is a difference of aspect between Ground and Cause; the latter is the *causa essendi,* the cause why a thing is what it is; the former is the *causa cognoscendi* — the cause of our knowledge of the event. A statement of a law may be a Ground, never a Cause, though the law may involve causal relations, and lay down what causes are followed by what effects.

In 'Causation in Logic', Keynes noted, 'Readiness to identify induction with determination of causes assisted by the tendency to confuse cause and ground. Induction is the determination of laws and laws are grounds, but *not* causes' (MSS, MLC, unclassified notes).

A second formulation of the contrast between the possible views of causality was based on Keynes' notion of 'dependence' (or 'independence' when the connection was denied). Stress could be placed, as he said in the Note of the *Treatise*, either on what is 'causally dependent' — that is the strictly material connection — or on what is 'dependent for knowledge' (or 'for probability'), that is the cognitive conditions of the connection being asserted and believed.

Keynes pointed out the possible mistake which might arise in mixing considerations of direct material connection with those of dependence for knowledge. 'Two events', he wrote, 'are not independent for knowledge merely because there is an absence of direct causation between them; nor, on the other hand, are they necessarily dependent because there is in fact a causal train which brings them into an indirect connection. The question is whether there is any *known* probable connection, direct or indirect' (CW, VIII, 182).

An implicit definition of 'dependence for knowledge' was to be found already in the conclusion of the Note of the *Treatise*. Reiterating his interest in the ordinary approach to cause, Keynes wrote:

> We wish to know whether knowledge of one fact throws light *of any kind* upon the likelihood of another and noted that the 'theory of causality is only important because it is thought that by means of its assumptions light *can* be thrown by the experience of one phenomenon upon the expectation of another' (CW, VIII, 308).

This definition has close similarities with that of probability set out in chapter 1, 'The Meaning of Probability': 'In the ordinary course of thought and argument, we are constantly assuming that knowledge of one statement, while not *proving* the truth of a second, yields nevertheless some ground for believing it' (CW, VIII, 5).

The same contrast concerning dependence was set out in chapter 16, this time directly opposing 'dependence of *events*' and 'dependence of arguments' (or of 'propositions'). Two *events* are dependent if the occurrence of one is a part cause or possible part cause of the occurrence of the other. In the example of the tossing of a coin, when we speak of dependence of events, we focus on the fact that the result is dependent on the existence of bias in the coin or in the method of tossing. This perspective focuses on the material connection of events. Two *arguments* or *propositions*, on the other hand, are dependent when the knowledge of one fact or event affords any rational ground for expecting the other. This view emphasises the actual cognitive conditions. In the case of the tossing of a coin, when we speak of dependence of arguments, we focus on the fact that a knowledge of the results of other tossings of it 'may be hardly less relevant' than a knowledge of the bias of the coin or the method of tossing it, as a knowledge of these results may be a ground or 'some reason' for a probable knowledge of the bias or of the method of tossing (see CW, VIII, 181-2).

Anti-empiricism

The cognitive approach behind Keynes' view of cause implied a general shift from the realm of empirical uniformity, recurrence or regularity of events, to that of the thinking agents' reasons and grounds for believing:[3] 'With the term "event", which has taken hitherto so important a place in the phraseology of the subject, I shall dispense altogether'. 'Writers on probability', he added, 'have generally dealt with what they term the "happening" of "events"': on the contrary, his concern was to deal with the 'probability of *propositions* instead of the . . . probability of *events*' (CW, VIII, 5).

In contrast to J. Venn, one of the leading figures of the late nineteenth-century frequency approach to probability, who asserted that 'experience is our sole guide' and that, if 'we want to discover what is in reality a series of *things*, not a series of our own conceptions, we must appeal to the things themselves to obtain it, for we cannot find much help elsewhere' (Venn, 1866, 74; quoted in CW, VIII, 93). Keynes maintained that

> where our experience is incomplete, we cannot hope to derive from it judgments of probability without the aid either of intuition or of some further *a priori* principle. Experience, as opposed to intuition, cannot possibly afford us a criterion by which to judge whether on given evidence the probabilities of two propositions are or are not equal. (CW, VIII, 94)

This attitude was even clearer in the early 1907 draft of *A Treatise on Probability*, where he wrote that the English empiricists,

> have entirely lost sight for all practical purposes of the relational nature of the conception [of probability]. Under the aegis of an empirical philosophy they have sought in probability a quality belonging to the entities of phenomenal experience and have imagined that events have probabilities just as men belong to nations. This realist view has been one of the most dangerous disillusions in the past and is not even now eradicated from English philosophy. (*MSS, MLC*, 1907 draft, 18)

The same negative attitude towards empiricism can also be found in his view concerning material external causal laws:

> Whether there are really material external causal laws, how far causal connection is distinct from logical connection, and other such questions, are profoundly associated with the ultimate problems of logic and probability . . . But I have nothing useful to say about them. Nearly everything with which I deal can be expressed in terms of logical relevance. And the relations between logical relevance and material cause must be left doubtful. (CW, VIII, 183)

The same applied to Keynes' refusal to consider cause as connected to empirical uniformity. According to him, 'states of the universe' identical in every particular, may never recur, and, even if identical states were to recur, we should not know it' (CW, VIII, 276).

Chance

Keynes' cognitive attitude can also be detected in his discussion of chance, a concept strictly related to that of cause. The problem of chance, according to Keynes, can be approached from different points of view, represented by various pairs of oppositions. The two main ones are:

(a) the opposition between objective probability and objective chance. Keynes took this opposition as similar to that between cause and chance, namely between 'events . . . which are causally connected and events which are not causally connected'. Clearly this distinction stood for the notions of dependence and independence of *events*, relative to what Keynes called in the Note *'causa essendi'*.

(b) the opposition between knowledge and ignorance; between 'events . . . which we have some reason to expect, and events which we have no reason to expect, which gives rise to the theory of subjective probability and subjective chance' (CW, VIII, 311).

The phrases 'we have some reason to expect' and 'we have no reason to expect' are to be taken as standing for Keynes' notions of 'dependence' and 'independence', and of 'relevance' and 'irrelevance' *for knowledge* or *for probability*; that is for his notion of cause as *'causa cognoscendi'*. Therefore the opposition between knowledge and ignorance depends on whether or not we have some reason to expect or to believe something.

Keynes took the interpretation of chance to be that represented in opposition (b) as fundamental, believing that the opposition between probability and objective chance should be reduced to that between knowledge and ignorance. He treated other possible pairs of oppositions, such as that between chance and design, that is between 'blind cause' and 'final cause', in a similar fashion.

In the light of this, a situation of 'objective chance' can always be translated into cognitive terms. It would appear as one of complete ignorance, in which we have no reason to expect a particular happening. In the example of the coin tossing, its outcome is 'a chance event if our knowledge of the circumstances of the throw is *irrelevant* to our expectation of the possible alternative results' (CW, VIII, 317); or in general, if 'it would be necessary to know a great many more facts of existence about it than we actually do know, and if the addition of a wide knowledge of general principles would be of little use' (CW, VIII, 457). This is the typical situation of ideal games of chance, which are governed, according to Keynes, by complete ignorance. He considered this case, as far as actual human practices were concerned, quite unusual. In their activities, people act in situations which, although of limited knowledge, still remain of knowledge, not of ignorance. In situations of very low knowledge, the addition even of a small piece of information increases, if not the probability, then the 'weight' of the argument, thus increasing confidence in it (see CW, VIII, 83-4, 356).

The Mathematical Theory of Chance

Though Keynes rejected crude empiricism, early in his career he also distanced himself from the opposite view, that of outright rationalism. This point has been overlooked, I think, in the literature on Keynes. We find here one of the peculiar features of Keynes' approach, the mixture of anti-empiricism and anti-rationalism which is typical of a common-sense and ordinary-language position. We have already come across Keynes' anti-rationalistic attitude when dealing with his dislike of the narrow usage of the term 'cause'. It is therefore not surprising that Keynes, though having implicitly attacked Hume as an empiricist, opened his critical remarks on the application of mathematical calculus to probability by agreeing with Hume's opposition to 'the conclusions of a science which claimed and seemed to bring an entire new field within the dominion of reason' (CW, VIII, 90). In Keynes' opinion, Hume, in his view of probability, stood 'for the plain man against the sophisms and ingenuities of "metaphysicians, logicians, mathematicians and even theologians" ' (CW, VIII, 56).[4]

According to Keynes, Hume rightly distinguished between what Keynes called, on the one hand, the method of Locke and the philosophers ('the inductive method based on the experience of uniformity') and on the other hand the method of Bernoulli and the mathematicians ('the mathematical method of counting the equal chances based on indifference'). He quoted from *A Treatise of Human Nature* where Hume argued that 'Probability or reasoning from conjecture, may be divided into two kinds, *viz.* that which is founded on *chance* and that which arises from *causes*' (Hume, 1739-40, Book I, part III, sect. XI). And he embraced Hume's conclusion that 'there must always be a mixture of causes among the chances, in order to be the foundation of any reasoning', commenting that 'chance alone can be the foundation of nothing' (CW, VIII, 90).

According to Keynes, 'the whole fabric of mathematical probability' rested on the principle of non-sufficient reason, 'extended by Bernoulli beyond those problems of gaming in which by its tacit assumption Pascal and Huyghens had worked out a few simple exercises' (CW, VIII, 89). By this principle a rule of equality between probabilities was set, which presupposed that, where no sufficient reason to think otherwise existed (that is in a state of ignorance), the given evidence was composed of a number of equally probable alternatives: a condition which Keynes thought transformed ignorance into knowledge, as it permitted the mathematical treatment of probability. Keynes thought that 'no other formula in the alchemy of logic has exerted more astonishing powers. For it established the existence of God from the premiss of total ignorance; and it has measured with numerical precision the probability that the sun will rise to-morrow' (CW, VIII, 89). Keynes, on the contrary, maintained that the principle required that there must be *no known reason* for preferring one set of alternatives to any other; namely it involved a direct judgement of indifference or irrelevance *for knowledge* (CW, VIII, 59). This is why he redefined it as the principle of indifference (CW, VIII, 44).

Keynes also refused to accept the synthesis which was brought about by Laplace in the late eighteenth century between alternative conceptions of probability, the empiricist and the mathematical. His criticism was based on the fact that, paradoxically, the Laplacian synthesis 'proved too much'. The simpler and less complex the data of experience considered, the better the theory was. Contrary to what one would expect, a state of ignorance or, in technical terms, an ignorance that appeared 'equally balanced' in the light of the principle of indifference, was better than a wide experience and a large amount of information (CW, VIII, 92).

Chance in Contemporary Science

Keynes' view of chance can be brought out more clearly by considering his attitude to contemporary developments both in the natural sciences, notably physics and biology, and in moral sciences. He was fully aware of the intellectual debate which at the turn of the century marked the crisis in the vision of the cosmic order inherited from Newton's classical mechanics, a point which seems often to be ignored. We know, for instance, that as early as 1905 he made a thorough study of Henri Poincaré's *La science et l'hypothèse* (1896) a major work on probability and chance in physics; his comments on this are to be found in the 1907 draft.[5]

The classical scientific vision of cause had been based on the conviction that it was always possible to isolate the system under observation in order to foresee in an unequivocal way the phenomena taking place in it and to trace a deterministic explanation for each occurrence; the scientist was conceived as always capable of framing theories of this type. The main consequence of its breakdown, with the abandonment of causation and necessity, was to bring chance and possibility, and so probabilistic laws, to the centre of the attention of the early twentieth-century scientists and philosophers (Duhem, 1906; Bridgman, 1927; Cassirer, 1920 and 1937).

The problem of how to interpret probabilistic laws and the role played by chance has long been discussed and appears to be still unsettled (Mellor, 1971; Popper, 1982a and 1982b). This is also true of the concepts of indeterminism and uncertainty, which cover the same semantic field as that of chance. Perhaps their meaning can be elucidated by reference to the interpretation of probability on which they rest (Black, 1967; Weatherford, 1983). This was certainly Keynes' view. As we have seen, his basic distinction was that between objective chance and subjective chance, i.e. between ontology and the conditions of our knowledge. The distinction may be applied also to the problem of indeterminism and uncertainty.

Keynes' 'cognitivist' attitude to chance led him to reject as irrelevant for the actual conditions of knowledge, the theory of objective chance, although he neither affirmed nor denied the existence of chance events. This explains his criticism of the objective statistical view of chance in both the physical and the social sciences, based on empirical frequency of events. According to Keynes, such an approach saw everything in terms of the ideal game of chance (CW, VIII, 458). As we saw, according to him, this situation — taken by the frequency statisticians as corresponding to the ontological structure of events — could be interpreted, in cognitive terms, as a situation of complete ignorance, which hardly ever occurred in the actual conditions of knowledge. Keynes wrote:

> The statistical result is so attractive in its definiteness that it leads us to forget the more vague, though more important considerations which may be, in a given particular case, within our knowledge. To a stranger the probability that I shall send a letter to the post unstamped may be derived from the statistics of the Post Office; for me those figures would have but the slightest bearing upon the question. (CW, VIII, 356)

The Atomic Hypothesis

Keynes was critical of attempts at representing subjective chance by a mathematical theory of chance, and held related views concerning scientific reasoning and its relationship with mathematics, logic, and probability. Here again — as with cause — Keynes concentrated on the actual cognitive practice of scientists, notably those abandoning mechanism and necessity. What he took into consideration were the reasons, grounds and hypotheses concerning reality 'on which scientists appear commonly to act' (CW, VIII, 276).

According to him, the commonest hypothesis in physics was that of seeing matter as constituted by 'the collisions and arrangements of particles between which the ultimate, qualitative differences are very few'. It was shared also by Mendelian biology, which derived 'the various qualities of men from the collisions and arrangements of chromosomes' (CW, VIII, 468). When dealing with the problem of natural laws, Keynes described this hypothesis as 'what mathematicians call the principle of the superposition of small effects, or, as I prefer to call it, in this connection, the *atomic* character of natural laws'. According to it, he added,

> the system of the material universe [consisted] of bodies which we may term . . . *legal atoms*, such that each of them exercises its own separate, independent, invariable effects, a change of the total state being compounded of a number of separated changes each of which is solely due to a separate portion of the preceding state . . . Each atom can, according to this theory, be treated as a separate cause and thus not enter into different organic combinations in each of which it is regulated by different laws.

This hypothesis was particularly crucial to science, as it justified that particular type of inference — the application of the calculus of probability — according to which 'the occurence of a phenomenon which has appeared as a part of a more complex phenomenon, may be *some* reason for expecting it to be associated on another occasion with part of the same complex' (CW, VIII, 276-7). If the general hypothesis fell, the inference which was based on it would fall too.

In Keynes' picture of the concept of nature held by contemporary scientists, one can easily recognise the standard tenets of the classical mechanist view. He appeared to be interested in pointing out the continuities rather than the breaks with that tradition. Notably, he stressed the fact that contemporary science, though abandoning mechanical determinism, retained the atomic hypothesis on which classical mechanics was founded. Contemporary scientists had replaced the old machine metaphor with a view of nature which, while maintaining its atomic attributes, was based on mathematical chance, rather than on universal causality: nature was seen as 'an urn containing black and white balls in fixed proportions' (CW, VIII, 468).[6] Just as the machine model had permitted the application of the mathematical analysis, now the urn model permitted the application of the calculus of probability. The classical view of nature as something which is capable of being mathematicised in its essential features was fully maintained, the image being adjusted to fit the new mathematical tool.

In Keynes' eyes, the new laws of chance appeared to be as naturalistic and beyond human control as the old ones of causality were, causal necessity having merely changed into statistical necessity. They too could serve to confine the future within the data supplied by the past; and they too, adapting the phrase Keynes used in reference to economists, permitted the exorcism of the future by 'false rationalisation' obtained from the 'hypothesis of a calculable future' (CW, XIV, 122). The notion of possibility, which had been creeping in along with chance, was substantially excluded again.

According to Keynes, contemporary science did nothing but extend to all fields of experience that calculus of probability which in the seventeenth and eighteenth centuries had been applied, in the frame of the atomic hypothesis, to gambling and games of chance. Therefore Keynes felt it quite appropriate to extend the anti-rationalist criticism that he had levelled against Bernoulli's and Laplace's probability theory to cover the key tools of contemporary science. This is clear in his analysis of the cognitive conditions under which the atomic hypothesis could be 'reasonably justified'.

Mathematics, Logic and Probability

According to Keynes, the atomic hypothesis would be reasonable in those cases where the world did actually seem to have the characteristics presupposed by the mathematicians: i.e. when it resembled an urn or a ballot box, but he felt the need to stress that the *blind* application of the calculus meant the attribution to every probabilistic statement of the limited and particular conditions which were presupposed in the use of that tool. We shall see later individual instances in which Keynes thought the atomic hypothesis did not work.

In order to grasp correctly the sense of Keynes' general position, one has to remember that he did not contrast scientific hypotheses to 'objective reality'. Control over the compatibility between hypothesis and material came, according to him, from within, rather than from outside, the process of knowledge. When we misapply the calculus of probability, he explained, we are giving 'the names of addition and multiplication to certain processes of compounding probability *in advance* of postulating that the processes in question have properties commonly associated with their names' (CW, VIII, 174). He added that this could be avoided only by paying attention to the actual conditions of knowledge and stressed that an intuitive, 'direct judgement' on the 'independence of arguments' was strictly required before applying mathematical reasoning to probability. 'Unless . . . we are dealing with independent arguments', he wrote, 'we cannot apply detailed mathematical reasoning, even when the individual probabilities are numerically measurable. The greater part of mathematical probability . . . is concerned with arguments which are *both* independent and numerically measurable' (CW, VIII, 176).

In other words, before applying mathematical reasoning, one has to decide that there are *no known* reasons to believe or to expect that the arguments advanced refer to events which are materially connected. If so, the problem will be urn-like. If not, the application of the calculus will lead to conclusions which are 'unreasonable'. In this case the calculus would be perfectly correct from the point of view of formal logic and mathematical truth. But, according to Keynes, its application would be 'artificial' or 'mechanical' (CW, VIII, 15, 56-7, 174). I shall discuss later the nature of Keynes' logic of probability, but here first it is necessary to clarify what Keynes did *not* mean by 'logic': formal internal coherence. As he wrote, we must 'distinguish the rational from the true' and 'there is no direct relation between the truth of a proposition and its probability. Probability begins and ends with probability' (CW, VIII, 273, 356). Here is also a possible key to what he meant when, in dealing with the use of the calculus of probability in contemporary physics and biology, he referred to its 'alchemy' and 'astrology', and spoke of the 'undeserved' success of statistics (CW, VIII, 89, 468).

This point bring us to the questions Keynes raised about the relations between mathematics and probability and between logic and probability. Concerning the former Keynes wrote that 'the architectural scheme of the mathematical theory of probability resembles closely to an inverted cone' and that probabilists thought 'the supporting apex more stable than it looks' (*MSS, MLC*, 1907 draft, 4). In stressing this point, Keynes was raising in the field of probability a question similar to that discussed in the field of the epistemology of mathematics around the turn of the century concerning the nature and validity of mathematical deduction and proof. One of the outcomes of the debate was Gödel's theorem (1931), according to which mathematics could not be completely and consistently formalised in one system adequate for number theory. This shattered the idea of mathematics as a perfect deduction from first principles. As it appeared internally ungrounded, it could only be supported from the outside, by a non-mathematical interpretation (Kline, 1972, 1206-7; 1980; Quine 1964, 24; 1978, 154). Later, Wittgenstein (1956) advanced the thesis that mathematics could only be grounded in ordinary language.

One would have expected this debate to have a notable impact on probability theory, all the more given that it was then moving towards a complete mathematicisation. Eventually, the axiomisation of the mathematical theory of probability put forward by Kolmogorov in 1929 was to make probability a branch of pure mathematics (Kolmogorov, 1933).[7] Thus, the epistemology of mathematics became relevant for the axiomatic theory of probability itself. Measure theory and the axioms of the calculus of probability appeared to be empty, unless a non-mathematical and external interpretation was applied to them. Actually, the problem was felt mainly by writers working outside the field of probability theory.[8]

Hence the retrospective interest of the fact that Keynes, in addition to being one of the few twentieth-century writers on probability who dared to throw a stone into the quiet pond of mathematicisation, subsumed the calculus of probability under a logic not susceptible to complete mathematicisation or identification with the atomic hypothesis on which the calculus was based.[9] Concerning the relationship between logic and the calculus, he wrote that 'the calculus of probability has received far more attention than its logic' and 'the logic of probability approximates rather to Metaphysics than to Mathematics' (CW, VIII, 22; *MSS, MLC*, 1907 draft, 2). Therefore he seems to have thought that 'the supporting apex' of the calculus of probability rested ultimately on a 'metaphysical' rather than a mathematical, ground, the more so since he was convinced that mathematics itself, as well all other sciences, followed inductive and analogical reasoning (CW, VIII, 269-71).[10]

Probability as Organic

Keynes conceived probability in terms which openly contrasted with the atomic hypothesis. 'A degree of probability', he wrote, 'is not composed of some homogeneous material, and is not apparently divisible into parts of like character with one another' (CW, VIII, 32). Probability was thought of as represented by magnitudes which were qualitative, transitory, organically dependent, unique and time irreversible. They were intensive, rather than extensive magnitudes, differing from those of Russell's atomistic logic. Keynes compared them to degrees of colour and similarity (CW, VIII, 49). The 'objective quality measured may not . . . possess numerical quantitativeness' (CW, VIII, 49). They were therefore nearer to the 'secondary qualities' than to the 'primary qualities'. All their attributes were grouped by the notion of 'complexity' (CW, VIII, 277).

It was because of the 'complexity' of the magnitudes involved that, according to Keynes, the knowledge of probability could not be completely dealt with in analytical terms. Actually, it was endowed with a direct, intuitive and synthetical character, which belonged to what formal logic would have called 'indefinables' (CW, VIII, 8-9, 15, 56, 293).

As he thought the logic of probability was constituted by non-demonstrative propositions, Keynes contrasted his 'relatival logic of inference and probability' to 'Mr. Russell's universal logic of implication' (CW, VIII, 129). He stressed the need for the logic of probability to be open, unlike artificial languages, which are composed of a finite number of members, with exhaustive alternatives. He wrote, 'a system of facts or propositions, as we ordinarily conceive it, may comprise an indefinite number of members' (CW, VIII, 279; see also 41). Furthermore, he described his logic of probability as not obeying the principle of non-contradiction, namely what in the jargon of mathematical probability is called the complementational principle for negation. He pointed out that '"practical certainty". . . differs from logical certainty since its contradictory is not impossible' and that in probability 'the number of contraries to any proposition on any evidence is always infinite' (CW, VIII, 47, 177). Hence the comparison he advanced between the logic of probability and that of colours, somewhat anticipating the twentieth-century version of the 'logic of colours' which was to be developed by Wittgenstein (1978) (see CW, VIII, 38). His logic of probability is therefore to be carefully distinguished from the later developments of probability worked out by Carnap, in the Russellian tradition; its open character and its tolerance of contradiction clearly separated it from the later attempts to force non-demonstrative arguments into formal logic.[11]

The 'logicist' interpretation of Keynes' theory is thus probably based on a hasty reading of Keynes' text. In various passages Keynes did indeed speak of the 'logical' character of his notion of probability. And his theory of probability was indeed a logic, concerning the relations between propositions and arguments rather than between events. But this fact does not mean necessarily that, as a logic, it was a logic of the formal type. In fact, it was an ordinary discourse logic. This may help to explain the fact, which may baffle the reader of *The General Theory*, that Keynes referred to his analysis as logical and at the same time attacked the mathematical approach.

If the atomistic conception of probability involved the use of mathematical and formal logic, Keynes' adoption of an organic approach involved the use of ordinary language.

In the *Treatise* the priority of ordinary language over mathematical language was unquestioned. 'I shall not cut myself', Keynes wrote, 'from the convenient, but looser, expressions, which have been habitually employed by previous writers and have the advantage of being . . . immediately intelligible to the reader'. In the footnote, he praised ordinary language in terms of its semantical character, contrasting it to the pure syntactical one of artificial mathematical languages (CW, VIII, 19-20). Just for its organic characteristics, its open structure and the non-finite number of propositions, its compatibility with contradiction and its semantic character, ordinary language permitted one to deal with phenomena presenting the attribute of 'complexity' (CW, VIII, 277).

Ordinary language could also cope generally with 'continuum and non-enumerable aggregates' (CW, VIII, 50). According to Keynes, these included not only probability judgements, but those concerning both goodness, which were considered as 'organic and indivisible' (CW, VIII, 343), and utility and price, (which were defined in the *Essay on Index Numbers* (1909), in line with *A Treatise on Probability*, in terms of intensive and organic magnitudes.[12] The laws of additivity and multiplication did not apply either to probability or to such aggregates. As Keynes wrote, 'the assumption . . . that degrees of probability are wholly subject to the laws of arithmetic, runs directly counter to the view which has been advocated in Part I of this treatise'. And 'even if we are able to range goods in order of magnitude and also their probability in order of magnitude, yet it does not follow that we can range the products composed of each good and its corresponding probability in this order' (CW, VIII, 344, 349). This approach to non-numerical magnitudes was to be the basis of Keynes' thesis about the so called 'fallacy of composition' or the 'paradox of saving', both in *A Treatise on Money* (CW, V, 158-60) and in *The General Theory* (CW, VII, 85).

Keynes thought that his approach to probability had a general applicability. He considered his theory of non-demonstrative arguments valid 'in metaphysics, in science and in conduct' (CW, VIII, 3). He thought that 'the conception of our having *some* reason, though not a conclusive one, for certain beliefs ... may prove important for the theory of epistemology'. 'The old metaphysics', he explained,

> had been greatly hindered by reason of its having always demanded demonstrative certainty. Much of the cogency of Hume's criticism arises out of the assumption of methods of certainty on the part of those systems against which it was directed ... The demonstrative method can be laid on one side, and we may attempt to advance the argument by taking account of circumstances which seem to give *some* reason for preferring one alternative to another. (CW, VIII, 266)

Thus Keynes seemed to see his work on probability as a sort of anti-*Discours de la méthode*, based on probability, ordinary discourse and common sense rather than on certainty and on analytical reason. In fact, his work appeared as a general approach to cognitive procedures involving uncertainty both in everyday experience and in the moral as well as the natural sciences. We can sum it up by saying that its logic was a logic of opinion, rather than of truth. Thus, his contribution was in the long intellectual tradition which stemmed from Aristotle's doctrines of rhetorical argument and practical wisdom and adopted the rule of reasonableness, as distinct from that of reason.

As we saw, though Keynes thought that no science could do without non-demonstrative arguments, he did not suppose that there were no circumstances in which the atomic hypothesis and the mathematical calculus were applicable. But the task of the deciding and controlling the application of the analytical approach was seen ultimately as resting on the synthetic logic of probability. As it were, certainty represented nothing but a limiting case of probability.

Already in *A Treatise on Probability*, Keynes stressed the difficulty of applying mathematical discourse particularly to the moral sciences and psychology. He declared: 'I . . . have not the same lively hope as Condorcet, or even as Edgeworth, "éclairer les Sciences morales et politiques par le flambeau de l' Algèbre"'. Concerning psychology he wrote:

> We should be very chary of applying to problems of psychical research the *calculus* of probabilities . . . If, therefore, we endeavour to *calculate* the probability that some phenomenon is due to 'abnormal' causes, our mathematics will be apt to lead us into unjustifiable conclusions. (CW, VIII, 334-9).

The polemical target, as far as psychology was concerned, was explicit in his essay on Edgeworth (1926):

> The atomic hypothesis which had worked so splendidly in physics breaks down in psychics. We are faced at every turn with the problems of organic unity, of discreteness, of discontinuity — the whole is not equal to the sum of the parts, comparison of quantity fails us, small changes produce large effects, the assumptions of a uniform and homogeneous continuum are not satisfied. (CW, X, 262)

The rejection of the atomic hypothesis in the moral sciences and in psychology was to be the natural premise of the rejection of the individualistic approach which had dominated economics at the end of the nineteenth century. We have already seen that, in his picture of the atomic hypothesis in science, Keynes referred to its 'legal atoms', stressing its implicit juridical connotation, and describing the behaviour of atoms as that of the individuals of a perfectly liberal state. Moreover, the emphasis he placed on ordinary language throughout the *Treatise* already evoked a view of beliefs as conventional, rather than natural, and as collective, rather than private. These hints in *A Treatise on Probability* were to be fully developed in Keynes' criticism, notably in *The General Theory*, of so called methodological individualism in economics.

Economic Method

As far as economics was concerned, the hints Keynes made in *A Treatise on Probability* were obviously to be integrated with the scattered observations he made in the rest of his works. But, though the picture became richer, it remained within the general frame outlined in the *Treatise*. So in various passages Keynes stressed that most of the economic material possessed the attributes of 'complexity' set out in *A Treatise on Probability*, and were therefore not immediately susceptible to analysis. (CW, VII, 247; XIV, 286, 300).

As far as method is concerned, in the Introduction to the Series of Cambridge Economic Handbooks, 1922-3, we read: 'The theory of economics does not furnish a body of settled conclusions immediately applicable to policy. It is a method, rather than a doctrine, which helps its possessor to draw correct conclusions' (CW, XII, 856). The passage throws light on the continuity between *A Treatise on Probability* and Keynes' economic works. Perhaps one should say the 'point of coincidence', because in the passage the distinction between method and doctrine is rejected. In fact economics was thought of as a method of non-demonstrative argument, just like the logic of probability on which it was based.

In his discussion with Roy Harrod in 1938, which represents his maturest and most outspoken methodological manifesto, he declared that 'economics is a branch of logic, a way of thinking', rather than a 'pseudo-natural science'. In doing this Keynes only restated his early position (CW, XIV, 296). He was using the term 'logic' in the sense we have seen set out in *A Treatise on Probability,* which, I repeat, did not coincide with that of formal logic.

Right from the beginning of his career as an economist Keynes openly rejected positivism. Already, in his 1912 economic lectures, dealing with the causes of the value of money, the forces which he pointed out as causes were not the material ones, referring to homogeneous bodies which were moved by the 'force' of classical mechanics, but were the various reasons, beliefs and opinions of individual people (see CW, XII, 731).

In his discussion with Harrod not only did Keynes confirm his early belief, contrasting Harrod's explanation based on material causes with his own based on reasons, openly manifesting his dislike for the analogy between economic behaviour and the mechanical movement of physical bodies (see Harrod, 1938), but he went so far as to reverse completely the positivist application of the Newtonian method of physical sciences to economics for, he joked,

Economics deals with motives, expectations, psychological uncertainty. One has to be constantly on guard against treating the material as constant and homogeneous. It is as though the fall of the apple to the ground depended on the apple's motives, on whether it is worth while falling to the ground, and whether the ground wanted the apple to fall, and on mistaken calculations on the part of the apple as to how far it was from the centre of the earth. (CW, XIV, 300).

Keynes believed that no universal and objective rule could exist for classifying economic material and variables. An element which was taken as being logically independent in a given context, might be given the attribute of dependent in a different one. Moreover, Keynes saw this distinction among variables as practical and depending on the actual purpose of his analysis. In *The General Theory* he decided to consider as independent those elements, 'which can be deliberately controlled or managed by central authority in the kind of system in which we actually live' (CW, VII, 247). Elsewhere Keynes referred, instead to 'hypotheses' and 'models', describing economics as the art of constructing models (CW, XIV, 296). For him the two terms were synonymous, as both were to be taken in the sense of *A Treatise on Probability*, namely as non-empirical, non-deductive and not to be subjected either to verification or falsification.

The distinction between variables was introduced in *The General Theory*, according to Keynes, in order to make the material more manageable to analysis. That such a step was made necessary by the vast 'complexity' of the economic material, namely its organic, rather than atomic, character, was apparent from the fact that the material still retained its complex character. 'Practical intuition', together with ordinary language, were the tools which permitted us to pass to the second part of the analysis, that in which the variables hitherto considered independent were reintroduced into the analysis (CW, VII, 249). They permitted us to keep ' "at the back of our heads" the necessary reserves, qualifications and the adjustments which we shall have to make later on' (CW, VII, 297), notably, the fact that the initial hypothesis concerning independent variables was indeed nothing but an hypothesis.

The adoption of a non-mathematical tool meant that, in both parts of the analysis, the interpretations of the connection between the variables remained only 'probable' (CW, VII, 297). The situation was constantly one of substantial 'complexity'. Had Keynes thought complexity could be eliminated, he would simply have considered all elements independent. But, on the contrary, he criticised throughout the entire work the assumption held by classical and neoclassical writers concerning the independence of elements, such as saving and investment, which he considered organically interdependent (CW, VII, 179-85).

Keynes said that his approach in *The General Theory*, unlike the mathematical approach, offered only 'provisory' conclusions, as it was not 'a machine, or a method of blind manipulation, which will furnish an infallible answer' (CW, VII, 297). In other words, the connections traced by him between elements of the economic complex had no necessity. We have already seen that Keynes' approach to causal attribution was utterly unconcerned with material connection between events. We can therefore sum up his causal approach in *The General Theory* by saying that it traced probable, rather than necessary, connections between arguments or propositions, rather than between events. This was the same as his approach in *A Treatise on Probability*.

Economic Belief

The affinity between Keynes' approach to probability and his approach to economics appears more clearly if we consider the emphasis he placed in all his economic writings on the connection between economic theory and intervention. This echoed the emphasis he had placed, in *A Treatise on Probability*, on the connection between probability judgements and practical action.

Keynes' approach to action paralleled his approach to probability judgements and was marked by the same anti-positivist attitude. He rejected the physical and causal explanation of action, and connected action to the cognitive reasons, grounds and hypotheses on which he thought probability judgements were based; at the same time, he refused once again to see the realm of reason either as being governed by deductive logical certainty or as being unconnected to or unconditioned by practical action.

This double bond between theory and action was already implicit in Keynes' approach to scientific theory, which was considered earlier. Its reasons, grounds and hypotheses too were in fact probability statements, based on ordinary language and rooted in action-oriented beliefs. According to Keynes, to have reasons or grounds or to express hypotheses was closely connected with belief and action. 'To believe one thing *in preference* to another', he wrote, '. . . must have reference to action and must be a loose way of expressing the property of *acting* on one hypothesis rather than another'. And 'the probable is the hypothesis on which it is rational to act' (CW, VIII, 339). He also quoted the eighteenth-century author Bishop Joseph Butler: 'To us probability is the very guide of life' (Butler, 1736, iii).

In this sense Keynes' approach to both probability and action was covered by one and the same analysis, that of probability beliefs. This is the reason why one could hardly expect him to give weight to deductive logical certainty or blind action. As in Keynes' view of science, there was hardly room for physical objectivity or pure calculability.

In fact, the emphasis on cause interpreted as *'causa cognoscendi'* and on ordinary language contained in the approach to probability statements and to action set out in *A Treatise on Probability* also defined the epistemological status attributed by Keynes to both the economic scientist and to economic agents. On the one hand, the economist's reasoning was bounded by limited knowledge and uncertainty. Perfect knowledge would be only that guaranteed by the acceptance either of cause as *'causa essendi'* or of chance seen as completely mathematicisable. This was, we have seen, just what Keynes rejected. What the economist put forward in his doctrines and policy suggestions were his probability judgements, the beliefs on which he based his theoretical practice, ranging from 'we have some reason to believe' concerning present or short-term events to 'we don't know' concerning future events. On the other hand, as far as the object of his study was concerned, economic agents were taken as knowing, believing and acting beings, rather than as passive and neutral physical bodies subjected to natural laws. They too were circumscribed by limited knowledge and uncertainty, but their behaviour was not thought of as being either blind or causally driven, or led in a deterministic way by their judgements about maximum expected profitability. It was guided by an ordinary logic which was reasonable and, to some extent, analysable. Similarly, their practical beliefs and expectations were seen as dictated by hypotheses, if sometimes unconsciously. Ideas were important, according to Keynes, as they guided practice (CW, VII, 383-4). He compared the economic agent's expectations concerning the future, what he called 'the practical theory of future', to the scientist's hypotheses (CW, XIV, 114). As we have seen, the comparison worked the other way round too. The scientist's procedure is more systematic than that of the economic agent, but not qualitatively different.[13]

Such a symmetry between the economic scientist and the economic agent was made complete by the fact that the economist's logic was thought of as being the same as that of 'ordinary men', 'modern mathematicians', 'Polish farmers' and 'savages' (CW, VIII, 271-4). In fact, it was the same as that set out in *A Treatise on Probability*. Thus, in his theoretical practice the economic scientist acted as the economic agent did in his practical expectations, and the economic agent reasoned in his practical expectations as the economic scientist did in his theoretical practice. Or, using Keynes' words: 'As living and moving beings, we are forced to act . . . Yet we must be guided by some hypothesis. We tend, therefore, to substitute for the knowledge which is not attainable certain conventions' (CW, XIV, 114).

The Sense of Possibility

Because Keynes thought the ground on which the judgements and practices of both the economic scientist and the economic agent rested was beliefs, rooted in opinion and in convention, rather than in universal, unchangeable truth, Keynes viewed them as changeable.[14] The tool of change was persuasion and ordinary language, rather than demonstration and formal logic. There Keynes' approach to economics showed its latent rhetorical bent. The relation between the economic scientist and the subject of his study tended to be the same as that between the writer and his audience.

Hence the peculiar interplay in Keynes' economic works between theory and intervention, and between the economic scientist and the economic agent. On the one hand, the economist was able to *verstehen* his subject of study. At the same time, he could influence it by his writings. He could change the social understanding of the economic agent and, consequently, change his behaviour and action too. Conversely, the economic agent could react to theory, thus influencing the economist's beliefs.

Theory and action being closely connected, neither of them was thought of as static or independent (see Habermas, 1979). Being wrapped up in a net of ideas and behaviour which was organic and collective — Keynes spoke of a 'psychology of society' and a 'public mind' (CW, II, 11; CW, VII, 373) — they were seen as changeable *en bloc*, through a process of intuitive switching from one 'twist in the mind' to another. (Harrod, 1951, 113).

He explicitly stressed the importance for economic theory and policy, and politics, of the fact that beliefs are changeable. If beliefs were unchangeable, economics and politics would be useless. In *A*

Revision of the Treaty (1922), he wrote of public opinion, saying that it was

> the mysterious entity which is the same thing perhaps as Rousseau's General Will. Yet, all the same, I do not attach to what they tell me too much importance. Public opinion held that Hans Andersen's Emperor wore a fine suit; and in the United States especially, public opinion changes sometimes, as it were, *en bloc.* If indeed, public opinion were an unalterable thing, it would be a waste of time to discuss public affairs. And though it may be the chief business of newsmen and politicians to ascertain its momentary features, a writer ought to be concerned, rather, with what public opinion should be. (CW, III, 125)

Since probability judgements were based on the shaky foundation of belief and ordinary language, Keynes was fully aware too that one can only convince or persuade, i.e. obtain the assent of the public or of the economists; one cannot demonstrate the truth of theories. 'In economics you cannot *convict* your opponent of error — you can only *convince* him of it' (CW, XIII, 470). The role of theory was therefore that of trying to influence beliefs and opinions. As he said in the preface to the *Essays in Persuasion* (1931), 'It was in a spirit of persuasion that most of these essays were written, in an attempt to influence opinion' (CW, IX, xvii).[15]

Keynes' emphasis on the importance of beliefs was complementary to his view of social and economic life as being open to the possibility of change. This in turn was reinforced by his opposition to the positivist approach based on empirical causality or on calculable chance (so vigorously expressed in his letters to Harrod in 1938). That is to say, referring again to the distinction set out in *A Treatise on Probability,* the interpretation of cause was as *'causa cognoscendi'* not *causa essendi.* Without rejecting the latter, Keynes could neither have seen social and economic life as effectively open and pliable, as human constructions comprising 'hypothesis' and experiment (CW, VIII, 306), nor have expressed the idea, as he did in *The General Theory,* that one could, if not change human nature, at least 'manage it' (CW, VII, 374). Nor could he actively oppose the naturalism and determinism implied in the 'laissez faire' theory, according to which economic intervention could only risk making things worse in comparison to the presupposed fixed or self-adjusting order of nature. As Keynes commented in the *Economic Possibilities for our Grand-children* (1930), this was just 'the pessimism of the reactionaries' which called for 'no experiments' (CW, IX, 322). In *The General Theory,* concerning underemployment equilibrium, he wrote: 'We must not conclude that the mean position thus determined by "natural tendencies" . . . is therefore established by laws of necessity. The unimpeded rule of the above conditions is . . . not a necessary principle which cannot be changed' (CW, VII, 254).

Physical or statistical necessity being rejected, change could therefore be seen as possible, through the positive condition represented by the mouldability of beliefs. However, just because it was not guaranteed by necessity, it could be fostered only by a voluntary action. This was indeed the role attributed by Keynes to those we have seen he called the 'writers'. As he wrote in *A Revision of the Treaty,* 'I seek by the proposal of this chapter, not to prescribe a solution, but to create a situation in which a solution is possible'; and 'I shall do better to construct an independent solution, which is *possible* in the sense that nothing but a change in the popular will is necessary to achieve it, hoping to influence this will a little' (CW, III, 115, 117). This was the reason why economists, according to Keynes, should always keep their eyes turned towards what he called 'the possibility of things' (quoted in Johnson, 1978, 32). Keynes' expression cannot but remind us of the title of a chapter of Robert Musil's *The Man without Qualities:* 'If there is such a thing as a sense of reality, there must also be a sense of possibility' (Musil, 1931, 11); or, closer to home, of one of Wittgenstein's aphorisms: 'The insidious thing about the causal point of view is that it leads us to say: "Of course, it had to happen like that". Whereas we ought to think: it may have happened like that — and also in many other ways' (Wittgenstein, 1980, 37).

In Keynes' approach, too, the sense of possibility was also valid for judging the past. In *A Treatise on Money* (1930), discussing the causes of the depression, he maintained that it was neither inevitable nor a result of a natural force or an accident!

> If then, these are the causes, was the slump avoidable? And is it remediable? The causes to which we have assigned it were the outcome of policy, and in a sense, therefore, it was avoidable. Yet it is evident that the policy could not have been radically different, unless the mentality and ideas of our rulers had also been greatly changed. That is to say, what has occurred is not exactly an accident; it has been deeply rooted in our general way of doing things. (CW, VI, 345)

His attitude towards contemporary economic policies rested on the same epistemological ground as that which he showed towards future ones. When he stressed the necessity, in economic thought, of 'taking wings into the future', he was fully aware, as he tried to show, that such an achievement needed a fresh look at the scientific status of economics — to be seen not as a 'pseudo-natural science' but rather as an 'art', which was based, as he wrote in the *Essay on Ramsey*, on 'theory and fact, intuitive imagination and practical judgement'(CW, IX,322;CW, XIV, 296; CW, X, 335).

Acknowledgement

I should like to thank Donald Moggridge of the University of Toronto for useful advice during the preparation of this chapter.

Notes

1. Keynes discussed cause and chance mainly in *A Treatise on Probability* (CW, VIII). The book was published in its final version in 1921. Two earlier typed drafts bearing the title 'The Principles of Probability' 1907 and 1908, together with manuscript notes, are still extant, and are now kept in the Marshall Library, Cambridge (*MSS, MLC*). Up to now the role of this work in framing Keynes' methodological attitude to economics has not been sufficiently stressed (Carabelli, 1982). Keynes' interest in the theoretical foundations of economics, which he always viewed as belonging to the 'moral sciences', was already manifest in his approach to probability as early as 1905, when he laid down a 'Scheme for an Essay on the Principles of Probability'. Chapter 14 of Part I bore the title 'The Application of Probability to Certain Questions in Economics' and Chapter 1 of Part II bore the title 'The Application of Mathematics to the Moral Sciences' (*MSS, MLC*, TP Box 7, fly-sheet).

2. With small changes the Note follows Chapter 12 'On Causation' of the 1907 draft and Chapter 16 of the 1908 draft (*MSS, MLC*, 1907 draft, 251-9 and 1908 draft, 253-60).

3. For a general view on causality see Bunge (1959). For causation as regularity, see Hume (1739-40), book I, part 3; Hume (1748), Sections 4-7; Hume (1740), (for Keynes' view of Hume see introduction pp. V-XXXII; now in CW, XXVIII, 373-390). For other views which are substantially in line with Hume, see Mill (1843), vol. 1, book 3, chs. 4-6; vol.II, book 3, ch. 21; Russell (1912-13).

4. The two passages can also be found in the 1907 version of *A Treatise on Probability* (*MSS, MLC*, 1907 draft, 76-7 and 103). The order of the two passages is inverted compared to the final version but their content, apart from some stylistic changes, remains unchanged. In the Preface to the 1908 version the same attitude was stressed again: 'It seemed that [the calculus of probability] might be the means of leading in the Age of Order and Reason' (*MSS, MLC*, 1908 draft, iv).

5. Keynes read the English translation of Poincaré's book, published in the same year (*MSS, MLC*, 'List of the books read during Easter vacation 1905'); for comments, see the 1907 draft, 79.

6. See for example Jevons (1874, 1907 ed., 150): 'Nature is to us like an infinite ballot-box, the contents of which are being continually drawn, ball after ball, and exhibited to us. Science is but the careful observation of the succession in which balls of

various character present themselves; we register the combinations, notice those which seem to be excluded from occurrence, and from the proportional frequency of those which appear we infer the probable character of future drawings'.

7. 'The calculus of probability . . . is no guide by itself as to which opinion we ought to follow, and is not a measure of the weight we should attach to conflicting arguments' (CW, VIII, 105, n.l.). According to A.J. Ayer (1972, 28), judgements based on the *a priori* calculus of chances are mathematical truisms.

8. The 'later' Wittgenstein, in a way similar to Keynes, thought that it would be absurd to require for probability statements, as well as for intentional statements which manifest will, desire etc., an analysis which fixes 'the degree' or 'the measurability' as within a calculus. Probability was seen by him, again in a way very similar to Keynes' organic relation of probability, as an *internal* relation between propositions: an expectation is embedded in a situation, which is rooted in human customs and ordinary language (Wittgenstein, 1953, n. 337, 445, 581; 1969b, 224-35; Waismann 1967, 81). On Wittgenstein's notion of probability and expectation see Kenny (1973, ch. 7) and von Wright (1969, 259-79).

9. The other disturbers of the peace were, in economics, F.H. Knight (1921), and in logic, W.E. Johnson (1921-4; 1932), H. Jeffreys (1931; 1939).

10. His approach anticipated those of J. Polya (1954a; 1954b) and I. Lakatos (1976; 1978).

11. Until quite recently Keynes' contribution was grouped within the logicist approach to probability, mainly thanks to R. Carnap's reading of it (Carnap, 1950, 31).

12. The class of 'intensive quantities', in contrast to that of 'extensive quantities' was discussed at length by Keynes in the 1907 draft of *A Treatise on Probability* (*MSS, MLC*, 1907 draft, 52-68, 119-24) and later, in a much shorter form in 1921 final version (CW, VIII, mainly in chs. 3 and 4, especially 30, 38, 50). In the 1907 version Keynes discussed critically Bertrand Russell's philosophy of measurement, in particular the measurement of *relations,* which Russell had put forth in his *Principles of Mathematics* (1903). Concerning utility and prices, in the *Essay on Index Numbers* (1909) Keynes wrote: 'There is an aggregate of utilities . . . but not a sum'; and he compared price relations to physical relations, like 'the quality of a substance, specific volume or specific density' (CW, XI, 59,57).

13. Examples of the attention Keynes paid to the concept of *'causa cognoscendi'* in his economic works can be found in the 1909 *Essay on Index Numbers*: 'there is no *a priori* reason for expecting . . . there may be reason, quite apart from what the actual result turns out to be, for trusting some observations more than others' (CW, XI, 87, 154-5; see also 89); in *A Treatise on Money* (1930): 'Unless there is a serious reason in the minds of the majority of those controlling funds for positively fearing . . .' (CW, VI, 320-1); in his writings concerning his activities as an investor (Memorandum 1931, CW, XII, 18); in *The General Theory* (1936): 'I must not be supposed to deny the possibility, or even the probability, of this outcome. For in such matters it is rash to predict how the average man will react to a changed environment' (CW, VII, 377). See also CW, XXIX, 100-106.

14. Keynes constantly focused the attention on beliefs, opinions, sentiments and feelings both of economic agents (entrepreneurs, speculators, consumers and institutions) and of politicians and of the public. See for example in the 1910 article on 'Great Britain's Foreign Investments': 'The feeling . . . in the mind of the investor' and 'the relative amount of foreign investment is determined . . . by what the average investors believe to be reasonable' (CW, XV, 46, 53); in *A Revision of the Treaty* (1922): 'the living, indefinite belief of the individual man' and 'two opinions, the outside and the inside' (CW, III, 2, 4); in *A Treatise on Money* (1930): 'the sentiment of the public', 'the financial sentiment' and 'the prevailing opinion comes to seem reasonable' (CW, V, 128, 229, 272); in *The General Theory:* 'optimistic and pessimistic sentiment' and 'average opinion' (CW, VII, 154, 156); in the 1937 article 'The Theory of Employment': 'conven-

tional judgement' (CW, XIV, 114; see also 124)
  15. This aspect is also connected with Keynes' notion of 'practical certainty'. It is interesting to note the similarity of Keynes' attitude towards persuasion to that of Wittgenstein in *On Certainty* (Wittgenstein, 1969a). One of Wittgenstein's aphorisms reads: '(612) I said I would "combat" the other man, but wouldn't I give him *reasons?* Certainly; but how far do they go? At the end of reasons comes *persuasion* (Think what happens when missionaries convert natives)'; see also aphorism (262): 'This would happen through a kind of *persuasion*'.

References

Ayer, A. J. (1972) *Probability and Evidence,* Columbia University Press, New York
Black, M. (1967) 'Probability', *Encyclopedia of Philosophy,* Macmillan, London, *VI,* 464-79
Bridgman, P. W. (1927) *The Logic of Modern Physics,* Macmillan, New York
Bunge, M. A. (1959) *Causality,* Harvard University Press, Cambridge (Mass.)
— — (1973) *Philosophy of Physics,* Reidel, Dordrecht
Burtt, E. A. (1925) *Metaphysical Foundations of Modern Physical Science,* London
Butler, J. (1736) *The Analogy of Religion, Natural and Revealed, to the Constitution and Course of Nature,* Knapton, London
Carabelli, A. (1982) 'J. M. Keynes e *A Treatise on Probability*' in *Modelli di razionalità nelle scienze economico-sociali* (Papers presented at the Conference on '*The Rationality in the Social Sciences',* held in Modena, 9-11 October 1980), Arsenale Cooperativa Editrice, Venezia, 115-137
Carnap, R. (1950) *Logical Foundations of Probability,* Chicago University Press, Chicago Ill.
Cassirer, E, (1920) *Zur Einstein'schen Relativitätstheorie,* Bruno Cassirer Verlag, Berlin
— — (1937) *Determinismus und Indeterminismus in der modern Physik;* English Translation. *Determinism and Indeterminism in Modern Physics,* Yale University Press, New Haven, 1956
Czuber, E. (1903) *Washrscheinlichkeitsrechnung und ihre Anwendung auf Fehlerausgleichung, Statistik und Lebensversicherung,* Teubner, Leipzig
Duhem, P. (1906) *La théorie physique, son object et sa structure,* Chevalier et Rivière, Paris; English translation *The Aim and Structure of Physical Science,* Princeton University Press, N.J. 1954
Habermas, J. (1979) *Communication and the Evolution of Society,* English translation and introduction by T. McCarthy, Heinemann, London
Harrod, R. F. (1938) 'Scope and Method of Economics', *Economic Journal, 48,* September 383-412
— — (1951) *The Life of John Maynard Keynes,* Macmillan, London
Hicks, J. R. (1979) *Causality in Economics,* Blackwell, Oxford
Hume, D. (1739-40) *A Treatise of Human Nature,* ed. by L. A. Selby-Bigge, Clarendon Press, Oxford 1888, repr. 1967
— — (1740) *An Abstract of A Treatise of Human Nature,* ed. by J. M. Keynes and P. Sraffa, Cambridge University Press, Cambridge 1938
— — (1748) *An Enquiry Concerning Human Understanding,* ed. by L. A. Selby-Bigge, Clarendon Press, Oxford, 2nd edn. 1902, repr. 1966
Jeffreys, H. (1937) *Scientific Inference,* Cambridge University Press, Cambridge
— — (1939) *Theory of Probability,* Oxford University Press, Oxford
Jevons, W. S. (1874) *The Principles of Science: A Treatise on Logic and Scientific*

Method, Macmillan, London 1907

Johnson, E. S. and H. G. (1978) *The Shadow of Keynes*, Blackwell, Oxford

Johnson, W. E. (1921-4) *Logic*, 3 vols., Cambridge University Press, Cambridge

— — (1932) 'On Probability', *Mind*, N.S. 42

Kenny, A. (1973) *Wittgenstein*, Allen Lane, London

Keynes, J. M. CW *passim*

— — (*MSS*) Marshall Library Cambridge (*MLC*)

Kline, M. (1972) *Mathematical Thought from Ancient to Modern Times*, Oxford University Press, Oxford

— — (1980) *Mathematics: the Loss of Certainty*, Oxford University Press, Oxford

Kolmogorov, A. N. (1933) *Grundbegriffe der Wahrscheinlichkeitsrechung*, J. Springer, Berlin; English translation *Foundations of the Theory of Probability*, Chelsea Pub. Co., New York 1956

Knight, F. H. (1921) *Risk, Uncertainty and Profit*, Houghton, Boston

Lakatos, I. (1976) *Proofs and Refutations. The Logic of Mathematical Discovery*, ed. by J. Worrall and E. G. Zahar, Cambridge University Press, Cambridge

— — (1978) *Mathematics, Science and Epistemology. Philosophical Papers*, ed. by J. Worrall and G. Currie, Cambridge University Press, Cambridge

Locke, J. (1690) *An Essay concerning Humane Understanding*, Th. Basset, London

Mellor, D. H. (1971) *The Matter of Chance*, Cambridge University Press, Cambridge

Mill, J. S. (1843) *A System of Logic*, J. W. Parker, London

Musil, R. (1931) *Der Mann ohne Eigenschaften*, Rowohlt Verlag, Berlin; English translation *The Man without Qualities*, Pan Books, London 1979

Pasinetti, L. L. (1974) 'The Economics of Effective Demand' in *Growth and Income Distribution. Essays in Economic Theory*, Cambridge University Press, Cambridge , 29-53

Poincaré, H. (1896) *La science et l'hypothèse*, Flammarion, Paris; English translation. *Science and Hypothesis*, Scott Publ. Co., London 1905 and The Science Press, New York, 1905

Polya, G. (1954a) *Mathematics and Plausible Reasoning*, Oxford University Press, Oxford

— — (1954b) *Induction and Analogy in Mathematics*, Oxford University Press, Oxford

Popper, K. R. (1982a) *The Open Universe: An Argument for Indeterminism*, ed. by W. W. Bartley III, Rowman and Littlefield, Totonea, N.J.

— — (1982b) *Quantum Theory and the Schism in Physics*, ed. by W. W. Bartley III, Rowman and Littlefield, Totowa N. J.

Quine, W. V. O (1964) 'Foundations of Mathematics' in *The Ways of Paradox*, Random House, New York, 1966, 22-32

— — (1978) 'Success and Limits of Mathematization' in *Theories and Things*, Harvard University Press, Cambridge Mass. 1981

Ramsey, F. P. (1926) 'Truth and Probability' in *The Foundations of Mathematics and Other Logical Essays*, ed. by D. H. Mellor, Routledge and Kegan Paul, London, 1978

Russell, B. A. (1901) 'Recent Work in the Philosophy of Mathematics', *The International Monthly*, 3; reprinted as 'Mathematics and the Metaphysician', in *Mysticism and Logic*, Allen and Unwin, London, 1917

— — (1903) *Principles of Mathematics*, Allen and Unwin, London

— — (1912-13) 'On the Notion of Cause' *Proceedings of the Aristotelian Society*, 13, reprinted in *Mysticism and Logic*, Allen and Unwin, London 1917, ch. 9

— — (1918-19) 'The Philosophy of Logical Atomism', *The Monist*, 28 and 29; reprinted in *Logic and Knowledge*, Allen and Unwin, London, 1956

—— (1919) *Introduction to Mathematical Philosophy*, Allen and Unwin, London

Venn, J. (1866) *The Logic of Chance*, Macmillan, London and Cambridge

Waismann, F. (1967) *Wittgenstein und der Wiener Kreis*, ed. by B. F. McGuinness, Blackwell, Oxford

Weatherford, R. (1982) *Philosophical Foundations of Probability Theory*, Routledge and Kegan, London

Wittgenstein, L. (1953) *Philosophical Investigations/Philosophische Untersuchungen*, ed. by G. E. M. Anscombe, Blackwell, Oxford

—— (1956) Remarks on the Foundations of Mathematics/*Bemerkungen über die Grundlagen der Mathematik*, ed. by G. H. von Wright, R. Rhees, G. E. M. Anscombe, Blackwell, Oxford

—— (1964) *Philosophical Remarks/Philosophische Bemerkungen aus dem Nachlass*, ed. by R. Rhees, Blackwell, Oxford, 1975

—— (1969a) *On Certainty/Über Gewissheit*, ed. by G. E. M. Anscombe and G. H. von Wright, Blackwell, Oxford

—— (1969b) *Philosophical Grammar/Philosophische Grammatik*, ed. by R. Rhees, Blackwell, Oxford

—— (1978) *Remarks on Colour*, ed. by G. E. M. Anscombe, Blackwell, Oxford

—— (1980) *Culture and Value/Vermischte Bemerkungen*, ed. by G. H. von Wright, Blackwell, Oxford

Wright, G. H. von (1969) 'Wittgenstein's Views on Probability', *Revue Internationale de Philosophie, 23*, 259-79

10 THE FOUNDATIONS OF KEYNES' METHODOLOGY: *THE GENERAL THEORY*

Lawrence A. Boland

Keynes said that the readers of *The General Theory* would have to endure a 'struggle of escape' if his assault upon them was to be successful. This chapter is about his 'assault' strategy, its comportment relative to common views of what Keynes was trying to do, and the logical possibilities of its success. Since Keynes was arguing against the then predominant Marshallian neoclassical method of economic analysis, we shall have to also give some time to considering the essentials of Marshall's methods in order to determine where Keynes might have thought he was placing the most telling blows.

General *vs* Special Cases

The claimed thrust of Keynes' assault was to show that 'classical' economic theory was merely one special case on a more general continuum of possible cases. Unfortunately, this way of presenting his assault can be very misleading. Whenever we are dealing with formal models we are always dealing with arbitrary frameworks defined in terms of specified sets of variables. What may be a special case in one framework of given exogenous and endogenous variables can often be seen as the general case in another merely by rearranging the allocation of those variables as endogenous or exogenous. I think the arguments of Patinkin and others have shown this. As long as the only variables allowed are natural 'givens' and the aims of individuals (i.e. no social variables are allowed if they are not reducible to the logical consequences of individual choices), this interpretation of Keynes' 'general-*vs*-special' case argument will always see Keynes' assault as a failure. For Keynes, generality refers to a methodological-cum-historical continuum. On this continuum any current state of equilibrium is a special case as it is merely one point on a historical time-continuum. Similarly, any realistic state of disequilibrium is also just a specific point on that continuum.[1]

In the other camp, which includes followers of Marshall and the so-

181

called Keynesian counter-revolutionaries, generality is seen differently because they are referring to a different continuum. It is different because it is a logical continuum of time-periods which runs from a zero point at the left end representing an infinitely small instant to a point at the right end representing an infinitely long period of time. For these Marshallian advocates of neoclassical economics, whenever one is considering points further to the right one is automatically considering periods of time which allow more and more variability — that is which allow for more time for all variables to change.

Since a longer time period is being considered whenever one adopts a methodological perspective further to the right on this continuum, more and more variables can be made endogenous instead of exogenous — that is more variables can be considered to have been chosen by maximising individuals whenever there has been enough time allowed to make any needed adjustments or 'substitutions' (to use Marshall's term).[2]

Generality from Keynes' Viewpoint

Keynes' argument was more than a petty dispute over historical *vs.* logical time-continuum viewpoints. He argued that there are important non-individualist, non-natural givens facing the real-time individual decision-maker. A main thrust of Keynes' argument is that these short-run 'macro' variables are necessary for adequate explanations even in the usual neoclassical micro-model (cf. Richardson, 1959). In particular, there are 'aggregate' variables such as GNP, the general price level and expectations which do not depend on any specific individuals' psychological state but on the behaviour and expectations of all other individuals. At any point of time, these are contemporaneously determined variables which the individual cannot choose yet they are variables whose states affect the decisions made.

Keynes' concept of generality seems to rest, then, on the methodological position that considers a model with more exogenous givens to be more general. Any methodological strategy that restricts the list of permitted exogenous variables would be considered a 'special case' in Keynes' classical framework. This is contrary to the usual neoclassical perspective which measures generality by the number of endogenous variables explained.

Whenever enough time is allowed in any neoclassical model, all variables, including 'aggregate' variables, depend ultimately on individual choice. But it is also important to realise that in Keynes' argument no amount of real time would ever be sufficient to explain 'aggregate' variables away as the neoclassical methodologists would have us do. So it is important to restrict Keynes' arguments to the Marshallian 'short-run' since it is short-run analysis which requires the needed exogeneity of variables.

Neoclassical Methodology and Psychologistic Individualism

It is a central methodological feature of neoclassical theory that the only exogenous variables allowed are those natural constraints such as resource availability and the naturally-given psychological states of individuals such as tastes or preferences. Methodologists call this 'psychologistic-individualism' in order to distinguish it from the weaker form which they call 'methodological-individualism' (Boland, 1982, ch. 2). Methodological-individualism is the view that only individuals make decisions. It does not require any commitment to reduce all economic explanations to matters of psychology as John Stuart Mill would have had us do.

According to psychologistic-individualism, all non-natural variables may be considered 'exogenous' only temporarily as an arbitrary matter of methodological perspective. For example, in a short-run model one will see many variables that cannot be changed in the short run (e.g., available capital, the income distribution, the interest rate, the market structure, etc.) and that are thus exogenous constraints for the individual decision-maker. Such a short-run perspective can never be adequate since neoclassical methodology requires that all such temporary, non-individualist variables should be transformed into endogenous variables by simply broadening one's logical time-horizons. As a consequence, the only acceptable neoclassical explanation will be a long-run model in which it is logically possible to reduce all endogenous variables to matters of individual choice guided by psychologically-given aims (Lucas, 1980).

In any Marshallian long-run model everything will be in equilibrium because there will be no non-natural constraints artificially preventing the individual from adjusting his or her situation to its optimum. Often, short-run constraints that are neither non-natural nor non-individualist will be explained away as being the results of past (optimising) choices. In neoclassical methodology, disequilibria caused by intervening constraints are either temporary states of affairs or they are illusions (see further, Archibald and Lipsey, 1958). In any neoclassical model, a disequilibrium is temporary merely because enough time has not been allowed to pass for the relaxation of the intervening non-natural constraints.[3] A disequilibrium will be an illusion in Coase's sense whenever it can be explained to be really an equilibrium which would be apparent if we were able to perceive that the intervening constraints are the logical consequences of the natural givens (i.e. of externalities).

Unfortunately, most neoclassical economists confuse psychologistic-individualism with methodological-individualism and the situation is not helped by Keynes' reliance on such things as subjective probabilities. In addition, when referring to his theory of the consumption function, he says 'This psychological law was of the utmost importance in the development of my own thought' (CW, XIV, 120). However, Keynes' insistence on taking a psychologistic view of decision-making may arise only because he wants his criticism to avoid the automatic rejection by neoclassical economists that abandonment of this view might seem to entail.

Keynes' Macro-variables *vs* Neoclassical Individualism

Keynes implicit insistence on the necessary role for macro-variables in the explanation of individual decision-makers could create methodological problems for any 'counter-revolutionary' Keynesian model. Macroeconomic variables (those whose values depend on the behaviour of all individuals in the economy) do not present a problem if we restrict our analysis to long-run equilibria. But this requirement supposedly leads to highly unrealistic models ('in the long run we are all dead') and thus the need to look at short-run models.

The important question here is whether restricting economics to short-run models necessarily violates the requirements of methodological-individualism. To say that Keynes insists on a short-run perspective for economic explanations is not to criticise Keynes for not being individualistic. In a very important way he was more individualistic than typical neoclassical economists. As Spiro Latsis (1972) has argued, the neoclassical maximisation model suffers from not truly allowing free choice by the individual decision-makers in question. If an individual in the long-run equilibrium is given a utility function by nature and the constraints are also given by nature, the choice option which maximises utility is mathematically predetermined and only needs to be found by the individual. There is no free choice in long-run equilibrium. The only question is whether the individual is smart enough to know when his or her utility is maximum. Of course, the concept of 'constrained maximisation' has always had its methodological problems.[4]

The Marshallian Background of Constrained-Optimisation Methodology

Latsis' view of neoclassical methodology may be too severe. Nevertheless, there is a difficulty with the neoclassical framework which makes 'constrained maximisation' the keystone, and this difficulty is one concern of Keynes' assault. The difficulty is that the neoclassical model cannot explain the existence of 'liquidity'. In neoclassical maximisation models all optima are necessarily points on a boundary formed by the natural constraints, much as a text book Production Possibilities Curve (PPC) forms the upper bound on the possible mixes of output combinations limited only by the available resources and technologies. We are to explain the state of an economy by showing that the economy is at a point on such a boundary and that the shape of that boundary at the chosen point explains prices. Why would anyone want to be on the boundary of their capabilities? This question, we shall see, reveals the importance of Keynes' idea of 'liquidity'. What if an individual chose some degree of 'liquidity'? By choosing to have liquidity, individuals deliberately choose not to operate on the boundary of production possibilities. But most importantly, there is no way to rationalise the choice of liquidity in a neoclassical framework since the existence of liquidity itself, I shall argue, is inconsistent with maximisation.

Before we examine the idea of liquidity we need to consider a world without liquidity — namely, the text-book world of Marshallian-neoclassical maximisation where all predictions and explanations are based on one or more boundary functions. We will do so by briefly looking at the object of Keynes' assault — Marshall's methodological approach to economic explanations that he presents in his *Principles*. Marshall's methodology there is quite straightforward. In his first preface he tells us exactly what he is about to do. He will apply the 'Principle of Substitution' and the 'Principle of Continuity' in his economic explanations. The 'Principle of Substitution' merely says that every individual makes a choice between options by selecting the one option which maximises a given objective function. The 'Principle of Continuity' is co-requisite with the other principle because deliberate maximisation presumes that the options lie on a continuum. Any finite endpoint usually represents one of the constraints facing the individual decision-maker. The chosen option must not be at one of the endpoints of that continuum — that is the chosen (maximising) option must be somewhere between the endpoints. If the optimum were at an endpoint it would not be clear whether the chosen option was desired or simply accepted. Much of Marshall's book up to Book V is devoted to showing that the second principle does indeed apply to all economic variables.

While Marshall's methodology of explanation appears to rest on his two principles, the task of using it runs into some procedural difficulties. One cannot explain everything in the universe all at once. Every maximisation situation involves constraints some of which are irrelevant endpoints and others which define the situation. For example, in the consumer maximisation model, the budget line is a constraint but is not always an exogenous variable. Given enough time, the individual consumer chooses it, too (cf. Clower, 1965). So Marshall's strategy is to lay out a continuum consisting of ever longer time-periods in which more variables become endogenous. It needs to be pointed out that when discussing long-run decisions — those which require a lot of time — the firm will always be in a position where it has been able to optimise with respect to the shorter-run variables. For example, the firm always adjusts the labour to fit the just chosen capital level but it may still be constrained to reside in the current industry if enough time has not been considered to allow such a long-run adjustment. One might say that Marshall's explanatory methodology is all a matter of peeling the temporal onion.

The Marshallian optimisation methodology always considers the decision-maker to be facing something like a short-run production-possibilities curve. The curve forms a continuum and its position is limited by given constraints.[5] In the case of the price-taking individual consumer with no market power, the possibilities 'curve' will always be a straight line since that individual does not affect the given prices. The location of the curve is determined or constrained by the limited available resources or income. The constraints may not be naturally given but only difficult to change in the time-period under consideration. But what is most important here is that the chosen option must be a point on the boundary formed by the curve.[6] If a point interior to the PPC were chosen then the relationship between prices and marginal productivities would break down. One way to be at an interior point is by not maximising with respect to all the givens. All of the neoclassical marginal productivity theories of income distribution would then also be in serious jeopardy if not completely lost if the individuals did not operate on their respective boundaries. This is the importance of Keynes' introduction of 'liquidity'. The usual neoclassical results can not be maintained if 'liquidity' is allowed for.

The Keynes-Hicks Methodology of Optimum 'Liquidity'

Let us now turn to the matter of Keynes' concept of liquidity. As a student I was once taught that 'liquidity' was the key contribution of Keynes. Later I was taught that liquidity was only important in terms of the effectiveness of monetary policy. Keynes would seem to have little to say except in a severe depression where interest rates were so low that further monetary stimulation of investment would not be possible. These views of Keynes' concept of liquidity are quite unsatisfactory. Nevertheless, the concept of liquidity is the source of all the alternative views which say that Keynes introduced one particular variable or another. For example, there is the claim that all that matters is Keynes' assumption that the labour market is not in equilibrium. It was some-times claimed that all that matters is the 'liquidity trap'. And, of course, many still claim it is just the recognition of 'expectations'. All of these can be seen to be merely instances of what Hicks now recognises as a general form of liquidity,[7] as I shall now try to show.

Hicks' Theory of Keynes' Liquidity Concept

I would argue that a more general view of the concept of liquidity is the key to the methodological strategy of Keynes. In his recent book, *Causality in Economics*, Professor Hicks has carefully explained his view of the concept of 'liquidity'. While Hicks is more concerned with the quasi-Austrian aspects of real-time decision-making, he reveals the importance of why there may be good reasons for an individual choosing an amount of liquidity. For our discussion, the importance of an individual's choosing an amount of liquidity would be that the individual is choosing to be inside his or her possibilities boundary.

The point raised by Hicks is that, in a world that is either static or moves in a sequential fashion (step by step, as in Marshall's world of comparative statics where there is always enough time allowed to make any adjustments), there is really no need for liquidity. However, in a world where many things are happening simultaneously, the presumption of optimisation in the usual sense (without due allowance for uncertainty) is misleading. Every decision involves an actual decision situation (a set of relevant givens — income, prices, technology, availability, etc.) and a time-lag. Since every decision takes time to implement, during that time the original givens (which depend on the actions of other people, see Richardson, 1959) might have changed and thus the implemented choice decision might not actually be the optimum for the new givens (see Hayek, 1933-9).

For example, if one thinks the future will favour large fuel-inefficient personal cars and that there will be an unlimited amount of fuel, then specialising in the production and marketing of such cars might be the optimum choice regarding one's production technology. If the market should suddenly shift in favour of small efficient cars or if the availability of cheap fuel disappears, then one's profit potential would be drastically altered. The same would be true in the less dramatic case where a certain size of market is anticipated but there is a sudden increase in demand as a result of a strike at a competing firm. If the previous level of output was the usual neoclassical long-run optimum (price equals average cost) then the firm would not be able to respond competitively by producing more unless there was more production capacity. To increase capacity would take time and might not even be optimal after the strike is over. It would seem that zero excess capacity for the firm in the Marshallian short run — that is no liquidity in the non-financial sense — would not be an optimum situation. However, the appropriate optimum (with regard to excess capacity or liquidity) may not be knowable by the firm since knowledge of it depends on the unknown contemporaneous actions of other people as well as on the unknown future.

Keynes' Use of Liquidity

Allowing for liquidity as a deliberate choice variable is central to Keynes' assault. From Keynes' viewpoint, such liquidity is simply good business. For example, usually, whenever the labour market is in a state of 'disequilibrium' where the current real wage is above the one which would clear the market, there is excess supply. Such excess supply may very well represent a desirable state from the standpoint of the employer. For some it is always desirable in order to be able to expand production immediately whenever necessary. Similarly, whenever the wage is below the market clearing wage, a 35-hour working week may be an optimum for an individual even though he or she could work a 60-hour week. Having some free time to pick up some emergency money on the side when it is needed may be more desirable than working to one's limits according to an inflexible contract.

Good business may require the ability to choose one's speed of adjustment to changing conditions. Sometimes, a quick response is better than a slow response and at other times it is the reverse. Flexibility is the key here. But it is not a variable that can be chosen in the same way one would choose a quantity of food or a quantity of capital to achieve a given current objective. The reason is that one's choice of liquidity, be it financial as Keynes discussed or non-financial as Hicks noted, always depends on variables which cannot be easily determined. However, knowledge of them would be essential for the usual neoclassical explanation.

The Consequences of 'Liquidity in General'

While Keynes focuses his idea of liquidity on the more narrow concept of financial liquidity, it is easy to see that the idea of liquidity can be extended to all situations where the decision-maker is placed inside the boundary of his or her capabilities. The classic example is that of 'excess capacity' which is a position where the firm has enough capital to increase production without raising unit costs (including infinitely rising cost at the absolute boundary of production capabilities). Whenever the firm operates with 'excess capacity' the economy must be inside the PPC and being inside, small adjustments in the chosen point may not affect the costs or productivities.

To understand the significance of stressing the desirability of liquidity we need also to see why it is not part of the usual neoclassical model. Consider again the PPC. This time we shall assume it refers to the production possibilities of a specific firm producing two goods, x and y. So long as more is always better, any individual facing the limitations represented by such a curve will want to be producing on the boundary of possibilities as represented by the curve. To produce on that boundary, all available resources will need to be fully employed (Samuelson, 1950). If one does not use all resources fully then necessarily the chosen point will be inside the boundary.

Whenever the firm is producing on its PPC optimally (i.e. maximising its 'profit' or net revenue) we know that the relative marginal productivities of those resources in the production of x will just equal the relative marginal productivities of those resources in the production of y since both ratios must be equal to given relative prices of those inputs.

Similarly, for any resource, the ratio of its marginal productivity in the production of x to that in the production of y must just equal the same ratio for any other input since these ratios will all equal the given relative price for the two products. What is significant about all this is not that these well-known equalities are achieved but that the individual's decisions must be responsive to changes in the given prices.[8] Whenever the given prices change there is an explainable shift from one point on the boundary to another on that boundary since we can calculate the point on the boundary at which all the equalities are satisfied. And almost always there will be a shift whenever one of the prices changes. The whole importance of the competitive market is that everyone should take prices as the appropriate signal concerning what to produce or buy. That the price of fuel-inefficient cars should be falling relative to efficient ones is important social information. By responding to such a price change by reducing the output of inefficient cars, the firm is doing what society wants — just as indicated by the change in relative prices.

Now what happens when the firm is not operating on its possibilities boundary — that is when, for example, it is deliberately providing liquidity in the form of excess capacity? For one thing, except by accident, not all the above equalities will be satisfied. Net revenue is therefore not being maximised with respect to all inputs. As a result the income distribution is not likely to reflect the indirect demand for productive services. Since there are many ways to be at an interior point (e.g., excess capital, excess labour or any combination of these) and since by being there the firm may not be maximising with respect to at least one of the inputs, predicting where the firm will be if it has chosen to respond to any change in the prices would be difficult. Similarly, if the firm has chosen a point inside the boundary, restricting any input may not have immediate effects on the individual firm's output level. For these reasons not only is there no guarantee that individual firms (or individual consumers) will be doing what society wants, but any attempt by government to alter their behaviour by changing tax rates or by manipulating interest rates may prove to be quite ineffective in the short run.[9]

Keynes' discussion of expectations (when expressed in terms of methodological and epistemological questions) raises similar issues. In his 1937 *Quarterly Journal of Economics* article about his *General Theory* he explicitly identifies decision processes which are not optimising. Collecting all the available information to make an investment decision may be uneconomical even if it is logically possible.

Simple rules-of-thumb ('conventional judgement') may be adequate but may not be optimising even for the state of limited knowledge. Follow-my-leader behaviour may be easier to justify than maximisation. Since all investment decisions involve estimations about future states of affairs, relying on the going interest rate as an indicator about the appropriate relative price for future-*vs*-present consumption decisions (following Irving Fisher) presumes that it has been determined in a free market of buyers and sellers with perfect foresight. If buyers and sellers are, instead, using information from sub-optimising decisions, what does the market interest rate indicate to an individual decision-maker? High interest rates may only reflect the current state of optimism rather than known investment possibilities.

On Effective Criticism

It is unfortunate that the so-called post-Keynesian as well as the counter-revolutionaries consider *The General Theory* to be a 'blueprint' for an alternative to neoclassical economics. There really is little in *The General Theory* to form a coherent alternative economic model. Despite what many critics of neoclassical economics might like to believe, the introduction of liquidity or excess capacity into an otherwise neoclassical model does not always conflict with the usual assumption of maximisation. For all we know the individual firm may have inadvertently chosen the optimum amount and thus have all its marginal productivities equal to their respective factor prices. That is to say, whenever there is excess capacity, maximisation is not logically precluded. What Keynes argued was simply that there is no good reason to think that they have consciously chosen the optimum amount in accordance with neoclassical models. Furthermore, to say firms may not be optimising does not deny any conscious attempt on their part to choose the optimum amount of liquidity — although, in the face of uncertainty, it is unlikely that they could ever succeed. In other words, all the usual elements of neoclassical choice theory and methodology are here since only individuals are making choices and those choices are intended to be optimising. For many objects of immediate choice (consumable goods, direct services, etc.) there is no good reason to doubt neoclassical maximisation. However, for objects of choice involving judgements about the future state of the economy (such as investments, capacity, etc.), it is difficult or impossible to see the decision process as that of straightforward maximisation. In the face of uncertainty, liquidity is a means of avoiding the difficult determination of maximising choices. Thus, when it comes to liquidity (which, in the face of uncertainty, is offered as a necessary short-run endogenous variable in *The General Theory*) there may not be any good reason to doubt the presumption that it has been chosen optimally — except one. If liquidity could be chosen like any other variable there would be no need for liquidity! So, I am arguing that Keynes' primary assault on neoclassical theory is based on the empirical claim that in any individualist model of an economy liquidity (or excess capacity) is a necessary object of choice. Thus all long-run models must be at best irrelevant or at worst empirically false.

The point of Keynes' assault is that he wishes to challenge the advocates of neoclassical economics *on their own terms* — namely, in a world where *only* individuals make decisions. If he were to try to criticise them on radically different terms, his views could too easily be dismissed as being irrelevant for questions addressed by neoclassical economics. In this case it is not clear that Keynes was successful, since the only change in mainstream economics since the publication of *The General Theory* has been the introduction into the curriculum of a course called macroeconomics and with it the implicit claim that Keynes was dealing with questions that are different from those addressed by microeconomics. Keynes is entirely to blame for this strategem for avoiding his criticism. He is the one who stresses the necessary role of macro-variables in the theory of the individual decision-maker. Perhaps he only introduced 'macro' variables because, while he accepted the psychologistic version of individualism that underlies all of neoclassical methodology, he knew the introduction of such variables was against the neoclassical methodological-individualist rules. Had he avoided psychologistic-individualism he would not have had to stress the 'aggregate' variables — that is, have had to emphasise the active role of variables which cannot be explained as being reflections of only the aims of individuals in real time.[11] But, of course, this conjecture is silly. Had he not followed psychologistic-individualism as most neoclassical theorists do, he would have been dismissed on those grounds alone — without his criticism ever being considered. I would therefore claim that until mainstream neoclassical economics drops its dependence on narrow psychologistic-individualism, Keynes' assault will not provide a struggle for neoclassical economic theorists.

Acknowledgements

I wish to thank Tereasa Chudy, Shyam Kamath and Chris Jensen for their extensive and timely help with the final revision of this chapter.

Notes

1. The typical labour market is a good example. Observable points (i.e. points representing levels of actual employment at the going wage-rate) will be located on the demand curve whenever the wage-rate is above the equilibrium rate and they will be on the supply curve when it is below that rate. The maximum observable level of employment (without exploitation) will be that one point where demand equals supply. There is then a continuum running from high wage-rates to low rates with just one rate being the equilibrium rate.

2. When we are discussing Keynes' assault it is important for us to keep the Marshallian logical continuum in mind since it is directly relevant to the significance of the 'Generality *vs.* Special Case' debate and it is indirectly but more fundamentally relevant to the intellectual background against which Keynes was directing his assault. The logical continuum is the foundation for Marshall's method of explanation which uses various temporal perspectives — 'market periods', 'short periods', 'long periods' and very long periods representing inter-generational differences.

3. All other variables are just 'independent' endogenous variables with respect to the individual decision-maker but 'dependent' endogenous for the system as a whole. Note also that in a broader sense (e.g., general equilibrium theory) only the variables which are exogenous in the long-run models are really exogenous (see Hicks 1979).

4. But not all of the problems usually discussed (see Boland 1981).

5. Note that the PPC represents the Pareto-optimal allocations of fixed resources as indicated by the size of an Edgeworth-Bowley box, e.g., in a two-factor world. Specifically, it is a one-to-one mapping between the points on a locus of tangency points between opposing production isoquant maps and points on the PPC representing the (maximum) output levels indicated by the two isoquants that are tangent. If the size of the box is increased, then the PPC will be located further from the origin. See further, Samuelson (1950) and Koopmans (1957).

6. In a set-theoretic sense, the PPC is the positive boundary of a convex set. The convexity of the set is logically provided in the usually Marshallian model by simply assuming all production functions exhibit diminishing marginal returns to all factors and there are no increasing returns to scale in any production process.

7. Specifically, he refers to 'financial' and 'non-financial' liquidity (Hicks, 1979, 94ff).

8. Note that this is why the issue of 'stickiness' of wages is so important, since whenever any price is artificially restricted from changing in response to different market conditions, that price no longer provides useful information for any decision-maker. Generally speaking, prices are easier to change than quantities, so that a fixed price only slows down any adjustment process. Although it may take a lot longer, in the usual neoclassical model it is at least logically possible to find values for the quantities such that all the equations can be restored as equalities.

9. Note that this is just the other extreme from the current arguments against governmental intervention of the Rational Expectations school. Their argument is that if you assume a sufficiently long time-period, the government could not really change any givens by fooling everyone. In the long run, supposedly, everyone can learn the true nature of the world (see further, Boland, 1982, ch. 4).

10. The reason why it is necessary is that so many of any individual's decisions depend on the status of what we might now call 'macro' variables — variables which depend on the contemporaneous actions of many other individuals. Stressing the aggregate or 'macro' aspect of the variables only emphasises this dependence.

11. An alternative would be to recognise non-individualist, non-natural exogenous variables (see Boland, 1982, ch. 11).

References

Archibald, G. C. and Lipsey, R. (1958) 'Monetary and value theory: a critique of Lange and Patinkin', *Review of Economic Studies, 27,* 1-22

Boland, L. (1981) 'On the futility of criticizing the neoclassical maximization hypothesis', *American Economic Review, 71,* 1031-6

— — (1982) *The Foundations of Economic Method*, George Allen and Unwin, London

Clower, R. (1965) 'The Keynesian counterrevolution: a theoretical appraisal', in F. Hahn and F. Brechling (eds), *Theory of Interest Rates,* Macmillan, London, 103-25

Coase, R. (1960) 'The problem of social cost', *Journal of Law and Economics, 3,* 1-44

Hayek, F. (1933) 'Price expectations, monetary disturbances and malinvestments', in *Profits, Interest and Investments*, 1939, Routledge, London

Hicks, J. (1979) *Causality in Economics*, Blackwell, Oxford

Keynes, J. M. (1937) 'The general theory of employment', *Quarterly Journal of Economics, 51,* 209-23 reprinted in CW, XIV, 109-23, 1973

Koopmans, T. (1957) *Three Essays on the State of Economic Science*, McGraw-Hill, New York

Latsis, S. (1972) 'Situational determinism in economics', *British Journal for the Philosophy of Science, 23,* 207-45

Lucas, R. (1980) 'Methods and problems in business cycle theory', *Journal of Money, Credit and Banking, 12,* 696-715

Marshall, A. (1926) *Principles of Economics,* 8th ed., Macmillan, London, 1964

Richardson, G. B. (1959) 'Equilibrium, Expectations and Information', *Economic Journal, 69,* 223-37

Samuelson, P. (1950) 'Evaluation of real national income', *Oxford Economic Papers N.S., 2,* 1-29

11 TIME AND THE WAGE-UNIT IN THE METHOD OF *THE GENERAL THEORY*: HISTORY AND EQUILIBRIUM

Victoria Chick

The purpose of this paper is to assert and support analytically a proposition about the implicit method of Keynes' *General Theory* (CW, VII). The proposition is that the device of the wage-unit is much more than a convenient way of measuring output without using a price deflator: the wage-unit is fundamental in creating a theory of output, employment and prices which, although using the technique of static analysis, nevertheless belongs amongst examples of economic theorising in historical time. This fact distinguishes Keynes' analysis sharply from neoclassical theories.

The body of the chapter will be occupied with showing exactly how the wage-unit allows a combination of static method and historical time, but first let us put the problem in its methodological setting.

Methodological Background[1]

It is generally agreed that the method of *The General Theory* is statics — a method strongly associated with analysis 'out of time'. Contrast is often made with the explicitly dynamic method of the *Treatise on Money* (CW, V, VI) in a way which suggests that the method of *The General Theory* is a retrogression. Yet the assertion that 'Keynes in *The General Theory* took time into account in a meaningful way' has become a post-Keynesian slogan, and Joan Robinson's contrast of historical with logical time is explicitly directed towards establishing *The General Theory* as an example of theory occupying the historical-time domain (Robinson, 1977).

The sense of paradox is heightened by a semantic difficulty: a central proposition of *The General Theory* is the possibility of under-employment equilibrium, yet the equilibrium method is contrasted — again by Joan Robinson (1974) and also by Kornai (1971) — with methods embodying historical time. But they mean General Equilibrium theory. Keynes' theory, though called General and dealing with equilibrium, was not of that type.

195

In the essay just referred to, 'History versus Equilibrium',[2] Robinson elaborated on the inability of neoclassical theory to deal with historical time chiefly in the context of capital accumulation and of problems in defining a long-term rate of profit. On the subject of *The General Theory* she stressed the significance of the essential assumption of the short run: that production and hiring decisions are made with a capital stock which is given in type and in distribution amongst producers: 'Past history is thus put into the initial conditions, so that the analysis is static in itself, and yet is part of dynamic theory' (Robinson, 1952, v).

That characterisation is correct but for several reasons does not clinch the point. First, the dynamic theory of which the theory of output and employment is a part, namely the theory of capital accumulation, is not explicitly dealt with in Keynes (the consequences of accumulation are the subject of Chapter 17). Secondly, it does not make the point that the theory of output is itself dynamic. Thirdly, one could argue that in the absence of a theory of accumulation there is nothing to stop one setting the initial conditions 'arbitrarily' rather than as given by history; that is precisely what General Equilibrium theory does.

Let us push the contrast with General Equilibrium theory a bit further than the distinction between arbitrary and historically-given initial endowments. General Equilibrium theory derives the level (and composition) of output and prices and the volume of employment from these endowments, technology and the preferences of consumers between goods and leisure. Assuming existence etc., a vector of wages and prices is found which ensures that the output will be produced at those wages and bought out of the resulting income at those prices. Thus the level of demand is generated *within* the model: there is no 'false production' — no general glut, no demand deficiency, no 'market failure'. Only one level of 'aggregate demand' (a slightly alien phrase in the context) is consistent with a particular set of endowments and tastes. To generate another level of demand, the initial endowments or tastes or technology must be altered — by us, the theorists.

In contrast, in *The General Theory* demand may vary independently of the capital stock (aggregate demand may vary in the short run). Hence the theory can be used to analyse cyclical fluctuations, booming and depressed areas, etc. Demand is separated from endowments by the agency of historical time: demand varies mostly through investment, yet the capital goods so demanded are not yet in place and working. Thus it is legitimate to treat the capital stock as fixed while demand is free to vary in a way which is impossible in General Equilibrium analysis. One can go still further.

This chapter puts the case that nested within the dynamics of capital accumulation, which Keynes put to one side when developing his theory of output (by his device of separating long-term from short-term expectations), there is another dynamic, also embodying a separation in time — though a short space of time in comparison to that relevant to investment — of money-wages and actual prices. This latter separation is inherent in the facts of what Keynes called in an early draft of *The General Theory* the 'entrepreneur economy' (CW, XXIX, 63, 67, 76-102),[3] an economy in which production for market sale is organised along capitalist lines. He also calls it a 'monetary, production economy' (CW, XIII, 408-11). The contrast is with the 'co-operative economy' or the 'real exchange economy' in which wages and prices are pre-reconciled and it is meaningful to speak of real wages in an objective sense. (To the entrepreneur economy real wages are *subjective*: the money-wage is deflated by *expected* prices, whether expected by the worker or the entrepreneur.)

A model of an economy in which wages and prices are determined at the same time — pre-reconciled as in General Equilibrium theory or through the device of agreeing to accept wages paid in kind — is what Keynes means by 'co-operative'. Compare the entrepreneur economy where the attempt to gain a certain real wage must proceed through a money-wage bargain, and the actual real wage cannot be known for certain at the time the money-wage offer is accepted. These features follow from two facts: that wages are both agreed and paid in money and that the hiring of labour must precede production of output which in turn precedes the offer of output for sale.

An entrepreneur economy thus by the very nature of its activities involves 'historical time'; time that goes in one direction and cannot be reduced to a point, reversed, or stopped and started up again. The result is a potential for surprise on both sides of industry. The actual real wage is an outcome of the effect of the actual level of demand on prices and entrepreneurial surprise comes in the form of unexpected profits or losses.

Historical time does more, however, than open up the potential for *unexpected* profit: the very possibility of 'excess' profits (quasi-rents) depends on the independence of some element of demand from endowments and tastes, or equivalently it depends on the absence of pre-reconciled prices and wages.

It is clear that historical time is here bearing the load of explaining the difference between General Equilibrium solutions and Keynes' solution. It is now time to demonstrate that historical time was enabled to play a role in Keynes' theory of output despite the apparent timelessness of Keynes' chosen method: statics. Part of the story — the part that is pretty well understood — is that the capital stock is taken as given by whatever in the past determined its accumulation up to that point. The part that has not been adequately explored (including in my recent book, Chick, 1983), concerns the development of a method which captures the historical-time attributes of production in a static model. The essential trick is the use of the wage-unit.

Time and the Wage-unit

Structure of the Argument

The argument proceeds in five stages. It should be said, as a plea for the reader's patience, that the *order* of the stages of argument could, probably, just as well be inverted; not until the entire picture has been drawn will the significance of the parts be very clear. This cannot be helped, for there is no logical priority in the argument; it stands or falls as a whole.

The five steps are these:

(1)   The activity of production for market sale has a typical time-structure in which costs are known before demand.

(2)   The essentially dynamic process of production is 'modelled' statically by Keynes in terms of aggregate supply (Z) and demand (D) functions. These are specified both in money terms and in wage-units; Z is contingent on the money-wage.

(3)   But the absolute level of money-wages depends upon the history of wages (and prices) and those factors which determine levels of money-denominated variables. Even over a short span of time there is no unique relation between wages and employment when there is involuntary unemployment, i.e. when one is 'off the labour supply curve' to the left: the movement of wages predicted by the theory depends on where one started from. It is desirable to allow for this fact, on the grounds of realism.

(4)   Translating Z and D in to wage-units (Z_W and D_W) makes these functions independent of the level of wages and hence independent of the historical component in their determina-

tion. Hence the wage-unit serves as a device which permits the statement of general principles (i.e. a theory), while allowing the historical element in wage determination to be preserved in the background.

(5) Z_W and D_W determine employment and the value of output in wage-units. The absolute levels of prices and output cannot be determined without determining the absolute levels of money-wages (that is, without reintroducing the historical component of wages). It is noted that Chapter 21 of *The General Theory* explores only the *elasticity* of the responses of output and prices to changes in the level of demand. This choice on Keynes' part supports the interpretation offered below in the section on the wage-unit.

The Time-shape of Production

As the discussion of the previous section should have made clear, the separation of entrepreneurial decisions into an output, pricing and employment problem dominated by short-period expectations taking the capital stock as given, and an investment decision based on long-period expectations, is fundamental. This chapter is concerned only with the former.

The object of this section is to demonstrate that to model the dynamic process of production in a static way, something has to be assumed not only about capital, but also about the level of money-wages.[4]

Consider the time-shape of a typical process of production for market sale. The essence of production for the market is that goods are produced on an *expectation* of demand. (This stands in contrast to production to order.) It is also typically true of industrial production that workers are paid frequently (weekly) — too frequently for it to be convenient to adjust production levels to alterations in labour costs within that time-frame. For this reason and others, wages tend to be set for some time in advance.[5] Except in casual-labour industries, offers of employment usually are also intended to apply to some considerable span of time.

It is easiest to think of these things in terms of a production period — some length of time over which management sets output and forecasts or sets prices on the basis of an estimate of demand. At the end of the period it reviews sales performance in the light of demand-expectations held at the beginning. It is a logical necessity that the labour used to produce output during the period must have been hired before the output was produced, and the output must be produced before it is sold.

At the end of the period, as sales data accumulate, producers discover whether they have estimated demand correctly and receive the profits they expected, and they are either pleasantly or unpleasantly surprised.

The profit-seeking nature of the firm I take for granted. (I shall take profit-maximising as a working assumption; the theory can be modified for other types of entrepreneurial behaviour.) Profits are a money sum, the difference between two other monetary magnitudes: revenue and costs. If producers are to maximise profit they must form an expectation of demand and also an expectation of the wages they will have to pay. Let us for the moment assume that the firm's best guess is that the money-wage at the beginning of the current production period will be the same as it was in the last period. This would have been a reasonable assumption in the 1930s though not in the 1970s or even now. However, we need some such assumption in order to get started, and this is the simplest.

Given the capital stock and technology, the estimate of money-wages provides a cost function and producers can establish a profit-maximising output and pricing strategy given their expectation of final demand. The plan to produce a given output implies an offer of employment.

Let us say, again only for argument's sake, that the offers of employment of all firms are accepted at the last period's wage, i.e. there is either involuntary unemployment (some labour willing to work is not taken up) or full employment. (Something has to be said about labour's price expectations here; again it is no longer reasonable to assume as Keynes did that the labour supply curve will not be shifting to the left on account of rising price expectations. All I require to keep things simple is that the curve does not shift so far to the left as to invalidate the assumption just made. Any 'involuntary over-employment' will only cause trouble in the *next* production period.)

Under the conditions specified, producers' expectations are not falsified by events in the labour market and production plans can be implemented without alteration. Thus the wage bill is now known for this production period. But income and profits are not known until the end.

Prices, too — at least some prices — will not be known at the beginning of the period, even by producers. One has considerable latitude in what one assumes about prices, for marketing practices differ. Producers may set the price which, if their estimate of demand is correct, maximises profits, and stick to that price. Deviations of demand from

the expected level are then reflected in inventory changes and in deviations of actual profits from the level expected. Or one can assume that
prices are allowed to respond to unexpected variations in demand.
(Keynes allowed both these possibilities in Chapter 5 but he has been
interpreted exclusively in terms of the former option.) Even in the case
in which prices are set by firms and stuck to, there is no reason to
assume that they are known to workers, who would not only have had to
make the same estimate of demand that producers made, but would also
need to know as much about the technical conditions of production as
firms do to derive their costs — not only the technology of the firm they
work for but those which produce the things entering into their calculation of 'real wages'. For completeness, they would also have to estimate
user cost in those industries!

The Static Representation of the Output Decision

The process described above was given static expression in *The
General Theory* by means of two functions of the level of employment,
N: aggregate supply, Z(N) and (producers' expectations of) aggregate
demand, $D^e(N)$, which jointly determine output, Q, employment and
prices, P, which producers anticipate or set.

Weintraub (1958) was, I believe, the first to set out the relationship
of Z(N) to the theory of the firm.[6] What is involved is a translation of the
conditions of profit-maximisation from the P,Q space with N implied
by Q to a PQ,N space with the division between P and Q left
implicit.

Assume small (but not price-taking!) firms. This is to many people a
contradiction in terms, but it is obvious that firms producing to an
anticipation of market demand cannot be price takers except in the kind
of equilibrium, to quote Joan Robinson again, that has been in existence
since the Fall of Man.

The elasticity of demand facing a firm depends on its size relative to
the industry (not on the property of 'price taking'). Thus P represents
(for the small firm) the expected level of demand to which it should
work, and profits are maximised by equating price and marginal cost in
the usual way. One might have said equating marginal cost and expected prices, though that would imply that producers have no power over
prices (no power to set either the right or the wrong price) and is thus
best avoided.

Despite the unfamiliarity of a small firm in doubt about its future
sales, the formal representation is standard. All production always
takes place in the short run, so Q = Q(N). Profits are maximised where

$w/Q'(N) = P$. Multiplying both sides of this expression by Q and making use of the symbol A for average product we have

$$PQ = \frac{wA}{Q'}\, N,$$

a Z function for an individual firm.

The above account may be generalised to larger firms by allowing for their facing a less-than-infinitely-elastic demand curve. Since in the non-atomistic case some degree of control over prices is conventionally assumed, specifying P rather than P^e would be the natural thing to do in that case, but it is equally a possibility for small firms.

Aggregation over firms is extremely tricky and must not detain us here (see Weintraub, 1958; Chick, 1983, ch. 5). Briefly, firms second-guessing each other, as in most oligopoly models, must be ruled out, and it is convenient to assume that the commodity-composition of output is kept constant. These assumptions allow the formulation of Z for an individual firm to hold in aggregate.

Now assuming producers know that the general level of demand will be related to employment and that they will share in the economy's fortunes or misfortunes, we can also postulate $D^e(N)$. If producers' forecasts are correct then at least locally $D^e(N)$ and $D(N)$ — the latter representing the actual demand function — coincide. Their coincidence is not, however, required for any given period or short run of periods: producers can make mistakes.

At the intersection of $Z(N)$ and $D^e(N)$, N and PQ are determined. The division of PQ into its components may be inferred from N, given Q is uniquely related to N in the short run.

Clearly this whole story depends on producers' assumptions about wages being met, which in turn depends on there being enough labour to satisfy demand at that wage. If those conditions are not met, money-wages may change, not only shifting Z but also (because of income redistribution) D — and D^e if firms have good forecasters.

The Determination of Money-wages

This brings us to wage determination, which is best approached in terms of the labour market. (It must be emphasised that to take this approach in no way invalidates the proposition that employment is determined in the market for output.)

The demand for labour is strictly derivable from the factors that determine Z, being the marginal value product of labour. The supply curve of labour is also traditional: it gives the *maximum* amount of labour obtainable at any given money-wage and price expectation on the part of labour. The difference — the vital difference — between Keynes and both his predecessors and most of his successors is that the supply curve need not enter into the determination of actual wages and employment. To most economists this suggests 'indeterminacy', but that view ignores the role of history in determining wages. (The whole point of most static analysis is to ignore history.) One can proceed, in Keynesian analysis, either analytically from an arbitrary starting point or empirically from the point representing the most recent past, and trace out a possible path of wages through time, as demand expectations change.

Although it may seem the less satisfactory alternative, let us begin arbitrarily, at a point of involuntary unemployment, B, in Figure 11.1. (The vertical axis is money wages in order to make price-expectation assumptions explicit.) One can then trace the effects of a rise (say) in product demand from that point. The demand for labour shifts in accordance with higher expected prices, and employment follows the path indicated by arrows from B. Small changes of demand in either direction are unlikely to alter money-wages though of course real wages are changing continuously unless there are constant costs. Falling real wages for the already-employed (e.g. between B and F) are not pleasant but are acceptable, since there is still an excess of wages over the marginal disutility of work. Until demand rises sufficiently to reach the labour supply curve, the assumption that yesterday's wage will persist today despite an alteration in the expected level of product demand is unexceptionable.

By this argument the arbitrary starting-point B is given historical significance: one begins the analysis from where one is or has just been. Our initial assumption, that yesterday's wage prevails, is now seen as more than just a way of getting started: between B and F or G in Figure 11.1 it is the most relevant assumption to make.

The above analysis in money terms breaks down when for any reason higher wages are necessary to get the labour which producers want. As explained earlier, both Z and D^e are liable to shift, with uncertain effects on employment and output. (This is the subject of *The General Theory*, Chapter 19.) All one can say unambiguously is that a rise in demand will cause prices to rise by more than they would have done had wages not risen. Output and employment will still rise as long as the money-wage rise is not so large as to remove all profit-incentive for expansion. (In contrast, the neoclassical instinct is to say that since we are at full employment prices will rise by the same proportion as wages, and output, employment and real wages will be unchanged. This is an assertion invalidly carried over from statics to answer a question about *change*, for which it is not equipped.)

Now suppose we are at G and aggregate demand falls. The demand for labour shifts downward accordingly, but wages do not fall or fall only slowly.[7] Once again we are on safe ground as regards the stability of D^e and Z, and wages are, as in the range BF, determined entirely by history: they are where they are because they rose, in the past, from F to G; and from G to C, yesterday's wage is once again the best prediction of today's.

Figure 11.1: A Possible Path of Money Wages.

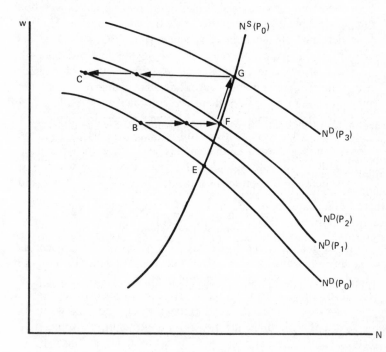

The Wage-unit

It is important of course to model producers' profit-seeking behaviour in money terms, for the reasons explained in the methodological section. But for several reasons the theory is incomplete or unsatisfactory if specified entirely in money terms.

Firstly, it would be unfortunate if a theory advertised as 'general' precisely in the sense that it incorporated both the unemployment and full-employment cases were restricted to the range over which the wage today could reasonably be expected to be the same as the wage yesterday.

Secondly, although firms are motivated by a desire for money-profit, demand is properly specified in 'real terms' (units of output). Keynes did not approve of using general price deflators (CW, VII, ch. 4) and the wage-unit is his preferred method for converting 'nominal' to 'real' magnitudes: the command over goods afforded by one labour unit (not quite the same thing as a unit of labour-time as we shall see in a moment).

Thirdly, although specifying Z in terms of wage-units begs all the interesting questions of producers' responses to changes in expected demand, it frees the theory from specific assumptions about diminishing or constant returns.

Let me expand briefly on each of these assertions, first defining the wage-unit and its counterpart the labour-unit. The wage-unit is the wage of 'ordinary labour'; skilled workers count as two or three or four labour-units as their wages are twice, thrice or four times that of ordinary labour. Coupled with the assumption that labour is paid its marginal product, the labour-unit is seen as an efficiency-unit. Further, where workers are not homogeneous in their ability to do a given task Keynes subsumes 'the non-homogeneity of equally renumerated labour-units in the equipment, which we regard as less and less adapted to employ the available labour-units as output increases' (CW, VII, 42).

If I understand the burden of these assumptions, variations in output per man due to diminishing returns and skill differentials have been removed from the labour-unit, such that the employment of one more labour-unit (*not* an increase in employment of one person or so many labour-hours) entails an increase in one unit of product measured in wage-units. Thus by construction the slope of $Z_w(N)$ is unity.[8] (If diminishing returns were not 'subsumed in the equipment', $Z_w(N)$ would be convex from below and only constant costs would give a unit slope. Only increasing returns would really cause any trouble, however. Small firms would not produce in that range but oligopolistic ones might do.)

The significance of the wage-unit device at one level is that it makes the supply decision commensurate with demand. It is of course essential to Keynes' argument that $D_w(N)$ cut $Z_w(N)$ from above, so that profitable expansion has a limit even when firms guess correctly about $D_w(N)$. With the slope of $Z_w(N)$ unity, all one needs is that the slope of $D_w(N)$ be less than one. Now one can understand why Keynes was so excited about his 'Fundamental Psychological Law' that the slope of the propensity to consume — a function which Keynes defined, for reasons indicated above, in wage-units — was less than one.

Not only does specifying the propensity to consume in wage-units approximate the 'real terms' which, though even more appropriate, are open to index-number objections; there is also an extra advantage: the function is *stable with respect to changes in the wage-unit*.[9] Thus all the problems of Z and D shifting due to changing wages are avoided by this device. (It is to be noted however that shifts in D_w due to altered income distribution can still be entertained.)

If Z_w and D_w are invariant with respect to the wage, plainly any result obtained with them can be obtained at any level of wages. We thus have a theory which is consistent with both unemployment and full employment, as I set out to demonstrate in this section.

In the argument of the previous section we began at an arbitrary point B and discussed the behaviour of wages consequent on changes in demand from that point. Clearly we could have chosen some other point, say C (Figure 11.1) or even E. From C we would also expect an insensitivity of wages to fluctuations in demand, but at a higher level of wages. Once involuntary unemployment is admitted there is no unique relation between wages and employment.

But that does not mean either that the theory is arbitrary or that, at any point in history, wages are indeterminate. In that section we began with an arbitrary wage, but in the first section started with the wage of the previous period, that is, we allowed immediately previous *history* to enter the picture and *choose* the point at which we began. We chose an under-employment point because we needed to have a stable wage in order to derive Z and D^e in money terms, but the choice between suitable alternatives in terms of Figure 11.1 — B or C — was not arbitrary, rather, we began from the point of immediate historical departure: we began from where we were. (Compare with neoclassical analysis, which will instinctively begin with the 'market-clearing' wage, at the intersection of supply and demand, whether one has just been there or has never been there. It is a natural instinct, for this theory pre-reconciles prices and wages. Nothing could better bring out the significance of ignoring history.)

Had we started with Z_W and D_W we should not have been confined to underemployment points as points of departure. (Remember the argument can proceed in any order.) We could as well start (in terms of Figure 11.1) at E or F. But this generality has its costs: nothing can be said, in wage-units, about prices or profits. For those one needs to know the level of wages and work in money terms.

Keynes' theory works in both sets of terms. The theory is general, abstract *and* historical. The static analysis necessarily ignores the historical. The process analysis necessarily includes it. The wage-unit provides a bridge between the two, making the modelling of a process in terms of statics feasible.

'The Theory of Prices'

I believe my interpretation to be vindicated by Chapter 21 of *The General Theory*. Although called 'The Theory of Prices', Chapter 21 is not concerned with the determination of the price *level* but rather with the determination of the implications of a *change* in (expected) aggregate demand for prices and output at the margin. Its freedom from absolute levels of any of the variables is achieved by the device familiar to every first-year student: all responses are formulated in terms of *elasticities*.

The elasticity formulation makes it a matter of indifference from the theoretical point of view whether a rise in demand corresponds to labour demand at point B or point C (of Figure 11.1): if the rise in demand is relatively small the elasticity of wage response is determined in the short run by the effects of changing capacity utilisation (or, equivalently, by the extent of diminishing returns). A rise in demand starting at E or F would have a different effect. But the history (whether one is at B or C to start with, or E or F) is put aside for the sake of deriving a theoretical framework, as it should be. *Applying* the framework, the theorist, empirical investigator or forecaster is thus free to start with the recent past as stylised facts or actual data, and that too is as it should be. That is where history comes back into the picture.

A contrast with neoclassical Keynesianism is perhaps unnecessary — it is all too familiar. Just recall that any extended IS-LM model (i.e. one which includes the labour market) purports to determine the *level* of wages and prices. A moment's reflection suggests that unless there is something immutable about the relation between money and prices — a proposition which even quantity theorists these days do not wish to defend — there is no way of knowing what those levels should be, without tracing the history of one or other of them back to the beginning of time. There are better things to do, and Keynes' way round the problem frees us to do them.

Acknowledgement

I wish to thank Colin Rogers for his most helpful comments.

Notes

1. This section draws almost exclusively on Joan Robinson's work because it is closest to the problem addressed in this paper.
2. To which the second half of the title of the present essay refers.
3. See the commentary on this by Torr (1980).
4. Changes in other variable-input costs, notably the cost of raw materials and running costs such as energy, are subsumed in *user cost* and omitted from both the aggregate demand and aggregate supply functions for reasons given in Keynes (CW, VII, 24, n.2).
5. The 'implicit contract' literature has elaborated on these.
6. The treatment here and in Chick (1983) differs from Davidson and Smolensky (1964), who embody expected demand in the aggregate supply function.
7. For a justification see Chick (1983, ch. 7).
8. Note that nothing is being said about the intercept of Z_w, only the slope.
9. This point can perhaps be better seen by analogy with the more familiar 'real' consumption function which, precisely because both consumption and income are deflated by prices, is stable when prices alter.

References

Chick, V. (1983) *Macroeconomics After Keynes: A Reconsideration of the General Theory,* Philip Allan, Deddington, Oxford

Davidson, P. and Smolensky, E. (1964) *Aggregate Supply and Demand Analysis,* Harper and Row, New York

Keynes, J.M. CW, V, VI, VII

Kornai, J. (1971) *Anti-Equilibrium,* American Elsevier, New York

Robinson, J. (1952) *The Rate of Interest and Other Essays,* Macmillan, London

— — (1974) 'History versus Equilibrium', *Thames Papers in Political Economy.* Reprinted in Robinson (1978) *Contributions to Modern Economics,* Blackwell, Oxford

— — (1977) 'What are the Questions?', in Robinson (1979) *Collected Economic Papers,* vol. V, Blackwell, Oxford

Torr, C.S.W. (1980) 'The Distinction between an Entrepreneur Economy and a Co-operative Economy' (Review Note), *South African Journal of Economics, 48*

Weintraub, S. (1958) *An Approach to the Theory of Income Distribution,* Chilton, Philadelphia

12 KEYNESIANISM IN GERMANY

Juergen Backhaus

Introduction

It is generally known, and Keynes himself was certainly not hesitant in recognising, that the first full-scale application of his *General Theory* had taken place in Germany well before the book was actually published. This is not surprising, since Keynes' influence in Germany had been significant ever since he wrote *The Economic Consequences of the Peace*. In addition, German economic policy for recovery during the crucial years 1932-5 had been shaped in a Keynesian mould almost single-handedly by one of the few German 'Keynesians': Wilhelm Lautenbach (1891-1948), a distinguished economist who worked in the Ministry of Economics. What is puzzling, though, is the role of the German academic community *vis-à-vis* these economic policies. When Keynes (in the preface to the German edition of *The General Theory* (CW, VII, xxvi)) asked whether he would be able to convince German economists that formal analytic methods could constitute an important contribution to interpreting contemporary history and the formation of economic policy, he had more than one good reason to be sceptical. The leading German academic economists (with a few notable exceptions) had vigorously opposed the deficit-based recovery policies. One would look for exceptions among the most prominent theoreticians in those research areas in economics that were to become macroeconomics. But the opposition to Keynesian employment policies included such outstanding economists as, for example, Schumpeter and Spiethoff, both leading authorities on busines cycle research.[1] Instead, the most prominent German professor in economics who vigorously pushed for Keynesian employment policies was undoubtedly Werner Sombart. Sombart was the leading exponent of the historical school, which has since literally disappeared from economics. In fulfilling Schmoller's programme and incorporating into it a strong dose of the Marxian legacy, he tried to advance systematic historical theories in economics (Schumpeter, 1927). In his time, Sombart's contributions enjoyed a worldwide appreciation and they proved goldmines for historical scholarship (Nussbaum, 1935; Krumme,

209

1968). But from today's vantage point, historicism tends to be regarded as a sterile chapter in the history of economics; while Sombart stressed 'verstehen' (understanding) over quantifiable analysis, his methodological antithesis in Cambridge prevailed, perhaps because those theories were more easily presented in quantifiable terms. After all, the rise of Keynesianism coincides with the emergence of modern econometrics.[2]

The aim of this chapter is to enhance our understanding of the rise of Keynesianism. This is, of course, not the first attempt. There are two reasons why I feel justified in adding to the rather well-stocked library on the same subject. First, there is no accepted theory that could account for the unprecedented transformation of economics that has sometimes been called the 'Keynesian Revolution'. Secondly, I take an approach that is different from all the others that I know.

My approach starts from the assumption that *The General Theory* was not an achievement so outstanding that its final acceptance was a foregone conclusion when it appeared in 1936. But what were the alternatives? This simple question does not, however, have a straightforward answer. There are two reasons for this difficulty. On the one hand, there is no undisputed interpretation of Keynes' *General Theory*. This means that it is almost impossible even among a small group of economists to establish agreement as to what the singular contribution of *The General Theory* has been. On the other hand, Keynesianism as a phenomenon distinct from the scientific content of *The General Theory* did not originate with the publication of Keynes' most important book. A study of the origins of Keynesianism must address both issues, but separately. Hence, in order to understand the Keynesian transformation of economics, it is important to consider the interdependence of these separate elements of what I hope provides a satisfactory explanation: (1) the contending paradigms in economics and the degree to which they could be made compatible with one another; (2) the exigencies of economic policy; and (3) the propagation of Keynes' theoretical contributions, of which *The General Theory* is but one element, and the theoretical developments that concurred with and built on Keynes' economics. The task of disentangling Keynes' economics and Keynesianism cannot be said to be a light one. But it is considerably facilitated if we geographically remove our analysis of the roots of Keynesianism away from Cambridge. This is not only required by the historical sequence of events, as mentioned in the introductory paragraph; it is also a way of focusing attention on alternative developments. By concentrating on the rise of Keynesianism in Germany, one hopes to obtain a fuller understanding of both the benefits and the costs of the Keynesian transformation of economics.

The present work may be seen as a preparatory step towards a more precise understanding of the methodological basis of Keynesianism, including the reasons for its astonishing success. The argument will be presented as follows. First, I shall try to determine what made Keynes' economics so pre-eminent. This is a problem to which Don Patinkin has devoted almost a lifetime of attention, most recently published in a book-length account as *Anticipations of the General Theory?*. This is the logical place to start my own analysis. As it turns out, the functional approach used by Patinkin is not suited to the German case. This eminent student of Keynes' work has developed an elaborate framework which leaves no room for the German antecedents of Keynesianism. The reasons for this peculiar exclusion lie principally in very specific assumptions about the organisation of scientific inquiry in economics, ones which did not fit the German case. In order to show that, contrary to Patinkin's assertion, there was a case at all, I resort to case studies.

My purpose here is not to give a full account of German Keynesianism, a task already accomplished by others (Bombach *et al.*, 1976; 1981). Rather, I want to emphasise contributions and contributors which describe German Keynesianism well while they cannot be captured by the measuring rod of Patinkin's approach.

This is why I focus on Sombart and Lautenbach. They are the leading protagonists in my story of the rise of Keynesianism in Germany. Sombart was the methodological antithesis to Keynes in Germany, the intellectual heir to the historical school as Keynes was to the tradition in Cambridge, a theoretical innovator as was Keynes, an authority who was also at the centre of many scholarly disputes. Lautenbach, on the other hand, literally used to be called 'the German Keynes'. He possessed none of the personal characteristics of Keynes, however. He was an impeccable civil servant, aloof, meticulous, personally modest, and yet presenting theoretical insights in part significantly different but partly very similar, often before Keynes. Once *The General Theory* had appeared, it met with a wave of critical reaction in Germany. I have listed much of this literature in the references.

Anticipations

Wherein lies Keynes' most important contribution to economics? Perhaps no one has tried to provide as clear-cut an answer as Don

Patinkin. Although Patinkin has not always enjoyed the agreement of all his colleagues, his recent book (Patinkin, 1982) shows again why it is impossible to ignore his opinion on any matter Keynesian. His authority is as much based on his erudition and expertise as it is due to the care and circumspection with which each argument is presented, all sources are checked and contexts analysed. Even if the author proves to have failed to convince with his central message, the book would still be important as a landmark in raising the professional standards in the subdiscipline of the history of economic thought.

The problem of anticipations in economics, and the problem of possible anticipations of Keynes' *General Theory* in particular, is a very important one for the historian of economic thought. Should it not be a matter of indifference to the professional economist who is looking ahead and trying to deal with today's macroeconomic problems whether the message of *The General Theory* had been anticipated somewhere at the outskirts of professional developments? Is it not important to concentrate only on the theory itself, once it has become the common property of the profession? The question is an old one, and we are reminded of a similar discussion between Jevons and Walras, to be found in their correspondence:

> M. Walras, on seeing the *Statistical Journal* for 1866, generously acknowledged my father's priority and published the correspondence in the *Journal des économistes* under the title 'Théorie mathématique de l'échange: question de priorité', though, as my father wrote, 'As to the question of priority of publications, it is, of course, of less importance than that of the truth of the theory itself.' (Jevons, 1934, 229)

It is indeed important that the theory prove to be correct. And the question of priorities could be altogether ignored if the resolution of this problem turned only on the vanity and satisfaction of individual researchers. But this is not at all the case. The question of anticipations is important because it helps us understand the conditions under which particular theories win general acceptance.

Thus my objective is to study Keynesianism in Germany, in order to answer, in particular, this question: What determined the sweeping success of Keynesian economics in Germany and elsewhere, despite the considerable initial resistance of the major part of the academic community there; and completely at the expense of the considerable body of Keynesian theory that had already existed in Germany? Don

Patinkin's studies provide a most welcome point of departure. They are welcome, because they speak to the salient points a study like this has to confront; and they do so in a fresh and up-to-date manner. On the other hand, they are but a point of departure, because, quite literally, I have to depart from his approach. The German case seems not to fit with his concepts and assumptions. Nevertheless, Patinkin's central message is convincing: Keynes' *General Theory* cannot be claimed to have been anticipated by either Kalečki or the Stockholm school. This message is important for two reasons: firstly, because of the way in which it is argued. And secondly, because of the particular result. I personally feel that in this case, the approach is even more important than the problem it serves to clarify: Who, among the three contenders appraised, actually won the prize for originality? With Patinkin as the umpire, the winner is, of course, Keynes himself.

In pursuing this question, Patinkin uses a functional approach. He refers to Robert K. Merton (1957)[3] in stating that science as an institution defines originality as a supreme value and consequently makes recognition of one particular researcher's originality a major concern. And rightly so. Because 'if the reward system of science is to function in a productive manner, its rewards must go to the true discoverers' (Patinkin, 1982, 85). This implies, as he further points out, two additional conditions: first, the scientist must himself be aware of the significance of the discovery and second, if the system is to function effectively, the originator must succeed in persuading others to follow his new research programme. From this it follows readily that the problem of anticipations of major breakthroughs in a science is a matter of the greatest importance for the smooth and effective operation of science as an institution. If we do not settle the question of who originated past discoveries, so Patinkin argues, we shall be less likely to witness future breakthroughs and progress in the discipline. As with all supply-side arguments, incentives assume a major importance. (The intrinsic rewards from scholarship and, perhaps, even ideological zeal (Schumpter, 1954) may often play an equally important role.) This logic has several rather startling consequences, one of which is that: even those economists who, today, would prefer to undo it, and reverse this particular process of intellectual development are well advised to concern themselves with how the Keynesian revolution came about.

What constitutes a 'new' theoretical achievement? 'The general type of answer that has on occasion been given, and that I would like to give here, is that a theory is "new" if it deals in a different manner with one of the central concepts of the science. Similarly, it is "new" if it stimulates concentrated research along hitherto neglected directions' (Patinkin, 1982, 169-170). As far as the 'central message' is concerned, Patinkin again acknowledges Merton's encouragement 'to make the "central message" my central message' (1982, x). This can be put in the form of a 'basic principle': 'that in studying a man's writings we must distinguish between that which was fully integrated into his conceptual framework and that which was not; between the systematic component of his thinking and the random component' (Patinkin, 1982, 16). In applying this principle, Patinkin designs a test consisting of three questions:

(i) What was the theoretical context in which the central message appeared?
(ii) How did this fit in the academic environment in which it developed?
(iii) Was the central message used systematically in order to derive policy implications?

In the case of Keynes' *General Theory*, Patinkin identifies the central message as having consisted of three parts. The first is, of course, the theory of EFFECTIVE DEMAND: 'The novelty of my treatment of saving and investment consists, not in my maintaining their necessary aggregate equality, but in the proposition that it is, not the rate of interest, but the level of incomes which (in conjunction with certain other factors) ensures this equality' (Keynes CW, XIV, 201-15). Second, he lists the notion of persistent unemployment as an UNEMPLOYMENT EQUILIBRIUM: '[T]he economic system may find itself in stable equilibrium with N [employment] at a level below full employment, namely at the level given by the intersection of the aggregate demand function with the aggregate supply function' (Keynes, CW, VII, 30). Finally, there is the concept of the MULTIPLIER: '[T]he major purpose of Kahn's article was to prove (by means of the multiplier formula which he developed) that not only would there be an increase in savings . . . but that this increase would exactly equal the initial increase in investment' (Patinkin, 1982, 27-8). This, in a nutshell, is the blueprint against which any claim of anticipation must be tested.

It is significant that if we apply Patinkin's standards, a mere demonstration that these ideas were present in the writings of somebody claimed to be an anticipator is not sufficient. Patinkin asks for more. An anticipation would require that the author placed the innovations squarely in the academic environment so they could be noticed by his peers. In testing a claim for anticipation, we should further have to ask:

(i) What aspects of his theoretical thinking did the anticipator-candidate choose for inclusion in professional journals?
(ii) How was his work perceived by his peers?
(iii) How did his work fare in reviews?
(iv) How is it reflected in the writings of others?

In the case of Keynes, the criteria which turn on the published record could provide some difficulties, since not all researchers can make themselves noticed with equal ease, a problem which Patinkin is quite prepared to acknowledge: 'There can be no doubt that Keynes — with his worldwide reputation, and situated at what was then the center of learning in economics — was in an ideal position to communicate his message to the profession as a whole' (Patinkin, 1982, 87). Patinkin deals with this sociological argument only to the extent of showing that Keynes' strategic position in the academic communications network cannot be said to have determined his success; both Kalečki and Ohlin had or gained access to the same communications network. They published in the same journals or went to similar international conferences. But Patinkin's way of handling the argument restricts its applicability to the two cases studied. It does not rule out the existence of anticipations which, for good reasons, occurred without the anticipators claiming their priority or trying to place their argument in the media of publication chosen by a particular school of thought. As these case studies show, Patinkin is incorrect in supposing that economics universally gravitated towards Cambridge (England).

With regard to Patinkin's third criterion and very much in line with his 'functional' approach to the history of thought, that the innovation should be tied to policy conclusions in order to prove its relevance: Did *The General Theory* have political implications? The answer is almost self-evident and a resounding yes.

In selecting possible anticipators of Keynes' *General Theory*, Patinkin was obviously guided by a perfectly reasonable interpretation of the contemporary literature. He chose those two economists who are most often claimed to have anticipated Keynes. Why a claim of anticipation is made, however, is not very obvious. With respect to Kalečki, I found G. C. Harcourt helpful when he wrote:

Keynes never succeeded completely in throwing off the effects of his neoclassical forebears, especially Marshall, and, moreover, his political temperament was such that as he grew older he dropped back into ways of thought that, politically, were less and less acceptable to his younger, more radical colleagues. Michal Kalečki, by contrast, was always a convinced socialist, with a healthy contempt for both capitalism and the Stalinist brand of communism. His political and analytical attitudes fit more comfortably with the attitudes of those who established the post-Keynesian school. (Harcourt, 1982, 387)

Ohlin, of course, took it upon himself to advance his own claim, though this claim is generally made on behalf of the Stockholm school (Ohlin, 1981; Hansson, 1982) as a whole. This school started with Wicksell and hence includes at least two generations. The problem, accordingly, involves a rather more 'complete study of the intellectual inter-relationships between Swedish and British economists in the interwar period' (Patinkin, 1982, 45), an enterprise which Patinkin certainly could not be expected to accomplish in passing. He adds an interesting aside which is relevant to the German case. After mentioning Lindahl, Robertson, Myrdal, Hawtrey, Kahn and Hicks, he goes on to say: 'Nor should we forget the crucial role Hayek played in the early 1930s in bringing the message of Wicksell to England via Austria' (1982, 46). Thus two separate schools might possibly be involved.

On the basis of the foregoing discussion, the reader will not be surprised to learn why Patinkin feels confident in rejecting both claims to originality:[4]

[It] is significant that in supporting her claim for Kalečki, Joan Robinson (1966, 336 bottom) singles out for mention his remarkable 1935 magazine article, 'The Mechanisms of the Upswing'. . . which — because of Kalečki's failure to include its analysis in his scientific writings as well — I have not considered to be part of his central message to the profession (just as I would not so consider a theory which an economist would present in, say, a *Newsweek* column and which did not have a counterpart in his scientific writings). Similarly, I have contended . . . that the passages Steiger cites from Myrdal's and Ohlin's writings as presenting the equilibrating role of changes in output were not part of their respective central messages. (1982, 85; see also 80-1)

In this context, Joan Robinson's dictum comes to mind that 'Hitler had already found how to cure unemployment before Keynes had finished explaining why it occurred' (Robinson, 1972, 8). After Warsaw, Cambridge and Stockholm, perhaps we should now turn to Berlin?

According to Patinkin there was reason to expect a multiple discovery of the central message of *The General Theory*:

> For, from the viewpoint of social needs, the pernicious problem of persistent depression and unemployment which formed the background of *The General Theory* was common to all of the Western world in the early thirties; while, from the viewpoint of internal dynamics, the state of economics as a science in several of these countries (e.g. Britain, United States, Sweden) was not basically different at that time. (1982, 5)

This I would take to mean that when looking for possible anticipators of *The General Theory*, we should keep in mind, as Patinkin suggested, the similarity of the economic conditions (notably the unemployment problem) that beleaguered the Western democracies. Significantly, the German-speaking countries are missing in his enumeration. The economic problems these countries faced were certainly not less pernicious than they were in the rest of the Western world, although perhaps economic conditions and certainly the academic environment differed from those of the English-speaking world.

In this respect, Professor Robinson's often-quoted remark ignores not only Keynes' considerable influence in Germany but also, more significantly, the fact that initially Hitler's economic policies were not really Hitler's. They were rather initiated by his predecessors before his rise to power; the dictator started by leaving economic policy to experts whom he encountered in the ministries and agencies, instead of either concerning himself with it or entrusting economic policy to party economists. What was the response to the economic crisis from economists in Berlin?[5]

Economics in the German universities of the twenties and early thirties was much more heterogeneous than it was in Britain, for example, with scholars as diverse as Friedrich August von Hayek, Ludwig von Mises, Wilhelm Lautenbach (1939, 1952), Emil Lederer, Wilhelm Roepke (1926, 1932), Joseph Alois Schumpeter, Werner Sombart (1927, 1928, 1929, 1930a and b, 1932, 1933), Arthur Spiethoff, etc., all publishing at the same time on topical issues. It is a pity that Patinkin did not consider seriously the possibility of Keynes' anticipations in

Germany,[6] the more so since the first full-scale experiment in Keynesianism was carried out in that country, prior to the publication of *The General Theory*.

Obviously, these political activities did not occur in a theoretical vacuum. Several scholars stand out for mention. Werner Sombart (1932, 1933) who, as a professor in the University of Berlin, was the leading spokesman of historical theorizing in the Wagner chair of Germany's leading university.[7] He also made the argument for credit-financed public re-employment programmes one of his central concerns, opposing, as he did, the majority of German academic economists and actively and successfully seeking access to political decision-makers. He, of course, is not a candidate for a Keynes anticipator; for the sake of his own effectiveness, he would not have chosen to associate himself with Keynes, since he pursued a rival theoretical approach.

Wilhelm Lautenbach, on the other hand, although he may indeed be called an anticipator on Patinkin's terms, since he integrated the three notions of an underemployment equilibrium, the macroeconomic theory of aggregate demand and the conception of a multiplier (Lautenbach, 1933), never claimed to be an original thinker but preferred to describe himself as a Keynesian. Again, this may have been a matter of modesty as much as a matter of professional effectiveness: Lautenbach had access to political power. He also had a Keynesian-derived theoretical conception, but initially he lacked authority, especially in comparison to such towering figures as Keynes and Sombart. Since his theoretical approach indeed owed much to Keynes, claiming priority would have compromised the political task at hand. Incidentally, Lautenbach also differed from Sombart in lacking access to the international media of communication. While Sombart frequently published in American journals and could count on his work being regularly reviewed, Lautenbach, for all he did to popularise and develop Keynesian theories in Germany, apparently could not even count on Keynes to acknowledge, let alone answer his correspondence.

The upshot of this discussion should not be misunderstood as a plea for adding further economists to an already sufficiently long list of Keynes' possible anticipators. I think the case for Lautenbach has been fairly convincingly made elsewhere (Landmann in Bombach *et al.*, III, 1981, esp. 253-308), while focusing attention on Sombart highlights developments in schools different from that at Cambridge. Differing schools define different professional standards, have different media of professional communication and emphasise different reward systems for successful scholars. These variations in the professional organisation of economics, across cultures and over time, are not captured by Patinkin's approach to studying anticipations of *The General Theory*. What is gained in the rigour of his analysis may be lost in breadth and scope. This is a real loss in our understanding of those factors which determined that, despite and at the expense of parallel theoretical work outside Cambridge and in very different scholarly contexts, it was Keynes who became the undisputed authority in the new subdiscipline of macroeconomics which he had helped initiate. Keynesian macroeconomics won the day. This Keynesian macroeconomic work in some respects is not as rich as that of some of the neglected contributors to early macroeconomics. Unless we can isolate and properly understand those factors, we cannot be certain that they have ceased to persist in slowing down the rate of growth of knowledge in the discipline.

Werner Sombart

Werner Sombart's Place in the History of Economic Thought: a Sketch

Werner Sombart is usually characterised as an economic sociologist in the tradition of the followers of the historical school, who stubbornly insisted on a romantic methodology and used concepts of changeable content (von Mises, 1960, e.g. 144, 200) in order finally to indulge in glorifying Nazism.[8] Yet, when we consider Germany's leading economists of the time, we find them almost invariably opposing Keynesian employment programmes, leaving the political arena wide open for activists[9] of many different persuasions. With these well-documented activisms I am not concerned, because the activists cannot be described as having developed theoretical concepts systematically in order to explain chronic underemployment or — on such a theoretical basis — to propose measures of Keynesian economic policy.

In making this point, I am not claiming that Sombart anticipated Keynes the theorist. Keynes' theoretical contributions were certainly instrumental in fostering Keynesianism, but they cannot be regarded as the only element that can serve to explain the rise of Keynesianism in the Western economies. Against this view it is often held, e.g. by Patinkin, that 'Keynes provided the theoretical underpinning for the policy of public-works expenditures which, though it had been advocated before (by himself as well), did not become widely accepted until after the acceptance of *The General Theory*' (Patinkin, 1982, p. xxi). From my reading of the historical record, this statement overemphasises the importance of Keynes' theoretical contribution for Keynesian economic policy making. In Germany, these policies were accepted conclusions from theoretical constructions other than *The General Theory*.

In the first place, policies of public works expenditure during depressions were already an integral part of the theory of economic policy. This is true for the academic tradition even in Britain, and well before Keynes. Recommendations for public works to reduce unemployment were proposed by Bentham,[10] later by Sidney and Beatrice Webb (1909). Ohlin (1981, 198) has documented further examples from Scandinavia and Germany. The *Handwoerterbuch der Staatswissenschaften*, a leading German scholarly encyclopaedia on a par with the *International Encyclopaedia of the Social Sciences*, in its 1929 supplementary volume (to the fourth edition) approvingly lists similar recommendations as a staple item in Roepke's article on 'State Interventionism' by referring to Mueller-Armack's article on 'Business Cycle Research and Policy' (1929); that article details various classes of projects and gives theoretical criteria (conditions of aggregate demand, labour mobility, capacity utilisation of state enterprises over the business cycle, etc.) under which their success was to be expected.

I take all this as evidence that the impediments to public works employment policies were not of a theoretical nature. Since lack of theory development cannot be argued in the German case, the emergence of Keynesianism is all the more remarkable. Against this historical background, a look at some of the other roots of Keynesianism besides Keynes' *General Theory* is clearly warranted. In this chapter I want to argue that the historical school, and Werner Sombart in particular, contributed to the rise of Keynesianism in Germany.

It was Sombart who stood out as an exception among German economics professors. Where all the senior members of the profession, with very few exceptions (notably Roepke and Wagemann) strictly opposed Keynesian public works employment policies, Sombart campaigned for their adoption. As a highly visible figure and an eloquent persuader, he made the critical underemployment problem a central focus of his scholarly activities.[11] He gave lectures in which he urged the government to adopt a particular programme;[12] he backed an influential group of activists who had the most detailed programme closest to his own approach;[13] he endorsed this programme with a separate expert opinion which was used to promote the initiative;[14] he wrote and published a monograph which was supposed to serve as the theoretical framework of his policy analysis;[15] and he based all this on his monumental analysis of modern capitalism, in particular its third volume (Sombart, 1927), which had appeared shortly before. All this he did in 1932, immediately prior to the adoption of measures similar to those which he had advocated. Thereafter, he devoted his attention to other subjects.[16]

What were his methods of analysis? When discussing Sombart's method and approach, it should be kept in mind that he wrote at a time when what is today separately dealt with in economics and sociology was still considered one and the same subject. Sombart, a student of Schmoller's and a 'descendent' (in Schumpeter's words) of the historical school, was at the same time deeply influenced by Karl Marx. Hence he tried to accomplish a twofold and bold task: to suggest a comprehensive theory of the development of socio-economic systems in general and of capitalism in particular. Not content with economic historiography and historical case studies, Sombart attempted to derive an evolutionary theory of economic organisation. It was for this unique combination of history and theory that Schumpeter credited Sombart with having overcome the dilemma posed by the *Methodenstreit* (Schumpeter, 1927, part II; also Mitchell, 1929, part VII). By virtue of his own example, he had changed the outlook of the discipline as a whole. Having thus accomplished what can certainly not be said to have been a minor achievement, Sombart is generally said to have failed in the very two respects which were the respective strengths of the two opposed camps in the *Methodenstreit*. While his theories were historically based, they were certainly not theories in the Austrian sense. And his use of historical sources was not always as discriminating as an historian's (Kuczynski, 1968, 58). At the same time, his theoretical constructions were hardly lightweight. All this led Schumpeter to note with a sigh of despair: 'If one could only mix Sombart and Edgeworth! But the future will do this anyway' (Schumpeter, 1927, 367; my translation J.B.). Sombart's method was not without an artistic quality, rich in posing new problems, successful in coining ideal types and relationships with strong suggestive explanatory power, elegant, fresh, stimulating and often daring. But he was neither rigorous nor thoroughly empirical.

His monumental *Modern Capitalism* may serve to illustrate this point. The book tries to explain the emergence of the modern business enterprise as the main constituent element for defining the capitalist period. The book to which von Mises, in paying one of his characteristically generous compliments, referred to as 'a historical monstrosity' (von Mises, 1978, 103), was criticised by professional historians, when it appeared, for not presenting genuine historical research, since it relies exclusively on secondary sources. Of course, Sombart's intention had not been to compete with historians in the game of unearthing new sources; rather his purpose was to use the historical material for a theoretical purpose, i.e. the explanation of the contemporary economy. But, unlike the classical economists, Sombart advocated a hermeneutical method, emphasising *verstehen*. In his book of 1930 *Die drei Nationaloekonomien* he distinguishes between *richtende* i.e. normative economics, *ordnende* in the sense of positive economics, as well as a third approach: *verstehende* or a type of economic theorising that enables us to understand processes and institutions as distinguished from a method that enables the researcher to classify correctly and predict a phenomenon without necessarily understanding it. While Sombart felt that classical and neoclassical economics were wrong in limiting economics to the use of the positive method which he felt was adequate only for the natural sciences, he preferred economics to be practised as a philosophy and an art stressing understanding in addition to categorising and predicting. This methodological difference in itself would be sufficient to explain why Sombart's prose looks fuzzy and imprecise to the modern reader. His literary and expository style helped to reinforce these traits. He offered impressions, surprising combinations of arguments that habitually tend to be separated from each other in the day-to-day practice of economic analysis, and he was always ready to test new explanatory constructions. At the same time, he was not dogmatic about any of these and willing to discard what proved no longer useful in probing a particular point. Thus Sombart's place in the history of the behavioural sciences is secure as that of an economist and sociologist who stimulated new lines of research, and gave the profession new arguments the corroboration or refutation of which involved the production of hitherto unavailable knowledge, and as one of the founders of what today is called 'comparative economic systems', i.e. the systematic comparison of different types of economies, where any particular real-world economy should be explicable by comparison to an appropriate ideal type (*Idealtypus*) in the Weberian tradition (to which Sombart belongs in this respect).

Sombart's Economic Analysis and Policy Recommendations in the Face of the World Economic Crisis

As noted above, Sombart advocated a systems approach to economic analysis. He opened the first substantive section in his lead article in the second volume of the *Economic History Review* with this characteristic statement:

> It is of primary importance for the historian to realize that, whether he is dealing with the conduct of an individual, or a political situation, or a number of successive events, he is concerned not with isolated facts but with connected systems (*Ganze*). (*EHR*, 1929, 2)

A system in Sombart's context is somewhat different from a system for example in cybernetics. The system in the social ('cultural') sciences, according to Sombart, has the task of finding 'ways and means by which to grasp cultural phenomena in their historical singularity' (1930, 196). Again, the methodological emphasis is on *verstehen*. This also defines the purpose of the economic system.

> By an economic system is understood a mode of satisfying and making provisions for material wants which can be comprehended as a unit and wherein each constituent element of the economic process displays some given characteristics. These constituent elements are the economic spirit or outlook — the sum total of the purposes, motives, and principles which determine behaviour in economic life — the form of economic life or the objective system of regulation of economic relations, and the technology employed in economic processes. Defined more precisely, an economic system is a unitary mode of providing for material wants, animated by a definite spirit, regulated and organised according to a definite plan, and applying a definite technical knowledge. (1930, 196)

In the context of this approach, capitalism is just one such economic system, and, of course, the one Sombart witnessed during his lifetime and therefore sought to understand (*verstehen*) and explain. True to his definition, three constituent elements have to be singled out in an analysis of capitalism; the capitalist spirit, the form of economic life, and capitalistic technology. The spirit of the capitalist system turns on the ideas of acquisition, competition, and rationality. In this context, it may be important to point out that while capitalism in Sombart's view requires rationality on the part of the economic agents, Sombart explicitly allows for a wide variety of different individual motives for economic activity. Distinguishing between the corporation (as one of the salient features of the form of the capitalist system) and the entrepreneur, he was anxious to point out that entrepreneurial motives such as the desire for power, the craving for acclaim, the impulse to serve the common good, the urge to act etc. (1930, 200) are disciplined by the corporate form which begins to lead a life of its own. Only if a profit is made can those farther reaching aspirations be fulfilled.

While the individual is disciplined to be purposeful and rational, irrationality characterises the results produced by the capitalist system as a whole:

> While individual action under capitalism is informed by the ideal of highest rationality, the capitalist system as a whole remains irrational, because the other dominant capitalistic idea, that of acquisition, of the unrestricted assertion by the individual of his powers leaves the regulation of the total economic process to the uncoordinated discretion of individual economic agents. From this co-existence of well nigh perfect rationality and of the greatest irrationality originate the numerous strains and stresses which are peculiarly characteristic of the economic system of capitalism. (1930, 200)

Sombart's historical perspective suggests a view where economic systems are not always apparent in their pure form. As they emerge, they co-exist with late phases of earlier systems, in order to develop fully into the pure type and then decline at a later stage, while new systems emerge. The pure form of capitalism at its full stage had at its centre the entrepreneur, who in his quest for acquisition bore considerable risk, subject as he was to unrestricted competition which in turn produced more and more rational (i.e. efficient) modes of organisation. The legal system, the form, reflected this fully, leaving a wide scope of activity to an entrepreneurial aristocracy operating in many decentralised loci of organisational power. The period of late capitalism, however, which Sombart dated from the beginnings of World War I and the emergence of a state-run war economy, is already quite distinct from full capitalism. Economic processes become more and more predictable, freedom from external restraint characteristic of full capitalism is suspended in the period of late capitalism by an increase in the number of restrictions until the entire system becomes regulated rather than free, flexibility is replaced by rigidities, and regulation of economic life and of the market mechanism gradually reduces the function of price, demand and supply in the allocation of resources. The market system is superseded by the price regulation of unions and cartels or even of the government. For this reason what had later been termed the Keynesian approach to economic policy is for Sombart a feature of late capitalism:

> The entrepreneurial group has been consciously striving for stability as in the cartels and trade associations. Public authorities have intervened to offset the business fluctuations by withholding orders in periods of prosperity and granting them more generously in periods of depression; this policy will play an increasingly important role: 'stabilization of business' seems to be both the slogan and the accomplishment of this period. (1930, 208)

The analysis which Sombart presented in the face of the world economic crisis in 1932 follows almost directly from this general theoretical approach. He begins by noting that the economy has entered the phase of 'late capitalism', where new forms of economic life have emerged that can not be counted among the capitalist forms and now appear side by side with the latter. In particular, he was thinking of producers' co-operatives, public enterprises and symbiotic forms such as mixed public-private corporations (1932, 7). These changes in form reflected changes in the spirit of the economy. The dialectic tension between the acquisitive and risk-averse 'bourgeois' on the one hand and the entrepreneur on the other resulted in more and more constraints on entrepreneurial activity, leading to a decline in innovation and trammelling growth. At the same time the level of some prices was kept artificially high and unemployment was rampant.

In Sombart's historical perspective, such a hybrid economic system cannot last. And this prompts the question about *The Future of Capitalism* which Sombart tried to elucidate in a monograph of that title.[17] He distinguished between three logically possible scenarios that the future course of capitalism might take: continuation of the *status quo*, retrogression, and progression. The first scenario implied that the contemporary situation of 1932 could somehow be retained. And he described the economic policies of the day as consisting of haphazard state intervention, state initiatives lacking co-ordination as they were taken in response to pressures from special interest groups, subsidies here, regulatory controls there, protection of farming and promotion of the export industries. This, of course, describes the situation of the

Reich in 1932, and Sombart was convinced that it was an untenable one. The second possibility involved a return to full capitalism, which was indeed implicitly favoured by the majority of German economists at the time. A return would have required above all sweeping changes in the legal structure, namely undoing the regulatory state, in order to free the entrepreneurial spirit. Sombart rejected this idea, too, because it had been rendered impossible by the very development of capitalism itself. The large conglomerated corporations, trusts and cartels had themselves created a system of rules which tended to obstruct entre-preneurial activity. In addition, the political interest groups had become too powerful to be ignored or over-ruled, and the sheer size of the capitalist corporation had made into a political unit what once could properly have been regarded as a private affair. In referring to the then recent bank collapse in Germany he noted that the failure of just one major bank had repercussions that the state could no longer ignore: ' No state can tolerate "sovereign industrial duchies" in its interior.' Thus, having rejected the possibility of either retrogression or else the main-tenance of the *status quo,* Sombart saw progression to a new economic order as the most likely outcome. His projection involved on the one hand a concerted approach to economic policy (a concept he called 'planning') and on the other a return to largely self-sufficient national economic development.

What Sombart understood by planning was very different indeed from collectivist socialism. He was mainly interested in a co-ordination of the various political interventions into the economy to fit one com-mon pattern, to harmonise the different legal developments, to use taxa-tion as an instrument of fiscal policy, not merely as a method of revenue generation, and to do this on the basis of the traditional political system that guarantees individual liberties. As Sombart was anxious to point out, this approach to 'planning' would not bring about the introduction of any new policy instrument that was not already in use; rather, it was the integrated coordination of all those approaches that were already being practised that was his own contribution.

Obviously, Sombart in 1932 was describing what is commonplace today. The second element of his scenario, however, his rather critical view of free trade, which led him to emphasise (relative) autarky, is somewhat more puzzling.[18] Sombart's argument is reminiscent of public policy debates in Europe and the United States today, but it has a special catch. He began by noting that development in the less-developed countries was picking up, and that consequently domestic industries faced increasing competition from abroad. Foreign competitors were able to replicate production processes which were once exclusive to the domestic sector, and they were able to do this at a lower level of wages and other input costs which reflected the artificially high input price level consequent on unionisation and other forms of cartelisation, the universal quest for security and fixed incomes. An export industry could, however, thrive only on the basis of continued innovations ('our intelligence', as he put it) but this was no longer feasible owing to the changes in capitalism itself which had stifled initiative and entrepreneurship. The argument is thus simple and straightforward. If exports decline, imports have to be reduced as well. And this means that those products which are essential and which tend to be imported, notably primary (agricultural) products, have to be produced at home. This is why Sombart called for 'internal colonisation', an increase in the agrarian population which would absorb more or less the currently unemployed. (1932, 44)

Sombart and Keynes in their Respective Research Environments

So far, I have argued that Sombart, as the leader of the historical school in the Germany of the early thirties, contributed to the rise of Keynesianism.[19] How does all this relate to Keynes? Perhaps the best way to approach this question is to return once more to Patinkin's 'basic principle': 'That in studying a man's writings we must distinguish between that which was fully integrated in his conceptual framework and that which was not; between the systematic component of his thinking and the random component.' (1982, 16) In applying this principle, we have to try to answer these three questions: What was the theoretical context in which the central message appeared, and of what did it consist? How did it fit in to the academic environment as it developed? And, was the central message employed systematically in order to derive policy implications?

As far as Keynes is concerned, Patinkin defined his central message (with reference to *The General Theory*) as consisting in three elements: the theory of effective demand, the notion of an unemployment equilibrium, and the concept of the multiplier. In Sombart's case, the central message consisted of his historical analysis of the capitalist system and the specific result that, owing to a change in the spirit, the form and the technology of capitalism, the capitalist system had entered into a stage of transition and was about to evolve into something else, the elements of which new system could already be discerned. Incidentally, the vision of the system about to emerge is remarkably similar to 'The

Social Philosophy Toward which *The General Theory* might Lead', with which Keynes concluded his classic work.

Present in Sombart's analysis is the notion of a persistent disequilibrium in the capitalist system, in contradiction to Say's law. Present is the notion of waning entrepreneurship, too, as well as an underlying movement towards stabilising the business cycle. While Keynes, however, sought to argue for the state taking over the programming of investment and thus being instrumental in stabilising economic fluctuations, Sombart in the third volume of *Der Moderne Kapitalismus* had concluded (by 1927) that capitalism had already begun moving towards this end (see Chapter 45). He cited five reasons for the observed stabilisation of the business cycle (1928, 701-10):

(1) improved economic forecasting;
(2) monetary policy;
(3) commercial and industrial concentration and the change in the corporate structure;
(4) state regulatory policy; and
(5) concerted attempts in the business community to contain the effects of economic fluctuations.

While Keynes argued for the fulfilment of these underlying currents in capitalist development and wished the state systematically to combine policy efforts at stabilising the business cycle, Sombart was interested in drawing the conclusions from this change in terms of the comparative analysis of economic systems. In assessing the 'meaning' or implications of the business cycle for the system as a whole he noted:

> Measures such as the one mentioned last breathe already quite a different spirit than is characteristic of high capitalism. In a certain sense this is true of every effort at stabilising the business cycle. These measures are actually rather ambiguous. On the one hand, they are the ultimate development in rationalising economic life. Consciously or unconsciously, capitalist interests push in this direction. On the other hand, these policies constitute a danger for the continued existence of capitalism in its present form. We have had several occasions to note that capitalism derived its strength from the rhythm of the expansionary business cycle. Nowhere does it become as apparent as here that what is true for human life likewise holds for economic systems: that in the final analysis, rationalisation means aging. Once economic life has become equilibrated, tem-

perate and measured, will it not have to fall prey to regulation and bureaucratic control? This is why the stabilisation of the business cycle must conclude our discussion of rationalisations of the market; here we have reached the threshold to a new era, where high capitalism progresses into late capitalism. (Sombart 1928, 711; my translation J.B.)

How did this theoretical analysis fit in the academic environment of his time?

There are certainly some striking similarities between Sombart and Keynes. These are not similarities in their method of analysis, of course, but rather in the role and position Keynes and Sombart played in their respective scholarly environments. Keynes struggled against what he labelled the 'classical' tradition, realising that, if he wanted to be at all successful in convincing the scholarly as well as the political community of his views, he would have to resort to casting his policy analysis in the mould of a new theoretical framework. This led to a resurgence of Cambridge economics. Similarly, Sombart systematically strove to carry out the mission of the tradition in which he stood and which he finally fulfilled. It was Sombart who arrived at a comprehensive historical economic theory and in so doing apparently exhausted the potential of the historical school's paradigm — awe-inspiring to admirers and detractors alike.

The elements of their analysis were as different as the paradigms. Savings, investment, aggregate demand and supply, the multiplier etc., i.e. the main building blocks of Keynes' analysis, are present in Sombart, but they assume very modest backstage roles. For example, Sombart is credited with an independent multiplier analysis well before Kahn but he did not use it when arguing for public works programmes (Sombart, 1928, 132; Krumme, 1968, 115). His theoretical approach, turning on the *spirit*, the *form*, and the *technology* of an economic *system*, had nothing but secondary use for Keynesian constructs. Both Keynes and Sombart responded superbly to their academic environments, but as the environments were different, so were their responses.

In looking at the criteria which Don Patinkin has formulated for analysing anticipations of *The General Theory*, we can note that both Keynes and Sombart were thoroughly aware of the novelty of their respective approaches. Both put their analysis squarely before their academic colleagues and published them in the central media of scholarly exchange, while the developmental state of professional economics had not yet determined one single centre towards which everything gravitated. Sombart and Keynes were leading and prominent in their respective professional networks, but the overlaps between the two professional groups were few and far between. Sombart's *magnum opus*, which also contained the theoretical analysis which he applied to the stabilisation problem, had appeared after 1902 with the prestigious publishing house of Duncker & Humblot, and after the completion of the third volume in 1927, the entire set of three (bound in six) volumes appeared in a superb edition in 1928. When the third volume which crowned the effort was finally out, it met with numerous reviews, some very long and sometimes in several instalments. Schumpeter's review article still stands out as a succinct assessment of the accomplishments of the historical school. It appeared in the leading professional journal, *Schmollers Jahrbuch.*[20]

In applying the theoretical analysis to the concrete policy problem of unemployment, Sombart not only prepared the expert opinion (see note 14) which was submitted to the Chancellor, but at the same time he published the slim book of 1932, which was based on a public lecture and eagerly reviewed in the daily press. This publication also provides the answer to the third question: Sombart used his central message systematically in order to derive the specific policy conclusions he stood and argued for.

Keynesianism as understood today developed in Germany earlier than it did in Britain. This development actually preceded *The General Theory,* which is often seen as the basis of Keynesianism. Rather it appears that it had various sources, some closely related to Keynes himself, and some less so. One of these sources is the historical school, and Werner Sombart, its leading representative in the early thirties, contributed towards the rise of Keynesianism. Sombart offered a historical theory of capitalism which distinguished different stages through which capitalism passes as well as the different policy scenarios that are required by these stages. Keynes developed a macroeconomic theory with an underemployment equilibrium, the theory of effective demand and the multiplier as central elements. This is not present in Sombart, nor was it close to his concern. However, the political implications of both these theories in the face of the same historical situation were almost identical. And this may explain why German economic policy between 1932 and 1935 looked Keynesian, while its roots were clearly in the tradition of the historical school.

Wilhelm Lautenbach

> One of the perplexing riddles in the history of social science is
> how a man of the intellect of Keynes could have laboured for
> years on what he considered to be a revolution without becom-
> ing aware of its multifarious antecedents, and how such a large
> segment of the English-speaking community of economists
> could have accepted his analysis and policy conclusions as
> such. (Garvy, 1975, 391)

Garvy's remark is well taken. Garvy, however, focused on the activists
and reformers at the expense of the theorists. And this has misled even
an authority on everything Keynesian of the stature of Patinkin to
believe that there were only activists and reformers (1982, 6). But there
was at the same time a substantial scholarly literature. By 'scholarly' I
do not mean 'purely theoretical'. There is no difference between
Keynes and the German Keynesians in their concern for the political
applications of economic reasoning. And I am not referring to jour-
nalism or even the politics of informed interest groups, but to research
published professionally — in learned journals and with the most reput-
able publishing houses.

Certainly, a large share of the credit for this has to go to Keynes himself, whose writings and public appearances commanded almost
universal attention in Germany. Keynes sought and on occasion had
access to government leaders not only in his own country but also, if
somewhat scantily, in the United States, and more extensively in Germany. In 1931, he gave the Harris lecture in Chicago and argued for
greater state involvement in order to overcome the severe economic
crisis and improve the employment situation. In Don Patinkin's words
he offered:

> three 'lines of approach' for achieving this objective: first, restoring
> confidence, about which not much can be deliberately done; second,
> carrying out a program of public investment, which has the practical
> drawback that 'it is not easy to devise at short notice schemes which
> are wisely and efficiently conceived and which can be put rapidly
> into operation on a really large scale'; and, finally, lowering the long-
> run rate of interest by a vigorous central bank policy of open market
> purchases. (1979, 217)

Germany's international obligations practically ruled out the third line of approach. So the difficult task remained of designing 'at short notice schemes which are wisely and efficiently conceived and which can be put rapidly into operation on a really large scale'. Hence in what follows I want to emphasise the policy-oriented discussions of learned economists in German academe and government before 1936. I do not have here the space to give a precise account of the whole spectrum of theoretical issues raised by the German Keynesians and by Lautenbach in particular. Rather, I want to focus on salient features of contemporary 'Keynesian' thought about economic policy analysis, and I single out four related items which seem to be particularly interesting for an understanding of Keynesian economic policies in Germany before 1936.

While academic economics and economic policy-making are often related to each other in only a rather loose fashion, in the case under consideration it is possible to single out one economist who was a scholar and a policy-maker simultaneously. It is for this reason that I shall focus on Wilhelm Lautenbach, who served as *Oberregierungsrat* in the *Reichswirtschaftsministerium* (Imperial Ministry of Economics) and drafted the programmes which were to be implemented in 1932 and 1933. When Hjalmar Schacht took office as Minister of Economics, in August 1934, he was surprisingly quick in presenting Lautenbach, who had by then risen to the rank of *Ministerialtrat*, with the following choice:[21] he could either take early retirement (at the age of 43) or, while retaining title and pay, accept a less significant position with the *Statistisches Reichsamt* (Imperial Statistical Office).[22] Lautenbach chose the latter, while Schacht[23] proceeded to pursue the plans Lautenbach had designed and started to implement (Neumark, 1981, 478-85).

Lautenbach is quite singular in that he was an eminent economist charged with economic policy in a country where lawyers tended, then as later, to predominate in the civil service. There were not many economists in government. At the same time, Lautenbach published regularly and rather frequently in scholarly journals and did much to propagate Keynes' economic theories in Germany. As a Keynesian, Lautenbach was not alone in Germany. There were not only a number of practitioners and activists, who drafted recovery programmes of uneven persuasiveness and realism, but also outstanding figures in academe who shared similar views, notably Wilhelm Roepke and Werner Sombart. Since as a result of Garvy's writing the practitioners and activists are somewhat better known, I shall not consider them here.

Lautenbach came in close contact with practically all the different groups of activists, since their petitions and programmes tended to end up on his desk for comment. He corresponded with some of them. I am focusing on Lautenbach not only because he was a remarkable economist but also because he served as a signal link between economic theory and economic policy, contributing significantly to both. On his desk the competing approaches, from Lederer to Woytinsky, Colm to Neisser and, of course, Hayek, were assembled side by side. The papers still survive with his marginal notes and memoranda. Not content with what these eminent economists offered, Lautenbach went out on his own and sought like-minded people, such as Gestrich and Roepke, with whom he engaged in long discussions, the results of which are reflected in an extensive correspondence (partly collected in Lautenbach, 1952). By showing that the approaches discussed here are important in Lautenbach's writings,[24] I suggest that they reflect strong currents in economic theorising in Germany as well as central ideas underlying economic policy-making during the early thirties.

Employment

In his widely-read study prepared for the League of Nations and subtitled *Inquiry into the Nature and Causes of the Poverty of Nations,* Gustav Cassel in 1927 claimed that monopolistic tendencies in commerce and industry were responsible for the slowing down of growth in the economy and for unemployment of the factors of production. He applied this diagnosis to labour in particular. Trade unions, he argued, had monopolised the supply of labour characteristically in the most productive sectors of the economy, restricting the amount of labour supplied and pushing up wages in those industries, while inducing a lower demand for labour in other sectors as well. The secondary effect was suggested to be of a supply-side nature. Too little production in the monopolised sectors meant that the existing resources could not sustain a demand sufficient for employment of all the factors of production and labour in particular. Hence decartelisation would strengthen sustained demand for goods and services leading to further production. The crisis occurred because too little was produced. Among the consequences of these monopolistic practices he listed:

(i) A level of output in these industries well below their productive possibilities; and

(ii) a redistribution of income from unemployed workers to those employed in monopolised industries at high wages. Likewise he noted that there was

(iii) redistribution from the general public to the beneficiaries of
monopolies in the form both of output foregone and of an
increased tax burden to support the unemployed.[25]

It is indeed noteworthy that this perfectly neoclassical view was shared
by most of the 'Keynesians' in Germany.[26] In their policy recommendations the Keynesians went, of course, beyond Cassel in advocating
the decartelisation of all markets, including the labour market, and pro-
posing a concomitant wage rate reduction, which they hoped would
result in a wage sum increase.

While taking the neoclassical approach as a starting point for their
analysis, the Keynesians took a basically microeconomic approach to
the economy at large. They argued that the entire economy was essentially like a firm with a U-shaped average-cost curve. Unemployment
signified that the economy was operating at a point somewhere to the
left of the cost minimum. There, the burden of fixed costs (private and
public capital) had to be borne by too few units of production. This
straightforward explanation is well expressed in a memorandum drafted by a group of Keynesian-minded businessmen, bankers, civil
servants, etc., the *Studiengesellschaft fuer Geld- und Kreditwirtschaft.* The group that had been exceedingly active in pushing for
Keynesian measures by working out, as a private initiative, an immense
potpourri of ready-to-implement programmes (Draeger, *et al.,* 1933,
see also note 25), i.e. those 'schemes which are wisely and efficiently
conceived and which can be put rapidly into operation on a really large
scale' which Keynes had talked about in his Harris lecture. The experts
of the *Studiengesellschaft* noted: 'From the point of view of a business-
man, Germany is a firm operating with a *large* share of fixed costs. Only
as long as the firm operated at full capacity, could everyone earn a living, and the budgets be balanced' (p.32; see also Draeger, 1932).

Lautenbach, working in the Economics Ministry, offered essentially
the same point of view, albeit in a slightly more sophisticated form. The
following is an extract from the first draft (Aug. 1931) of his expert
opinion 'On the Basic Features of the Future Economic and
Financial Policies':

> The fact is that at the moment we have an extraordinarily large
> foreign trade surplus . . . On the other hand, there are still persistent
> difficulties right across all lines of production to sell what is produced,
> so that there is unsold output in spite of a large balance of trade
> surplus, and in spite of sharply reduced levels of production. All this

shows that there are large unused production possibilities. It is entirely rational and from an economic point of view entirely unobjectionable to use these unused capacities to launch projects, financed by credits, which are economically sensible and required for public purposes. (Lautenbach, 1952, 148-9; my translation, J.B.)

Lautenbach had explained the type of projects he had in mind a couple of pages earlier. The list of projects submitted by the *Studiengesellschaft* strikes me as passing a test which he formulated in the following way (I am now quoting from the revised and enlarged version of the same expert opinion as of 9 September 1931):

> To find a use for these production surpluses is the essential and most urgent task of our economic policies, and it is, in principle, a rather easy one: surpluses of goods, dormant units of production and idle labourers can be used to fulfill a new economic need: which, from the point of view of the entire economy, are investments. Here I am thinking of such projects as described in the Brauns Commission report, i.e. public or publicly assisted works which constitute an increase in the wealth of the economy and which will have to be carried out anyway after returning to normal economic conditions. (Lautenbach, 1952, 143; my translation, J.B.)

The Brauns Commission report (which owed more to Lautenbach than to anyone else) had also referred to investment, mostly in the public domain. The term 'investment' was not merely political rhetoric, but stems from an analysis of how to convert inventories, surpluses and involuntary savings into investment and capital formation. This is emphasised in Lautenbach's interpretation of the Brauns Commission report:

> What used to be desired and pursued by politicians in the interest of a healthy growth of the economy: surpluses of production over current demand = savings now appears as a symptom of a fatal disease. Why? We have no cause but this: they [the surpluses] are not employed appropriately. They are not tapped for investments. Surpluses over current demand can only be turned into 'savings' and 'capital' if they are employed as 'capital', i.e. only when they are employed as operating capital. (Lautenbach, 1952, 131; my translation, J.B.)

That any re-employment programme had to pass the test of economic profitability (in the sense of an overall balance of costs and benefits) was an opinion held by virtually all advocates of these programmes. The monograph published by the *Studiengesellschaft fuer Geld- und Kreditwirtschaft* contains this basic principle (italicised in the original):

> The law of economic profitability is the basic law of any economic activity. This law necessitates in the most stringent way this principle: The first commandment of any re-employment programme is the restitution of profitability in agriculture and industry. (Draeger *et al.*, 1933, 9)

It is instructive to compare this with Keynes' more lenient views with respect to profitability and economic efficiency:

> In other words, the Government must itself promote a programme of domestic investment. It may be a choice between employing labour to create capital wealth, which will yield less than the market rate of interest, or not employing it at all. If this is the position, the national interest, both immediate and prospective, will be promoted by choosing the first alternative. But if foreign borrowers are ready and eager, it will be impossible in a competitive open market to bring the rate down to the level appropriate to domestic investment. Thus the desired result can only be obtained through some method by which, in effect, the Government subsidizes approved types of domestic investment or itself directs domestic schemes of capital development. (Keynes, CW, VI, 337-8)

Credit, Saving, Demand and Reparations

Given that there were in Germany a number of advocates of Keynesian policies, though with a particular emphasis on productivity and efficiency, and given that they were scattered all along the political spectrum, the question arises as to why these policies were not implemented earlier. (Neither the von Papen nor the von Schleicher programme met with much public response.[27] Funds were left largely untapped and these programmes became effective only later, when the first and the second Reinhardt programmes were launched in and after 1933.)

There are several answers to this question, some relating to historical circumstances, some pertaining to the history of thought about expansionary macroeconomic (or in that sense 'Keynesian') policies. To begin with, a number of internationally binding restrictions, including the stipulations of the Young plan, the protocol of The Hague and the Bank Law, made it extremely difficult for the government to embark upon an active policy of credit expansion plus stimulation.[28] How intensely these restrictions were felt by the responsible politicians is revealed in the following quotation:

> In his memoirs, Bruening recalls that he had attempted in a lengthy conversation (Jan. 11, 1932) to convince Professor Keynes that in advocating inflationary techniques he was undermining any kind of reasonable financial policy for Germany. The audience which heard his Hamburg address had mistakenly concluded that the British government shared his views. When I asked him how he thought (in applying his policy recommendations to Germany) of getting around the stipulations of the Young plan with regard to the German currency, it turned out that he had not considered them at all.[29]

The quotation reveals, of course, not so much Keynes' ignorance of international treaties — a surprising assertion, indeed, given that his popularity in Germany stemmed in part from his book *The Economic Consequences of the Peace* — as Bruening's belief that expansionary policies had to be inflationary.[30] This belief was strongly disputed by the investment and productivity oriented German Keynesians, as will be discussed shortly.

Apart from the legal and political obstacles to Keynesian policies just mentioned, the leading economists did not favour expansionary policies either. When Ernst Wagemann published his proposal in January 1932, no less than 32 economics professors (i.e. half of Germany's total at the time) signed a memorandum in opposition (Krohn, 1981, 163). Gustav Stolper,[31] editor of the influential periodical *Der Deutsche Volkswirt* and close friend of Schumpeter, feared a massive exodus of capital as a consequence of expansionary policies if pursued by Germany *alone,* and not co-ordinated on an international scale. This international co-ordination was hoped for by Keynes (CW, VI, 335 ff) and Lautenbach alike. Arthur Spiethoff, after Sombart the leading representative of the historical school,[32] editor of *Schmollers Jahrbuch,* and an internationally renowned authority on business cycle research, reasoned that a crisis which had no monetary causes could not have monetary cures either.[33] A more substantial, somewhat Austrian, argument was also offered by Spiethoff: expansionary policies would affect all sectors of the economy alike, while a crisis which revealed structural deficiencies of the economy should be tackled with specific policies aiming at precisely those structural problems. While in Britain expansionary policies were criticised for their allegedly inflationary effect, with a view to the exchange rate, the perspective in Germany was quite different. A complex web of political and economic considerations entangled the early expansionary moves, such as the initiatives of the Brauns Commission (1931) or the Wagemann proposal of 1932. First, memories of the disastrous landslide effects of hyperinflation were still very fresh. Inflationary policies were thus impossible either at home or abroad, because of the reparations issue. Secondly, the crisis was widely perceived as reflecting the structural problems of the entire economy, produced by politically established but lagging heavy industries and successful export-orientated light industries. Thirdly, the latter were most likely to produce an export surplus as a consequence of expansionary policies, which, again, would be politically inopportune in terms of Germany's attempts to demonstrate that she was unable to service the (international) war debt. These international financial obligations were repealed in mid 1932. 'The need for an impressive demonstration', of which Keynes had spoken in his Hamburg address, was no longer present, and a major obstacle to the implementation of deficit-based employment policies had been removed.

Another point is of interest. The arguments mentioned thus far implied that expansionary policies would be confined to policies of easy money. Correspondingly, in November 1932 the president of the German central bank (Reichsbank) announced that the entire 700 million RM, the amount set aside by the government in September, was still available (Hans Luther, quoted by Draeger *et al.,* 1933, 45). Economic policies based merely on theory set out in terms of economic aggregates had already proved to be futile.

A different argument, which was critical of *any* type of intervention, claimed that the crisis was the natural process for curing an unhealthy economy. Thus it was argued that the economic situation should not be tampered with artificially. This view was held by many in the economics profession, but certainly not *faute de mieux,* as the above discussion shows. It is unlikely that it could have prevailed had it not been for that fear of inflationary consequences which concerned all politicians alike. This fear has already been illustrated by the previous quotation from Bruening's memoirs, and it was shared also by most other leading politicians, including Hitler, even after the summer of

1932. Hitler did not lose his apprehension of inflation until much later, perhaps as late as 1939.[34]

In June 1933, however,

> it was a historic moment when this man [Lautenbach], this fiery man with his sharp tongue and mind, who dominated any discussion with his temper and the maturity of his thoughts was officially dispatched in the late spring of 1933 to explain to Hitler the economics of combating crisis by credit expansion. This was reported to have been one of the rare encounters with Hitler in which the latter had to refrain from his customary monologue. As he interjected that credit expansion amounted to inflation, Lautenbach offered this reply: 'Herr Hitler, you are now the most powerful man in Germany. But one thing you cannot do: under the present circumstances, you are not able to engineer an inflation, as hard as you may work at it.'[35]

This cannot but impress us, however, as a Keynesian assessment. But the somewhat surprising reason for his certainty was based on the German Keynesians' conviction that the projected policy of productive credit expansion would be financed through increased savings.[36] Consider these arguments:

> The inflationary effect of certain expansion results in 'involuntary saving'. People, who don't want to save, suffer a reduction in their real incomes as a result of price increases. Thus, they are required to save as productive capacity is transferred from consumption of goods to productive facilities. This insight corrects the often repeated allegation by Ricardo that capital cannot be increased through banking operations. This is true, in principle; but banking operations can make available the finance required to increase the stock of real disposable productive capital.[37]

A somewhat different effect of savings on anti-trust policies was what Lautenbach had in mind. As mentioned in the section on employment above, cartelisations and monopolisations in the labour market were not regarded as exceptions with respect to anti-trust policies:

> Wages have to become more flexible, more elastic, and partly they must be reduced ... Both measures [reduction of monopolistic prices and wages] are pivotally important in order for the stimulation

policies to result in a healthy development based on workable markets. They will, in particular, lead to reduced operating costs in industry . . . This is not only true in the formal sense that economies in production, due to our price and wage policies, can now be used for additional production; at the same time, there will be true economic capital formation. Reduction of monopolistic prices will mainly result in a reduction of the prices of raw materials and intermediate products. The worker as a consumer will only minimally gain from these reductions; even minimal wage increases will be real wage decreases. This sacrifice on the part of workers is 'saving' for the economy as a whole; these saved resources can be used as new capital in order to re-employ workers for the accomplishment of public works. (Lautenbach, 1952, 148)

If these theoretical arguments failed to convince, some rough calculations such as those prepared by the *Studiengesellschaft* showed that, fiscally, the re-employment programmes could be financed by drawing on funds

(a) from unemployment insurance;
(b) from the von Papen and von Schleicher programmes, which were merely programmes of credit expansion without a demand component and remained largely untapped (in late 1932 and early 1933); and
(c) by resorting to policies of short-term revolving credits.

Indeed, some similarly rough calculations seem to indicate that the programme of productive credit expansion was a bargain in purely fiscal terms — and conceived that way. Until 1936, when rearmament programmes superseded re-employment programmes, roughly 6 billion RM had been spent on them, while roughly 7 billion RM had been gained in enhanced tax revenues and reductions in unemployment benefit expenditures. This entirely ignores the value of the public works accomplished.[38]

Thus far, the picture includes credit, with which to set off the programmes; savings, on which to base the credit; and demand, i.e. public demand, in the absence of private initiative and confidence, in order to bring about the *Initialzuendung* i.e. initial ignition (Roepke) for productive re-employment. One further factor, however, rendered the circumstances for implementing the German programmes of 1932 and 1933 decisively different from similar economic crises: her international obligations under the system of agreements that stemmed from the Treaty of Versailles.

In perfect agreement with the Keynes of the *Treatise*, there was a generally held conviction among advocates of the programmes of productive credit expansion that such programmes had to be internationally orchestrated and simultaneously implemented in all capitalist economies alike. Again, in Germany, Lautenbach was very articulate in pressing this point.[39] He argued that providing long-term capital to Germany in order to finance re-employment programmes was in the interest of lenders, who hitherto held short-term claims against an ever weaker economy. It became, however, painfully apparent in 1932 that there was to be no international movement to re-establish full employment. In this situation, the theoretician Lautenbach altered his position and the civil servant argued for internal German credit expansion.[40] Thus he took up a side-line which Keynes had also provided in the *Treatise*. Lautenbach noted that orthodox policies called for a continuing increase in Germany's balance of payments surplus. As mentioned above, there was reason for concern on this point. Given the prevailing economic conditions, it would result in an end to the renewal of the short-term foreign debt; this in turn would induce a capital exodus from Germany and lead to further economic stagnation, a collapse of the public finances, and internal political strife. At the same time, the balance of payments surplus would further whet the appetite for additional reparations payments. The same result would occur if long-term credits could be obtained for an internationally orchestrated employment programme, since the inflowing foreign currencies would first be used to pay off short-term debts. This, in turn, would result in increased pressures on the government for reparations as a consequence of its improved credit status.

The odd result with which we are left is that the lack of international co-operation and the stubbornness of the victorious powers over the reparations issue finally triggered off the programmes of productive re-employment, at almost the same time as the reparations were cancelled and the German politicians were thereby reasonably assured that they could retain the benefits from these programmes.[41]

The Market and the Government

Keynesianism is often perceived as amounting to interventionism. While Keynes himself did not favour *ownership* of the means of production he argued, both in *The General Theory* and in his policy statements thereafter, for two-thirds to three-quarters of total investment to 'be influenced by public or semi-public bodies' (CW, XXVII, 322).

This distinction between public ownership and Keynesian socialisation of (aggregate) investment should not be taken as mere sophistry as is shown by Keynes' approving quotation of Hubert Henderson, who favoured

> an arrangement under which the State would fill the vacant post of entrepreneur-in-chief, while not interfering with the ownership or management of particular businesses, or rather only doing so on the merits of the case and not at the behests of dogma. (CW, XXVII, 324)

The German Keynesians, and Lautenbach in particular, held views more like those of Keynes himself than those conventionally labelled Keynesian. However, in the writings of the German Keynesians we frequently detect a twist absent from Keynes' work. In line with Germany's historical performance in the area of public finance and public entrepreneurship, the German Keynesians, who believed in fiscal prosperity and economic efficiency, saw the government's role not as that of an invervener in the market order but as an entrepreneur within the rules of the market, who (not least for fiscal reasons) appeared as a powerful consumer at times of low prices and abundant supplies, not tampering, however, with the market and its *modus operandi*.

> There is a characteristic difference between the crisis which we are currently experiencing and those crises which the capitalist economy has repeatedly overcome in such a striking manner. In the latter there existed precise targets for production, while in the former there is simply the goal to increase production without any knowledge as to precisely what should be produced in larger quantities. We only know that we want to, and should, produce more. Yet the market, the only regulating mechanism in a capitalist economy, does not give us any indication whatsoever, and so entrepreneurs are in the dark. (Lautenbach, 1952, 139)[42]

What was required, then, was not a Keynesian socialisation of investment, but a strong state acting as an entrepreneur in the economy, and thus defining demand.

This distinction can hardly be overemphasised. It already reflects Hayek's later criticisms of Keynes.[43] As is well known, Hayek's work of the last three decades turns on the distinction between rule-making and policy-making government, and his insistence that the two different functions should not be the responsibility of the same decision-making body (Hayek, 1973, 1976, 1979). This is, of course, precisely what happens with conventional Keynesian policies. Pursuit of the two tasks begets conflicts which compromise the attainment of either goal. A similar problem arises when the state combines the function of economic policy-making with economic entrepreneurship. The first is rule-making in the economy, the second is participation in an economy the rules of which are accepted as given. Obviously, a state which is a strong participant in the economy may try to bend the rules in favour of state enterprises. The German Keynesians addressed this problem by focusing on the state as an entrepreneur, while today Keynesianism is seen as referring to economic and in particular fiscal policy making. But, as the last quotation from Lautenbach suggests, it was *not* macroeconomic policy based on influencing economic aggregates which the extraordinary crisis was interpreted as calling for, but specific entrepreneurial guidance. In practice, this guidance was to be exercised through the established forms of public enterprise, and through some new (and sometimes rather ingenious) institutional constructions created for the specific purpose of carrying out the public works programme within the rules of the framework of international agreements detailed above. Not aggregate demand, but the demand for specific commodities, was lacking, since 'entrepreneurs are in the dark'. And the motives for policy making differed, too. While in Keynesian discussions the problem of unemployed labour is perceived as a political challenge which requires extraordinary political steps, the German Keynesians, while not at all oblivious to the plight of the unemployed worker, focused on the fiscal advantage of using the state's purchasing power in times of underemployment in order to buy cheap and invest in the infrastructure of the economy, where public enterprise had traditionally been strong, with the certainty that not only would the investments stand on their own, but that they would also, by virtue of the multiplier, trigger off economic recovery.[44]

In conclusion, let me underline these findings. The early German version of Keynesian economics is different from the later developments of Keynesianism. The earlier doctrine, surveyed in this chapter, emphasised the full employment of all factors alike without specifically singling out labour. It emphasised productivity, capital formation, fiscal conservatism and an entrepreneurial approach to the attainment of public purposes. It was not designed for intervention but participation in the market.

Acknowledgements

Over the past several years, I have received many helpful suggestions for improving the manuscript. While, unfortunately, all the remaining inaccuracies are altogether my fault, I should like to acknowledge support from several anonymous referees; the following persons have also helped me considerably with their criticism of various drafts: Gary Anderson (George Mason), Donald Bellante (Auburn), Knut Borchardt (Munich), Donald Elliott (Ottawa), David Felix (New York), Roger Garrison (Auburn), Geoffrey Harcourt (Cambridge), Carl-Ludwig Holtfrerich (Berlin), Michael Hudson (Leeds), Terence W. Hutchison (Birmingham), Randall Holcombe (Auburn), David Whitten (Auburn), and Leland Yeager (Auburn).

Notes

1. The director of the German Institute for Business Cycle Research, who also held a chair in economics in the University of Berlin while at the same time serving as the president of the German Statistical Office, was Ernst Wagemann. In 1932, he advanced a pioneering deficit financed re-employment plan of his own (Wagemann 1932a), which ran into the stiff opposition of the otherwise rarely united German academic economists (Landauer, Hahn and Stolper, 1932). Consequently, and in view of Wagemann's official position, the German government saw a need to disassociate itself from the plan. In 1933, Wagemann resigned from the Statistical Office.

2. On Keynes' somewhat ambiguous position towards econometrics, see e.g. Patinkin 1982, 1984. While Keynes' position towards econometrics remained one of scepticism, his fierce critic Schumpeter was among the co-founders of the Econometric Society. The situation is truly ironic, in that Sombart can certainly not be called anti-empirical. On the contrary, his work abounds with empirical information of an astonishing and rather uneven variety.

3. Patinkin's approach is, however, significantly different from Merton's; this point proves to be important in studying the German case. See Patinkin's conclusions (1982, 80-1).

4. Michal Kalečki, 'The Mechanism of the Business Upswing', in Kalečki, *Studies in the Theory of Business Cycles: 1933-1939.* Basil Blackwell, Oxford: 1966.

5. A detailed discussion of German Keynesianism and reprints of many documents are now available (see Bombach *et al.,* 1976, 1981). A critical review of the third volume is pertinent to this discussion: Borchardt, 1982, 359-70.

6. Patinkin explicitly dismisses this avenue of investigation and cites Garvy in support: '[Since] so many claims of anticipation of the General Theory turn out on closer examination to be claims that public works were advocated before Keynes (cf. e.g. Garvy 1975), let me in particular emphasize that Keynes could not possibly have perceived this advocacy as constituting the major contribution of his book' (Patinkin, 1982, 6). Garvy cannot be cited in support of a view that the German Keynesians were just advocates of public works programmes. Many were, and therefore this is the focus of his article, since he is dealing with the 'activists', e.g. Woytinsky. His footnotes and bibliography contain some references to the theorists, too. See Garvy, 1975, 391-405.

7. There is an excellent epistemological study of most aspects of Sombart's theoretical approach, especially his notion of 'economic systems' by Weippert (1953).

8. Despite Sombart's rather cynical remarks about Nazism, and despite sharp criticisms which his allegedly pro-Nazi book of 1934 drew from the official party press, this view seems to be the accepted opinion about everywhere. See for instance Krause and Rudolph (1980) and Kuczynski (1968) for the Marxist camp or, in the mainstream, the biography by Blaug and Sturges (1983) or the textbooks by Seligman (1962) and Spiegel (1981).

9. See the account by Garvy (1975) and Bombach *et al.* (1976, 1981), in particular Vol. II; also Hudson (1982), section III.

10. Jeremy Bentham, Commonplace Book, 1776; quoted from W. Stark (1952, 13).

11. A lively description can be found in Bonn (1955, 322).

12. One of these lectures was held on 29 February 1932.

13. He backed the programme of the *Studiengesellschaft fuer Geld und Kreditwirtschaft* and was the only scholarly economist to sign a petition of this activist group of bankers, industrialists and economic publicists. The petition was presented to the Chancellor on 10 August 1932 and was signed by eleven persons, of whom four were private entrepreneurs, three bankers, two economic journalists, one a retired civil servant and one, Sombart, a university professor.

14. The programme itself consisted of a list of public works that should be carried out; it contained nineteen very detailed feasibility studies showing the short-term nature of the required deficits, since the protagonists insisted on an economically viable programme involving investment. The expert opinion elaborates on this particular requirement in some detail. It may be found in BA (Federal Archives) R 43 I /2045. The expert opinion was appended to the aforementioned petition.

15. Sombart (1932), on which the February lecture, for example, was based.

16. None of his later works is devoted to similar problems.

17. This is the literal translation of the title of his 1932 monograph.

18. Note the similarity with Keynes who was also in favour of restraining imports in order to stimulate employment at home (Patinkin, 1982, 209-10).

19. A similar point has been argued for America by J. Ronnie Davis (1971) who suggested that the 'new economics' could build on the teachings of the 'old economists'.

20. The companion article is his *Gustav Schmoller und die Probleme von heute*, which appeared in the same journal a year earlier. See also Mitchell (1929).

21. Decree of 19 September 1934 (AZ: H.B.L.14. R *Der Reichswirtschaftsminister und Preussische Minister fuer Wirtschaft und Arbeit*).

22. There, he served first as director of foreign statistics until 1941, then as director of money and credit, balance of payments and international debts. He was recalled to the Economics Ministry in January 1944. He never joined the National Socialist Party.

23. Knut Borchardt has observed that there is no documentary proof of Lautenbach's authorship of the programmes of 1932 and 1933. In particular, the collection of memoranda of the *Reichswirtschaftsministerium* is incomplete in the archives in Potsdam. Lautenbach himself states that he worked on the basic problems of employment measures and the techniques of their financing for both the Economics Ministry and the Ministry of Labour. He mentions that he wrote several internal essays about the problem, and that in June 1933 he was chosen to explain the issues to Hitler, with Minister Seldte and State Secretary Krohne present during the meeting (Wilhelm Lautenbach, 'Meine persoenlichen Verhaeltnisse', 3 March, 1941, BA Koblenz Nachl. Lautenbach fol. 1). In October 1933 and, again, in the Spring of 1934 he was instructed to design 'an economic policy programme of reconstruction'. In order to be able to devote himself completely to this task, he was relieved of all other obligations by internal decree of 3 October 1933 (H.B. 504). He was promoted on 20 April 1934. In these circumstances, I personally feel that the incomplete state of the files in the Potsdam Archives is not sufficient reason for casting doubt on Lautenbach's own account, which could have readily been challenged at the time of his writing. The decrees survive, and we know the dates of his promotions and the persons whom he chose as his references (namely his superiors at the time, notably Minister Schmidt, Schacht's predecessor). Also, as I understand that Schacht wanted to take credit for these policies, it would have been surprising if he had left Lautenbach's pertinent memoranda in the collection once he was in control of the Ministry. But these are personal views. It is my impression that historians familiar with time and circumstances tend to side with Professor Borchardt.

24. This should not be interpreted as implying that it reflects fully the breadth and depth of his contributions. See Olivier Landmann in Bombach *et al.* (1981, III, B I 2).

25. Cassel (1927). See in particular chapter 2 'Restrictions of Competition in the Labour Market', chapter 6 'Wages' and chapter 8 'Conclusions with Respect to Monopolization'.

26. Significantly, this is not true for the group of Keynesian economists working around Wladimir S. Woytinsky of the Trade Union Congress. Woytinsky tried to enlist Keynes' support for his politically motivated activities of combining employment policies with high wage rates. In this case, Keynes responded to Woytinsky's overture, gracefully declining. This correspondence is reproduced in Garvy (1975).

27. Franz von Papen and Kurt von Schleicher were the German chancellors immediately preceding Hitler.

28. This resulted from the interplay between the protocol of The Hague, the Young plan and the Bank Law (section 31) which was made a part of the international agreements. See details in Knut Borchardt, *Zwangslagen und Handlungsspielraeume in der grossen Wirtschaftskrise der fruehen dreissiger Jahre: Zur Revision des ueberlieferten Geschichtsbildes.* In Becker and Hildebrand (eds), (1980, 287-325 (297 fn. 29)). See also Heilfron and Nassen (1931). Sec. 31 of the old Bank Law remained unchanged in the new Bank Law (enacted after the Young plan agreements) in 1930. On the Bank Law see the commentary by Hans Neufeld (1925).

29. Heinrich Bruening, centrist chancellor ruling under extraordinary powers countersigned by the president for lack of backing in parliament, staunchly pursued policies of budgetary contraction, witnessing ever increasing rates of unemployment. The quotation is from Garvy (1975, 402 fn. 24). Garvy translates from Heinrich Bruening (1970, 137).

30. To be more precise, Bruening at least reckoned that these policies would be perceived as inflationary by leaders of international public opinion and thus jeopardise his attempts to have the reparations cancelled. This belief was not unfounded. When Ernst Wagemann, economics professor at the University of Berlin and leading expert on empirical business cycle research, who at the same time served as the president of the Imperial Statistical Office, published his own stimulation programme in early 1932, the German government, which had not authorised publication of Wagemann's document, met with furious reactions on the part of the international banking community, reactions which were felt to have impaired Germany's credit standing. The criticisms were articulated, by e.g. Chase International's economic advisor, Anderson. For this and similar reasons, upwards price stability was a binding constraint on *any* counter-cyclical stimulation programme that was intended to be taken seriously by politicians.

31. Gustav Stolper also orchestrated a virtual campaign in print against Wagemann after the latter had published his proposal. See Landauer, Hahn and Stolper's *Anti-Wagemann* (1932).

32. Spiethoff was a leading representative, of course, along with Werner Sombart, who, in many respects, had gone further in developing the historical school's method and approach.

33. Edgar Salin (1928, 12) approvingly reported this conviction. However, Salin practiced Keynesianism on a small scale in the metropolitan region of the city of Basel. On this see Netzband (1984).

34. Schacht (1966, 154) with his amusing egocentricity, gives a precise date: 19 January 1939, the day of his dismissal as president of the central bank. Since Schacht had repeatedly warned of the inflationary consequences of government policies, unwelcome warnings which finally led to his dismissal, we can safely assume that Hitler's fear of inflation had subsided earlier than this.

35. Roepke in Lautenbach (1952, p. X, my translation J.B.). Although Roepke relates this incident in a somewhat anecdotal style ('Herr Hitler' etc.), we know from Lautenbach that the meeting actually took place and who participated in it.

36. This was, of course, precisely what Bruening tried to achieve by relying on opposite means.

37. Schumpeter (1917-18, 706-7, my translation J.B.). This quotation was chosen because *Das Socialprodukt und die Rechenpfennige* at that time was the only published account of Schumpeter's theory of money, and was often referred to, e.g. by the practitioners in the *Studiengesellschaft fuer Geld- und Kreditwirtschaft.*

38. I am relying on figures contained in a publication by the *Deutsche Bau- und Bodenbank'.* 5,093 million RM had been spent on re-employment by the end of 1935. Further statistical data are reported in Grotkopp (1938, 55 and *passim*).

39. Notably in several articles on foreign capital as a catalyst in 1931 and 1932 (Lautenbach, 1952, 129-37). This corresponds to Keynes' position. See Moggridge and Howson (1974).

40. Lautenbach was by no means insensitive to political matters. Apart from being an outspoken democrat, which was not the rule among German civil servants during the days of the Weimar Republic, he was a member of the Democratic Club in Berlin (until its dissolution); he repeatedly received letters of recognition from his ministers praising his skillful efforts at international negotiations.

41. The Lausanne agreement dated 9 July 1932; the Papen programme was launched shortly thereafter.

42. Crises of the second type refer to war economies as well as to post-war and post-disaster reconstruction.

43. While Hayek failed to influence Cambridge Keynesianism, he made an impact in Germany and on Lautenbach in particular. His thirteen-page expert opinion on the second Brauns Commission Report entitled *Konjunkturankerbelung durch Investitionen* was found among Lautenbach's papers (BA NL Lautenbach, fol. 16).

44. His multiplier analysis is contained in Lautenbach (in Bombach *et al.*, 1981, 302-8), *Auswirkungen der unmittelbaren Arbeitsbeschaffung.*

References

Abraham, D. (1981) *The Collapse of the Weimar Republic: Political Economy and Crisis,* Princeton University Press, Princeton

Amonn, A. (1938) 'Keynes' Allgemeine Theorie der Beschaeftigung', *Jahrbuecher fuer Nationaloekonomie und Statistik 147,* 1-27

Backhaus, J. (1983) 'Economic Theories and Political Interests', *Journal of European Economic History, 12,* Winter, 661-7

Barkai, A. (1977) *Das Wirtschaftssystem des Nationalsozialismus,* Verlag Wissenschaft und Politik Berend von Nottbeck, Koeln

Becker, J. and Hildebrand, K. (eds) (1980) *Internationale Beziehungen in der Weltwirtschaftskrise 1929-1933,* Ernst Vogel, Munich

Bernhard, E. (1930) 'Das Arbeitsbeschaffungsprogramm von 1930', *Soziale Praxis, 9,* 18

Bieri, H.G. (1983) 'Professor Dr. Alfred Amonn zum 100. Geburtstag', *Schweizerische Zeitschrift fuer Volkswirtschaft und Statistik 119* (2), 109-12

Binder, P. (1953) 'Wilhelm Lautenbach und die moderne Nationaloekonomie' *Finanzarchiv 14,* 178-90

Blaich, F. (1970) 'Kapitalistische Planwirtschaft: Ein ordnungstheoretischer Versuch zur Ueberwindung der Weltwirtschaftskrise', *Schmollers Jahrbuch 90,* 43 ff

Blaug, M. and Sturges, P. (1983) *Who's Who in Economics. A Biographical Dictionary of Major Economists 1700-1980,* MIT Press, Cambridge (Mass.)

Boehler, E. (1933) *Moeglichkeiten der Krisenbekaempfung,* Zurich

Boese, F. (1937) *Geschichte des Vereins fuer Socialpolitik,* Duncker & Humblot, Berlin

Bollert, G. (1934) *Arbeitsbeschaffung durch Errwerbslosenbeschaeftigung: Zwei hilfswirtschaftliche Vorschlaege der Professoren Graham und Lederer in ihrer allgemeinen Bedeutung,* dissertation, University of Berlin

Bombach, G. *et al.* (1976, 1981) *Der Keynesianismus,* Springer, Berlin, Vol. I, II, 1976, Vol. III 1981

Bonn, M. J. (1955) *So macht man Geschichte? Bilanz eines Lebens,* List, Munich

Borchardt, K. (1980), 'Zwangslagen und Handlungsspielraeume in der grossen Weltwirtschaftskrise der fruehen dreissiger Jahre: Zur Revision des ueberlieferten Geschichtsbildes,' in Becker, J. and Hildebrand, K. (eds.) (1980) 287-325

— — (1982) *'Konnte und sollte Deutschland Grossbritannien folgen und 1931 den Goldstandard verlassen?'* mimeograph, University of Munich

— — (1982) 'Zur Aufarbeitung der Vor- und Fruehgeschichte des Keynesianismus in Deutschland', *Jahrbuecher fuer Nationaloekonomie und Statistik 197,* 359-70

Bramstedt, P. (1909) *Das Problem der Beschaffung von Arbeit durch Staat und Gemeinden,* dissertation, University of Kiel

Brandis, R. (1983) *Marx and Keynes? Marx or Keynes?* Proceedings of the Conference on Marx and Keynes, Northern Kentucky University, Highland Heights, Oct. 29

Bruening, H. (1970) *Memoiren 1918-1934.* DVA, Stuttgart, 137

Cassel, G. (1927) *Neuere monopolistische Tendenzen in Industrie un Handel: Eine Untersuchung ueber die Natur and die Ursachen der Armut der Nationen,* Julius Springer, Berlin

Coats, A.W. (1983) *The Relevance of the 'Strong' Program in the Sociology of Knowledge for HOPE,* History of Economics Society Annual Meetings

Davis, J.R. (1971) *The New Economics and the Old Economists,* Iowa State University Press, Ames

Draeger, H. (1932) *Arbeitsbeschaffung durch produktive Kreditschoepfung: Ein Beitrag zur Frage der Wirtschaftsbelebung durch das sogenannte Federgeld,* Eher, Munich

— — *et al.* (1933) *Arbeitsbeschaffung: Eine Gemeinschaftsarbeit,* Reimar Hobbing, Berlin

Engels, F. (1972) 'Ergaenzung und Nachtrag zum III. Buche des "Kapital"'. in: Karl Marx, *Das Kapital: Kritik der politischen Oekonomie III,* Dietz (East) Berlin: 895-919

Epstein, M. (1941) 'Obituary' (Werner Sombart), *Economic Journal 51,* 523-6

Feder, G. (1919) *Das Manifest zur Brechung der Zinsknechtschaft des Geldes,* Eher, Munich (repr. 1926)

Feiler, A. (1931) 'Auslandskredite — Arbeitsbeschaffung', *Soziale Praxis, 5,* 28

Feldstein, M. (1981) 'The Retreat from Keynesian Economics', *The Public Interest 64,* Summer, 92-105

Fick, H. (1932) *Finanzwirtschaft und Konjunktur,* Fischer, Jena

Foehl, C. *Geldschoepfung und Wirtschaftskreislauf,* Duncker & Humblot, Munich, Leipzig

Fried, F. (1931) *Das Ende des Kapitalismus,* Diederichs, Jena

— — (1932) *Autarkie,* Diederichs, Jena

— — (1942) *Die soziale Revolution,* Goldmann, Leipzig

Forstmann, A. (1938) 'Arbeit oder Beschaeftigung? Kritische Betrachtungen zu John Maynard Keynes' Allgemeiner Theorie der Beschaeftigung, *Finanzarchiv N.F. 5,* 375-487

Garvy, G. (1975) 'Keynes and the Economic Activists of Pre-Hitler Germany', *Journal of Political Economy 83,* 391-405

Der Gehreke Plan (1933) *Die Wirtschaftswende* (Special Issue) Edited by Robert Friedlaender-Prechtl. (This issue — the last one before the journal had to cease publication due to censorship — contains contributions by Draeger, Friedlaender-Prechtl, Mayer zu Schwabediessen, Luebbert, Sachsenberg, Schotte, Sombart, and Woytinsky)

Gourevitch, P.A. (1983) Book Review: 'The Collapse of the Weimar Republic' by David Abraham, *American Journal of Sociology 88*, 777-9.

Grotkopp, W. (1932) *Die Gefahren des Preisabbaus*, Stilke, Berlin

— — (1938) *Frei vom Golde: Bemerkungen zum Thema Wirtschaft und Waehrung*, Haude & Spenersche Buchhandlung, Berlin

— — (1954) *Die grosse Krise. Lehren aus der Ueberwindung der Wirtschaftskrise 1929/32*, Duesseldorf

Haberler, G. (1936) *Prosperity and Depression*, League of Nations, Geneva

Halm, G. N. (1951) *Economic Systems: A Comparative Approach*, Rinehart & Co., New York

Hansson, B. J. (1982) *The Stockholm School and the Development of Economic Method*, Croom Helm, London

Harcourt, G. C. (1982) *The Social Science Imperialists*, Routledge & Kegan Paul, London

Harris, S. E. (1955) *John Maynard Keynes: Economist and Policy Maker*, Scribner's, New York

Harrod, Sir R. (1961) *The Life of John Maynard Keynes*, Oxford University Press, London

Hayek, F. A. von (1929) 'Gibt es einen Widersinn des Sparens?' *Zeitschrift fuer Nationaloekonomie 1*, 187-229

— — (1931) *Preise und Produktion*, Springer, Vienna (repr. 1976; engl.: *Prices and Production*, 1940)

— — (1973, 1976, 1979) *Law, Legislation, and Liberty I-III*, The University of Chicago Press, Chicago

Heilfron, E. and Nassen, P. (1931) *Der neue Plan: Young Plan und Haager Vereinbarungen nebst den deutschen Ausfuehrungsvorschriften*, Berlin

Heimann, E. (1931) 'Zur Problematik und Begruendung der Notstandsanleihen', *Soziale Praxis 5*, 5

Hohn, H. W. (1973) *John Maynard Keynes und Carl Foehl: Eine vergleichende Darstellung ihres Beitrages zur Entwicklung der modernen Beschaeftigungstheorie*, dissertation, University of Munich

Hudson, M. (1982) 'German Economists and the Depression of 1929/33', manuscript, The University of Leeds

Hutchison, Terence W. (1979) *On Revolutions and Progress in Economic Knowledge*. Cambridge

— — (1980) *The Limitations of General Theories in Macroeconomics*, Washington D.C.: American Enterprise Institute for Public Policy Research (AEI Studies No. 285)

— — (1981) *The Politics and Philosophy of Economics*, New York, London: New York University Press

Jeidel, E. (1933) *Oeffentliche Auftraege als Mittel der Konjunkturpolitik: Das Problem der Krisenbekaempfung durch Arbeitsbeschaffung*, dissertatrary, University of Frankfurt

Jevons, H. W. (1934) 'William Stanley Jevons: His Life.' *Econometrica 2*, 229

Johannsen, N.A.F.L. (1903) *Der Kreislauf des Geldes und der Mechanismus des Soziallebens*. Berlin: (publ. under 'J.J.O. Lahn')

— — (1908) *A Neglected Point in Connection with Crises*, New York

— — (1913) *Die Steuer der Zukunft*, Berlin

Keynes, J. M. CW VI, VII, XIV, XXVII

Kindleberger, C. (1973) *The World in Depression 1929-1939*, University of California Press, Berkeley, Los Angeles

Klein, L. B. (1951) 'The Life of John Maynard Keynes,' *Journal of Political Economy 59*, 443-51

Kraemer, C. (1937) 'John Maynard Keynes ueber Kapitalersparung und -anlegung: Ein Vortrag', *Schmollers Jahrbuch fuer Gesetzgebung, Verwaltung und Volkswirtschaft 61*, 315-28

Krause, W. (1962) *Werner Sombarts Weg vom Kathedersozialismus zum Faschismus,* (East) Berlin

Krohn, C. D., (1981) *Wirtschaftstheorien als politische Interessen: Die akademische Nationaloekonomie in Deutschland 1918-1933,* Campus, Frankfurt

— — (1982) '"Oekonomische Zwangslagen" und das Scheitern der Weimarer Republik', *Geschichte und Gesellschaft, 8,* 415-26

Kroll, G. (1958) *Von der Weltwirtschaftskrise zur Staatskonjunktor,* Berlin

Krumme, G. (1968)'Werner Sombart and the Base Concept', *Land Economics XLIV,* 115 ff.

Kuczynski, J. (1968) 'Werner Sombart', *International Encyclopedia of the Social Sciences 15,* 57-9

Lampe, A. (1927) *Notstandsarbeiten oder Lohnabbau: Kritik der Wirtschaftstheorie an der Arbeitslosenpolitik,* Jena

Landauer, C., and Hahn, L. A. Stolper, G. (1932) *Anti Wagemann: Drei Kritiken,* Verlag des Deutschen Volkswirts, Berlin

Lautenbach, W. (1931) 'Konjunkturankurbelung durch Investitionen', *BA Koblenz,* Nachlass Lautenbach, fol. 16

— — (1933/34) 'Massnahmen zur Belebung der Wirtschaft, auch zur Arbeitsbeschaffung: Verschiedene Plaene und Ausarbeitungen, auch von Lautenbach (?)'. (1933-) 1934 *BA Koblenz,* Nachlass Lautenbach, fol. 16

— — (no date) 'Deutschlands Betriebskapital: Ein fehlerhafter Versuch' *BA Koblenz* Nachlass Lautenbach, fol. 40

— — (1932-34) 'Denkschriften des Oberregierungsrates Dr. W. Lautenbach (Reichswirtschaftsministerium)', *ZStA Potsdam,* Reichswirtschaftsminiterium, (31.01) 9930

— — (1933) 'Auswirkungen der unmittelbaren Arbeitsbeschaffung', *Wirtschaft und Statistik 13,* Nr. 21, reprinted in Bombach *et al.* (III, 1981, 302-8)

— — (1939) 'Geldschoepfung und Wirtschaftskreislauf,' *Weltwirtschaftliches Archiv 49,* 117-21

— — (1952) *Zins, Kredit, und Produktion,* Tuebingen: Mohr/Siebeck

Lenel, H. O. (1952) 'Wilhelm Lautenbach's Beitrag zur Nationaloekonomie', *Ordo 5,* 327-30

Mahlberg, W. (1931) *Arbeitsbeschaffung und fixe Kosten,* Leipzig

Marcon, H. (1974) *Arbeitsbeschaffungspolitik der Regierungen von Papen und Schleicher: Grundsteinlegung fuer die Beschaeftigungspolitik im Dritten Reich,* Frankfurt

Marx, K. (1971) *Das Kapital III,* Dietz, Berlin

Merton, R. K. (1957) 'Priorities in Scientific Discovery', *American Sociological Review,* 22, 635-59

Von Mises, L. (1960) *Epistemological Problems of Economics,* Van Nostrand, Princeton

— — (1978), *Notes and Recollections,* Libertarian Press, South Holland

Mitchell, W. C. (1929)'Sombart's Hochkapitalismus', *Quarterly Journal of Economics 43,* 303-22

Mitzman, A. (1973) *Sociology and Estrangement: Three Sociologists of Imperial Germany,* Knopf, New York, 133-264

Moggridge, D. E. and Howson, S. (1974) 'Keynes on Monetary Policy 1910-1946', *Oxford Economic Papers 26,* 226-47

Mombert, F. (1933) 'Arbeitsbeschaffung mit Kreditausweitung', *Die Wirtschaftskurve 11*

Muehlenfels, A. von (1930)'Allgemeine Theorie der Beschaeftigung, des Zinses und des Geldes', *Schmollers Jahrbuch fuer Gesetzgebung, Verwaltung und Volkswirtschaft 62,* 221-9

Mueller-Armack, A. (1929) Art. 'Konjunkturforschung und Konjunkturpolitik', *HdSW* Suppl. Vol. (4. ed.), 645-77

Neisser, H. (1930) 'Arbeitsbeschaffung durch Bauprogramme', *Magazin der Wirtschaft 7*, Nr. 18

— — (1931) 'Ankurbelung oder Inflation: Eine Entgegnung', *Der deutsche Volkswirt 6*, (3), Oct. 16, 80-4

— — (1946) 'Keynes as an Economist', *Social Research 13*, 223-35

Neufeld, H. (1925) *Das Bankgesetz*, Carl Heymanns Verlag, Berlin

Neumark, F. (1981) 'Hjalmar Schacht: Leben und Werk einer umstrittenen Persoenlichkeit', *Finanzarchiv N.F. 38*, 478-85

Netzband, K. B. (1984) 'Zum zehnten Todstag Edgar Salins: Aus Zeugnissen seines Nachlasses', *List Forum 12*, 205-27

Nussbaum, F. L. (1935) *A History of the Economic Institutions of Modern Europe: An Introduction to Der Moderne Kapitalismus of Werner Sombart*, F.S. Crofts & Co., New York

Oakeshott, M. (1938) 'Review of Sombart (1937) *New Philosophy', Economic Journal*, 537

Ohlin, B. (1981) 'Stockholm and Cambridge: Four Papers on the Monetary and Employment Theory of the 1930s', *History of Political Economy 13*, 189-255

Parsons, T. (1927-8) 'Capitalism in Recent German Literature: Sombart and Weber.' *Journal of Political Economy 36/37*

Patinkin, D. (1979) 'Keynes in Chicago', *Journal of Law and Economics 12*, 213-32

— — (1982) *Anticipations of the General Theory? And Other Essays on Keynes*, The University of Chicago Press, Chicago

Peter, H. (1937) 'Zu Keynes' "Allgemeiner Theorie der Beschaeftigung, des Zinses und des Geldes"', *Jahrbuecher fuer Nationaloekonomie und Statistik 146*, 60-83

Raphael, K. (1930) 'Wirtschaftende Arbeitslosenfuersorge als Spitzenausgleich der Arbeitslosigkeit', *Soziale Praxis 9*, Nr. 18

Reithinger, A. (1932) 'Stand und Ursachen der Arbeitslosigkeit in Deutschland', *Vierteljahreshefte zur Konjunktur forschung*, Special Issue 29

Richter-Altschoeffer, H. (1936) *Volkswirtschaftliche Theorie der oeffentlichen Investitionen: Eine Untersuchung ueber die theoretische Stellung der oeffentlichen Investitionen in der Dynamik der modernen Verkehrswirtschaft*, Duncker & Humblot, Munich, Leipzig

Robinson, J. (1966) 'Introduction', to: Michal Kalečki, *Studies in the Theory of Business Cycles: 1933-1939*, Basil Blackwell, Oxford

— — (1972) 'The Second Crisis in Economic Theory', *American Economic Review, Papers & Proceedings 62*, 1-9

Roepke, W (1926) 'Kredit und Konjunktur', *Jahrbuecher fuer Nationaloekonomie III-69*

— — (1929) Art 'Staatsinterventionismus', *HdSW*, Suppl. Vol. (4th ed.), 861-82

— — (1931) 'Das Brauns-Gutachten und seine Kritiker', *Soziale Praxis 5*, Nr. 21

— — (1931) 'Praktische Konjunkturpolitik', *Weltwirtschaftliches Archiv*

— — (1931) 'Die Angst vor der Produktion', *Frankfurter Zeitung* °260, 9 April

— — (1932a) *Die Konjunktur*, Gustav Fischer, Jena

— — (1932b) *Krise und Konjunktur*, Quelle & Mayer, Leipzig

— — (1933) 'Trends in German Business Cycle Policy', *Economic Journal*, September

— — (1936) *Crises and Cycles*, Hodge, London

Rogin, Leo (1933) 'Werner Sombart and the "Natural Science Method" in Economics', *Journal of Political Economy 41*, 222-36

— — (1941) 'Werner Sombart and the Uses of Transcendentalism', *American Economic Review 31*, 493-511

Ruestow, H. J. (1951) *Theorie der Vollbeschaeftigung in der freien Wirtschaft*, Mohr-Siebeck, Tuebingen

— — (1978) 'The Economic Crisis of the Weimar Republic and How it was Overcome:

A Comparison with the Present Recession', *Cambridge Journal of Economics 2*, 409-21

Salin, E. (1928) *Theorie und Praxis staatlicher Kreditpolitik der Gegenwart*, Mohr/Siebeck, Tuebingen

— — (1932) *Wirtschaft und Staat*, Hobbing, Berlin

Schacht, H. (1932) *Grundsaetze deutscher Wirtschaftspolitik*, Stalling, Oldenburg

— — (1966) *Magie des Geldes*, Econ, Duesseldorf

Schefold, B. (1980) 'The General Theory for a Totalitarian State? A Note on Keynes's Preface to the German Edition of 1936', *Cambridge Journal of Economics 4*, 175-6

Schneider, E. (1953) 'Wilhelm Lautenbach in memoriam', *Weltwirtschaftliches Archiv 71*, 1-3

Schotte, W. (1932) *Die Finanzierung der Arbeitsbeschaffung*, Berlin

Schumpeter, J. A. (1917/18) 'Das Sozialprodukt und die Rechenpfennige: Glossen und Beitraege zur Geldtheorie von heute', *Archiv fuer Socialwissenschaft und Socialpolitik 44*, 627-715

— — (1927) 'Sombarts Dritter Band', *Schmollers Jahrbuch fuer Gesetzgebung, Verwaltung, und Volkswirtschaft im Deutschen Reiche 51*, 349-69

— — (1931) 'Dauerkrise?' *Der deutsche Volkswirt 6*, 418-21

— — 'Weltkrise und Finanzpolitik, *Der deutsche Volkswirt 6*, 739-42

— — (1936) 'Book Review of John Maynard Keynes, *The General Theory of Employment, Interest and Money', Journal of the American Statistical Association 31*, 791-5

— — (1946) 'John Maynard Keynes 1883-1946', *American Economic Review 36*

— — (1954) *History of Economic Analysis*, Oxford University Press, New York

— — (1970) *Das Wesen des Geldes*, Vandenhoeck & Ruprecht, Goettingen

Seligman, B. B. (1962) *Main Currents in Modern Economics: Economic Thought Since 1870*, The Free Press of Glencoe, New York

Shackle, G. L. S. (1967) *The Years of High Theory: Invention and Tradition in Economic Thought*, Cambridge University Press, Cambridge

Simons, H. C. (1948) *Economic Policy for a Free Society*, The University of Chicago Press, Chicago

Skidelsky, R. (1984) *John Maynard Keynes: Vol. I Hopes Betrayed, 1883-1920*, Macmillan, London

Sombart, W. (1909) *Socialism and the Social Movement*, translated from the sixth (enlarged) German edition with introduction and notes by M. Epstein, J. M. Dent & Co., London

— — (1913) *The Jews and Modern Capitalism*. ('Die Juden und das Wirtschaftsleben', 1911) Translated by M. Epstein

— — (1902/1927/1928) *Der Moderne Kapitalismus*, Duncker & Humblot I, II, 1902: I (rev.) 1916; II (rev., 1917; III, 1927; I-III, 1928, Berlin

— — (1929) 'Economic Theory and Economic History', *The Economic History Review 2*, 1-19

— — (1930a) 'Capitalism', *Encyclopaedia of the Social Sciences*, Vol. III, 195-208

— — (1930b) *Die drei Nationaloekonomien: Geschichte und System der Lehre von der Wirtschaft*, Duncker & Humblot, Munich, Leipzig

— — (1932) *Die Zukunft des Kapitalismus*, Buchholz & Weisswaage, Berlin

— — (1933) 'Zum Problem der Arbeitsbeschaffung', *Die Wirtschaftswende*, special issue, No. 2

Spiegel, H. W. (1983) *The Growth of Economic Thought*, Duke University Press, Durham, N.C.

Spiethoff, A. (1909) 'Der Kapitalmangel in seinem Verhaeltnisse zur Gueterwelt', *Jahrbuch fuer Gesetzgebung, Verwaltung und Volkswirtschaft N.F. 33*, 117-37

Spliedt, F. (1932) 'Probleme der Arbeitsbeschaffung und der Arbeitsmarktpolitik', *Die Arbeit 9*, No. 8, 457-67

Stark, W. (ed.) (1952) 'Introduction', *Jeremy Bentham's Economic Writings*, George Allen and Unwin (for the Royal Economic Society), London

Steiger, O. (1976) 'Bertil Ohlin and the Origins of the Keynesian Revolution,' *History of Political Economy 8*, 341-66

Stephan, W. (1929) 'Ausgleich von Konjunkturund Saisonschwankungen mit Hilfe oeffentlicher Auftraege', *Reichsarbeitsblatt 11*

Stern, H. (1932) 'Arbeitsbeschaffungsprogramme', *Wirtschaftskurve 11*

Stuetzel, W. (1959) 'Wilhelm Lautenbach', *Handwoerterbuch der Sozialwissenschaften, 538*

Turban, M. (1982) 'Grundlinien des oekonomischen Denkens in Deutschland', *Jahrbuecher fuer Nationaloekonomie und Statistik 197*, 265-70

V. (1902/03) [Thorstein B. Veblen?], Book Review: 'Der Moderne Kapitalismus' by Werner Sombart, *Journal of Political Economy 11*, 300-5

Wagemann, E. (1932) *Geld- und Kreditreform*, Reimar Hobbing, Berlin

Webb, S. and B. (1909) 'The Minority Report': *Report of the Royal Commission on the Poor Laws and Relief of Distress*, Vol. III, Separate Report, London

Weippert, G. (1953) *Werner Sombarts Gestaltidee des Wirtschaftssystems*, Vandenhoeck & Ruprecht, Goettingen

— — (1956) 'Werner Sombart', *Handwoertenbuch der Sozialwissenschaften IX*, 298-305

Wilhelmi and Albrecht (1924) *Oeffentliche Notstandsarbeiten*, Berlin

Wissman, H. (1932) *Organische Waehrungs- und Wirtschaftspolitik*, Hoppenstedt, Frankfurt/Berlin (Das Spezialarchiv der deutschen Wirtschaft)

Worswick, D. and Trevithick, J. (eds) (1984) *Keynes and the Modern World*. Proceedings of the Keynes Centenary Conference, Kings College, Cambridge, The University Press, Cambridge

Woytinksy, W. S. (1931) *Die internationale Hebung der Preise als ein Ausweg aus der Krise*, Buske, Leipzig

— — (1931) 'Wirtschaftspolitik', *Die Arbeit 8*, No. 6, 414-40

— — (1932) 'Wann kommt die aktive Wirtschaftspolitik? *Die Arbeit 9*, No. 1, 11-31

— — (1932) 'Arbeitsbeschaffung und keine Inflationgefahr!' *Die Arbeit 9*, No. 3, 142-54

Yeager, L. (1982) 'Clark Warburton 1896-1979', *History of Political Economy 13*, 279-84

CONTRIBUTORS

Juergen Backhaus	Department of Economics, Auburn University, Alabama, USA
Lawrence A. Boland	Department of Economics, Simon Fraser University, Canada
Anna Carabelli	Istituto di Scienze Economiche e Statistiche, Università di Pavia, Italy
Victoria Chick	Department of Political Economy, University College London, UK
Alexander Dow	Department of Economics, University of Stirling, UK
Sheila Dow	Department of Economics, University of Stirling, UK
Geoff Hodgson	Faculty of Professional Studies, Newcastle-upon-Tyne Polytechnic, UK
Johannes J. Klant	Faculty of Economics, University of Amsterdam, The Netherlands
Tony Lawson	Faculty of Economics and Politics, University of Cambridge, UK
Hashem Pesaran	Trinity College, Cambridge, UK
John Pheby	Department of Government and Economics, City of Birmingham Polytechnic, UK
Ron Smith	Department of Economics, Birkbeck College, University of London, UK
Simon Wren-Lewis	National Institute of Economic and Social Research, London, UK

AUTHOR INDEX

255

SUBJECT INDEX